UNIVERSITY OF NORTH CAROLINA
STUDIES IN THE ROMANCE LANGUAGES AND LITERATURES
Number 77

AN INQUIRY INTO LOCAL VARIATIONS IN
VULGAR LATIN

AN INQUIRY INTO LOCAL VARIATIONS IN VULGAR LATIN

AS REFLECTED IN THE VOCALISM OF CHRISTIAN INSCRIPTIONS

BY

PAUL A. GAENG

CHAPEL HILL

THE UNIVERSITY OF NORTH CAROLINA PRESS

DEPÓSITO LEGAL: V. 4.279 - 1968

ARTES GRÁFICAS SOLER, S. A. - JÁVEA, 30 - VALENCIA (8) - 1968

I wish to express my gratitude and appreciation to the Montclair State College Development Fund, Inc. for financial support in connection with the publication of this study.

PARENTIBUS RARISSIMIS

ACKNOWLEDGEMENTS

This study is the complete text of a doctoral dissertation presented at Columbia University. In this connection, it gives me great pleasure to express my very profound gratitude to my sponsor and mentor, Professor Mario A. Pei, under whose direction it was undertaken. Professor Pei not only suggested the topic for this study of inscriptional material, supervising every step of its preparation with painstaking care, suggestions and constructive criticism but, throughout my graduate studies, provided me also with the necessary philological training and theoretical background that enabled me to tackle the task. For his interest, enthusiasm and the everpresent readiness to lend a helping hand, without regard to his own time and convenience, I am in his debt.

I also owe a debt of appreciation and gratitude to two distinguished members of the Columbia University faculty, Professors Frederick H. Jungemann and William G. Diver, who had kindly consented to act as my advisors and were most generous with constructive suggestions and criticism.

Finally, I wish to express my sincere and heartfelt appreciation to the Chairman of the Department of French and Romance Philology, Professor Lawton P. G. Peckham, for the sympathetic interest shown in my study.

PRELIMINARY NOTE

1. *Symbols and Abbreviations*

Most of the symbols and abbreviations used in this study are those found in the standard manuals on General and Romance Linguistics, such as Robert A. Hall, Jr., *Introductory Linguistics* and W. D. Elcock's *The Romance Languages*, to name but two of the more recent ones.

Latin etyma and inscriptional examples are given in small letters to conform to Diehl's presentation, rather than in capital letters as is sometimes the custom to do. For the sake of convenience, furthermore, a distinction is made between the vowel symbol *u* and the consonant symbol *v*.

The following symbols used in the inscriptional examples call for the special comment:

(a) Letters enclosed in square brackets [ ] are those supplied by the editor, although known to have formed part of a mutilated inscription.

(b) Letters enclosed in parentheses ( ) have been added by the editor to facilitate comprehension, even though nothing is missing on the original stone.

(c) A word appearing in parentheses immediately following a garbled or misspelled form, e. g. *quisscenti* (= *quiescenti*) has been supplied by us for clarification.

A symbol such as /ĕ/>*e* used in the tables means that the classical Latin short /e/ phoneme is represented by the letter *e*, while the symbol /ĕ/>*i* means that the same phoneme appears spelled with *i*.

2. Percentage Figures

As regards these figures we have generally omitted them when they represent

(a) a single deviation, unless there is a progression of a certain phenomenon over the centuries, in which case the figure is given in parentheses.

(b) two or more deviations found in the same inscription, since, just as in (a), they may represent only a single man's orthography,

(c) deviations occurring in one and the same form only, unless that form also appears correctly spelled, i. e. an orthographic hesitation that may have phonological or morphological implications.

(d) deviations that were felt not to be particularly reliable, such as in a proper, particularly Germanic name.

Sometimes, indeed, a high percentage figure may be due only to a few occurrences of a given phenomenon, so that even a single deviation might give an erroneous impression, as when we find that, for instance, out of two occurrences of Latin /ĕ/ in a certain position, one appears spelled with *i*. Although mathematically this would mean a 50 % deviation, it might, nevertheless, be inaccurate, and even misleading, to reach a conclusion on the basis of such scanty sampling. In such instances, percentage figures have generally also been omitted and only deviations were given.

Inscriptions followed only by a number, e. g. D3500 (from the Diehl collection) or V350 (from the Vives collection) are not dated.

CONTENTS

	Pages
ACKNOWLEDGEMENTS ...	9
PRELIMINARY NOTE ...	11
A SELECTED BIBLIOGRAPHY ...	15
PART I: INTRODUCTION ...	21
PART II: ORTHOGRAPHY AND PHONOLOGY ...	41

Chapter I: The Accented Vowels

1. Latin /ă/ ...	41
2. Latin /ĕ/ ...	41
3. Latin /ē/ ...	48
4. Latin /ĭ/ ...	58
5. Latin /ī/ ...	69
6. Latin /ŏ/ ...	74
7. Latin /ō/ ...	79
8. Latin /ŭ/ ...	87
9. Latin /ū/ ...	100

Chapter II: The Unaccented Vowels ... 102

1. Latin /ă/ ...	103
2. Latin /ĕ/ ...	108
3. Latin /ē/ ...	129
4. Latin /ĭ/ ...	146
5. Latin /ī/ ...	175
6. Latin /ŏ/ ...	184
7. Latin /ō/ ...	193
8. Latin /ŭ/ ...	210
9. Latin /ū/ ...	234

Chapter III: Diphthongs

1. Latin /aj/ ...	240
2. Latin /oj/ ...	256
3. Latin /aw/ ...	259

Chapter IV: Some Vocalic Phenomena

1. Prothesis 263
2. Apheresis 266
3. Syncope 267
4. Anaptyxis 272

Part III: Summary of findings and conclusions 275

A SELECTED BIBLIOGRAPHY

Note: This bibliography comprises only those sources and works that have been consulted in connection with this study. They will generally be referred to, either in the body of the text or in footnotes, by the name of the author, followed by an abbreviation of the title of his work, when necessary.
Works referred to only occasionally are cited in full in the notes.

I.—*Sources with Abbreviations*

C. I. L. = *Corpus Inscriptionum Latinarum.* Berlin, 1862-1943.
DIEHL, AI = Diehl, Ernst (ed.), *Lateinische altchristliche Inschriften.* 2nd ed., Bonn, 1913.
DIEHL, ICLV = Diehl, Ernst (ed.), *Inscriptiones Latinae Christianae Veteres.* Berlin, 1924-1931.
DIEHL, VI = Diehl, Ernst (ed.), *Vulgärlateinische Inschriften.* Bonn, 1910.
DÍAZ Y DÍAZ = Díaz y Díaz, Manuel C. (ed.), *Antología del latín vulgar.* Madrid, 1950.
MULLER-TAYLOR = Muller, Henri F. and Taylor, Pauline, *A Chrestomathy of Vulgar Latin.* New York, 1932.
MATEU Y LLOPIS = Mateu y Llopis, F., *Catálogo de las monedas previsigodas y visigodas del Gabinete Numismático del Museo Arqueológico Nacional.* Madrid, 1936.
VIVES = Vives, D. José (ed.), *Inscripciones cristianas de la España Romana y Visigoda.* Barcelona, 1942.

II.—*Chief Works Cited with Abbreviations*

BATTISTI = Battisti, Carlo, *Avviamento allo studio del latino volgare.* Bari, 1949.
BLOCH = Bloch, Raymond, *L'épigraphie latine.* Paris, 1952.
BLOOMFIELD = Bloomfield, Leonard, *Language.* New York, 1933.
BOURCIEZ, *Éléments* = Bourciez, Édouard, *Éléments de linguistique romane.* 4th ed. revised. Paris, 1956.
BOURCIEZ, *Phonétique* = Bourciez, Édouard, *Précis historique de phonétique française.* 9th ed. revised. Paris, 1958.
CARNOY = Carnoy A., *Le latin d'Espagne d'après les inscriptions.* 2nd ed. Louvain, 1906.

Cooper = Cooper, Paul J., «The Language of the *Forum Judicum*.» Unpublished PH.D. Dissertation, Department of French and Romance Philology, Columbia University, 1952.
Cross = Cross, Ephraim, *Syncope and Kindred Phenomena in Latin Inscriptions*. New York, 1930.
Diehl, *De m finali* = Diehl, Ernst, *De m finali epigraphica*. Leipzig, 1899.
Elcock = Elcock, W. D., *The Romance Languages*. London, 1960.
Entwistle = Entwistle, William J., *The Spanish Language*. 2nd ed. London, 1962.
Ewert = Ewert, Alfred, *The French Language*. 2nd ed. London, 1943.
Grandgent = Grandgent, C. H., *An Introduction to Vulgar Latin*. Reprint. New York, 1962.
Hall, *Linguistics* = Hall, Robert A., Jr., *Introductory Linguistics*. Philadelphia, 1964.
Jennings = Jennings, Augustus Campbell, *A Linguistic Study of the Cartulario de San Vicente de Oviedo*. New York, 1940.
Jungemann = Jungemann, Frederick H., *La teoría del sustrato y los dialectos hispano-romances y gascones*. Trans. D. Emilio Alarcos Llorach. Madrid, 1955.
Kaufmann = Kaufmann, Carl Maria, *Handbuch der alkristlichen Epigraphik*. Freiburg i. Breisgau, 1917.
Kieckers = Kieckers, Ernst, *Historische lateinische Grammatik*. München, 1931.
Krepinsky = Krepinsky, Max, *Inflexión de las vocales en español*. Trans. Vicente García de Diego. Madrid, 1923.
Lattimore = Lattimore, Richmond, *Themes in Greek and Latin Epitaphs*. Urbana, 1962.
Lausberg = Lausberg, Heinrich, *Romanische Sprachwissenschaft*. 3 vols. Berlin. 1956-62.
LeBlant = LeBlant, Edmond M., *L'épigraphie chrétienne en Gaule et dans l'Afrique romaine*. Paris, 1890.
Lehmann = Lehmann, Winfred P., *Historical Linguistics*. New York, 1962.
Lindsay = Lindsay, W. M., *The Latin Language*. Oxford, 1894.
Löfstedt, *Late Latin* = Löfstedt, Einar, *Late Latin*. Oslo, 1959.
B. Löfstedt = Löfstedt, Bengt, *Studien über die Sprache der langobardischen Gesetze*. Stockholm, 1961.
Martinet = Martinet, André, *Économie des changements phonétiques*. Bern, 1955.
Maurer, *Gramática* = Maurer, Theodoro Henrique, Jr., *Gramática do Latim Vulgar*. Rio de Janeiro, 1959.
Maurer, *O Problema* = Maurer, Theodoro Henrique, Jr., *O Problema do Latim Vulgar*. Rio de Janeiro, 1962.
Menéndez Pidal, *Gramática* = Menéndez Pidal, Ramón, *Manual de gramática histórica española*. 10th ed. Madrid, 1958.
Menéndez Pidal, *Orígenes* = Menéndez Pidal, Ramón, *Orígenes del español*. 4th ed. Madrid, 1956.
Meyer-Lübke, *Einführung* = Meyer-Lübke, W., *Einführung in das Studium der romanischen Sprachwissenschaft*. 3rd ed. revised. Heidelberg, 1920.
Meyer-Lübke, *Grammaire* = Meyer-Lübke, W., *Grammaire des langues romanes*. 4 vols. Trans. Eugene Rabiet. Paris, 1890-1906.

MILES = Miles, George C., *The Coinage of the Visigoths of Spain: from Leovigild to Achila II.* New York, 1952.
MOHL = Mohl, Friedrich Georg, *Introduction à la chronologie du latin vulgaire.* Paris, 1899.
MOHRMANN, *Latin vulgaire* = Mohrmann, Christine, *Latin vulgaire, latin des chrétiens, latin médiéval.* Paris, 1955.
MULLER, *Chronology* = Muller, H. F., «A Chronology of Vulgar Latin,» *Zeitschrift für romanische Philologie,* Beiheft 78. Halle (Saale), 1929.
MULLER, *Époque mérovingienne* = Muller, H. F., *L'Époque mérovingienne: essai de synthèse de philologie et d'histoire.* New York, 1945.
NAVARRO TOMÁS = Navarro Tomás, T., *Manual de pronunciación española* (Publicaciones de la Revista de Filología Española, No. 3). 9th ed. Madrid, 1959.
NIEDERMANN, *Phonétique* = Niedermann, Max, *Précis de phonétique historique du latin.* 3d. ed. revised. Paris, 1953.
NIEDERMANN, *Recueil* = *Recueil Max Neidermann* (Recueil de travaux publiés par la Faculté des Lettres). Neuchâtel, 1954.
PALMER = Palmer, L. R., *The Latin Language.* London, 1954.
PAULY-WISSOWA = *Paulys Real-Encyclopädie der Altertumswissenschaft.* Neue Bearbeitung. Herausgegeben von Georg Wissowa. Band IV. Stuttgart, 1901.
PEI, *Texts* = Pei, Mario A., *The Language of the Eighth-Century Texts in Northern France.* New York, 1932.
PEI, *Italian Language* = Pei, Mario A., *The Italian Language.* 2nd ed. New York, 1954.
PEI, *Linguistics* = *Invitation to Linguistics: a Basic Introduction to the Science of Language.* New York, 1965.
PEI, *Studies* = Pei, Mario A., *Studies in Romance Philology and Literature* (University of North Carolina Studies in the Romance Languages and Literatures, No. 44). Chapel Hill, 1963.
PEI, *Voices* = Pei, Mario A., *Voices of Man: the Meaning and Function of Language.* New York, 1962.
PIRSON = Pirson, Jules, *La langue des inscriptions latines de la Gaule.* Bruxelles, 1901.
PISANI, *Grammatica* = Pisani, Vittore, *Grammatica latina storica e comparativa.* 3rd ed. revised. Torino, 1962.
PISANI, *Testi* = Pisani, Vittore, *Testi latini arcaici e volgari con commento glottologico.* 2nd ed. revised. Torino, 1960.
POLITZER, *Study* = Politzer, Robert L., *A Study of the Language of Eighth Century Lombardic Documents.* New York, 1949.
POLITZERS, *Romance Trends* = Politzer, Frieda N. and Politzer, Robert L., *Romance Trends in 7th and 8th Century Latin Documents* (University of North Carolina Studies in the Romance Languages and Literatures, No. 21). Chapel Hill, 1953.
PRINZ = Prinz, Otto, *De O et U vocalibus inter se mutatis in lingua latina.* Halle, 1932.
PROSKAUER = Proskauer, Carola, *Das auslautende -s auf den lateinischen Inschriften.* Strassburg, 1909.
RICHTER = Richter, Elise, «Beiträge zur Geschichte der Romanismen: I. Chronologische Phonetik des Französischen bis zum Ende des 8. Jahhunderts,» *Zeitschrift für romanische Philologie,* Beiheft 82. Halle, 1934.
ROHLFS, *Grammatik* = Rohlfs, Gerhard, *Historische Grammatik der italienischen Sprache und ihrer Mundarten.* 3 vols. Bern, 1949-54.

Rohlfs, *Diferenciación* = Rohlfs, Gerhard, *Diferenciación léxica de las lenguas románicas*. Trans. Manuel Alvar. (Publicaciones de la Revista de Filología Española, No. 14). Madrid, 1960.
Sas = Sas, Louis Furman, *The Noun Declension System in Merovingian Latin*. Paris, 1937.
Schiaffini = Schiaffini, Alfredo «Problemi del passaggio dal latino all'italiano (evoluzione, disgregazione, ricostruzione),» *Studi in onore di Angelo Monteverdi*. Modena, 1959, pp. 691-715.
Schmeck, *Vulgärlateinische Forschung* = Schmeck, Helmut, *Aufgaben und Methoden der modernen vulgärlateinischen Forschung*. Heidelberg, 1955.
Schuchardt = Schuchardt, Hugo, *Der Vokalismus des Vulgärlateins*. 3 vols. Leipzig, 1866-68.
Silva Neto = Da Silva Neto, Serafim, *História do Latim Vulgar*. Rio de Janeiro, 1957.
Sittl = Sittl, Karl, *Die lokalen Verschiedenheiten der lateinischen Sprache mit besonderer Berücksichtigung des afrikanischen Lateins*. Erlangen, 1882.
Sittl, *Jahresbericht* = Sittl, Karl, «Jahresbericht über Vulgär-und Spätlatein 1884-1890,» *Jahresbericht über die Fortschritte der classischen Alterthumswissenschaft*, LXVII (1892), 226-286.
Sofer = Sofer, Johann, *Zur Problematik des Vulgärlateins: Ergebnisse und Anregungen*. Wien, 1963.
Sommer = Sommer, Ferdinand, *Handbuch der lateinischen Laut- und Formenlehre*. 3rd ed. Heidelberg, 1948.
Straka = Straka, Georges, «La dislocation linguistique de la Romania et la formation des langues romanes à la lumière de la chronologie relative des changements phonétiques,» *Revue de linguistique romane*, XX (1956), 249-257.
Sturtevant = Sturtevant, E. H., *The Pronunciation of Greek and Latin*. 2nd ed. Philadelphia, 1940.
Väänänen = Väänänen, Veikko, *Introduction au latin vulgaire*. Paris, 1963.
Väänänen, *Inscriptions* = Väänänen, Veikko, *Le latin vulgaire des inscriptions pompéiennes*. Helsinki, 1937.
Vidos = Vidos, B. E., *Manuale di linguistica romanza*. Trans. G. Francescato (Biblioteca dell'«Archivum Romanicum»). Firenze, 1959.
Vossler-Schmeck = Vossler, Karl, *Einführung ins Vulgärlatein*. Herausgegeben und bearbeitet von Helmut Schmeck. München, 1953.
v. Wartburg, *Ausgliederung* = Wartburg, Walther, *Die Ausgliederung der romanischen Sprachräume*. Bern, 1950.
Weinrich = Weinrich, Harald, *Phonologische Studien zur romanischen Sprachgeschichte* (Forschungen zur romanischen Philologie, Heft. 6). Münster (Westfalen), 1958.
Zamora Vicente = Zamora Vicente, Alonso, *Dialectología española*. Madrid, 1960.

III.—*Reference Grammars and Dictionaries*

Allen & Greenough = *Allen & Greenough's New Latin Grammar*, ed. J. B. Greenough, G. L. Kittredge, A. A. Howard and Benj. L. D'Ooge. Revised edition. Boston, 1903.
Du Cange = Du Cange, D. D., *Glossarium Mediae et Infimae Latinitatis*. 8 vols. Reprint of 1883-87 edition. Graz, 1954.

A SELECTED BIBLIOGRAPHY

LEWIS & SHORT = Lewis, Charlton T. and Short, Charles (ed.), *A Latin Dictionary. Founded on Andrew's Edition of Freund's Latin Dictionary. Revised, enlarged and in great part rewritten.* Oxford, 1958.

MEYER-LÜBKE, REW = Meyer-Lübke, W., *Romanisches etymologisches Wörterbuch.* Heidelberg, 1911.

SCHÖNFELD = Schönfeld, M., *Wörterbuch der altgermanischen Personen- und Völkernamen.* Heidelberg, 1911.

THESAURUS = *Thesaurus Linguae Latinae.* Leipzig, since 1900.

PART I

INTRODUCTION

1. *Nature and Purpose of This Study*

The present study, concerned with the vocalism of Latin Christian Inscriptions from those parts of the Western Roman World where Romance speech developed, [1] is an outgrowth of extensive investigation

---

[1] For the purposes of this study we have limited our field of inquiry to a thorough investigation of the vowels and diphthongs in both stressed and unstressed positions, as a self-contained unit. We are, of course, very much aware of the fact that our material may provide some valuable information in other areas as well, such as, for instance, the local and chronological aspects of such important consonantal phenomena as the voicing of intervocalic stops, palatalization and assibilation, gemination and simplification, the fall of final consonants, etc., even though some of these have already been treated in individual studies (cf. *infra*, footnote #6) and, more recently, have been given a comprehensive treatment in an unpublished PH.D. dissertation by Carl J. Odenkirchen, entitled «The Consonantism of Later Latin Inscriptions: A Contribution to the «Vulgar Latin» Question» (University of North Carolina, 1952).

As to the area of morphology, while no attempt at an organic treatment has been made, some problems involving mainly nominal and verbal endings have been raised, nevertheless, seeing that in the discussion of unstressed vowels in the final syllable these have been dealt with separately, according to whether they appear in morphological or non-morphological endings, cf. *infra*, p. 107.

In view of the strongly formulaic nature of inscriptional material, in general, and ours, in particular, the difficulties involved in obtaining a true picture of the syntactic structure of the Latin language therefrom have already been pointed out by Carnoy, when he said «Les textes épigraphiques offrent bien peu à glaner au point de vue de la syntaxe. C'est qu'ils sont en général très courts et se composent de formules stéréotypées et de noms propres.... Les textes versifiés sont aussi empruntés souvent à des manuels....» (p. 266).

of inscriptional material in connection with a seminar in Vulgar Latin conducted by Professor Mario Pei.

The study of Pompeian graffiti, pagan and Christian inscriptions and other so-called Vulgar Latin documents [2] has made us aware of

---

Information on the vocabulary of Christian inscriptions is given by Betty Knott in «The Christian «Special Language» in the Inscriptions,» *Vigiliae Christianae*, X (1956), 65-79. However, a study of the proper names, especially the Germanic ones, is, to our knowledge, not yet available.

It is our intention to pursue some of these areas further in subsequent studies.

[2] The lack of agreement among Latin and Romance scholars as to the term «Vulgar Latin» is probably best illustrated by the following statement by the British scholar L. R. Palmer, namely «we cannot hope to seize so Protean a phenomenon in a firm terminological grip. Many attempts at definition have been made but «Vulgar Latin» remains a shimmering mirage (p. 149). Cf. this statement with Sittl's definition of more than half a century ago: «Das Vulgärlatein, mit welchem die Latinisten operieren, ist ein Phantasiegebilde» in his *Jahresbericht*, p. 226.

For a critical review of some traditional definitions (among others Grandgent's concept of Vulgar Latin as being «the speech of the middle classes as it grew out of early Classic Latin» (p. 3), suggesting a unified, almost abstract speech form of which the Neo-Latin languages are but a modern phase), as well as an attempt at placing Vulgar Latin in proper perspective, cf. the chapter entitled «Qué é Latim Vulgar» in *História do Latim Vulgar* (pp. 11-37) by the Brazilian scholar Silva Neto. He himself proposes the expressions *latim usual, corrente, cotidiano,* de *conversação* (p. 33) to replace the traditional term of *latim vulgar,* evidently under the influence of the French historian Ferdinand Lot who, in his much quoted article «À quelle époque a-t-on cessé de parler latin?» (*Bulletin Du Cange*, VI (1931), 97-159) suggests that «le latin dit vulgaire c'est le latin parlé, évoluant suivant des lois inconscientes, mais implacables, au cours des siècles. C'est le latin en usage dans toutes les classes de la société, en haut comme au bas de l'échelle, c'est le latin tout court» (p. 102).

For a summary of views on this subject expressed by various scholars within the last two decades, cf. H. Schmeck, *Vulgärlateinische Forschung,* p. 6, footnote #4. The author's comments regarding the lack of agreement on the concept of Vulgar Latin is also of interest: «Abgesehen von Gemeinplätzen.... ist es doch so, dass jeder Forscher auf dem Gebiete des Vlt. zunächst in der Theorie des Begriffes eine Stellung einnimmt, die sich schwerlich mit der gleichgesinnter Weggenossen deckt» (p. 6), and concludes: «eine einheitliche Auffassung ist praktisch unmöglich, weil der Terminus «Vulgärlatein» in Theorie und Begriff allzu sehr schillert. Wo liegen die Grenzen? Wo Anfangs-und Endpunkt?» (p. 7). (Schmeck's monograph also includes a concise summary of the history of Vulgar Latin studies but makes no mention of the important studies by H. F. Muller and his school).

On the occasion of the «centennial» of Vulgar Latin studies, i.e. the publication of Hugo Schuchard's epoch-making *Vokalismus des Vulgärlateins* almost a century ago, the Viennese scholar Johann Sofer published a monograph entitled *Zur Problematik des Vulgärlateins,* a sort of *état de la question,*

INTRODUCTION   23

the importance of documentary research in the field of Romance Philology³ and it was felt that a further investigation of hitherto untapped or, at least, insufficiently studied inscriptional sources might yield some additional data for our knowledge of spoken Latin, especially as far

---

which is all the more interesting since it lists geographically the important centers at which such studies have been and are still being undertaken. Sofer, of course, cannot avoid the controversy surrounding the question of terminology either; in fact, thus the author tells us, one of the first postulates for coping with the whole problem of Vulgar Latin is the necessity of a precise terminology and he suggests emphatically: «man möge nicht mehr den nicht eindeutigen Terminus Vulgärlatein verwenden, sondern statt seiner lieber die Bezeichnung Sprechlatein gebrauchen, als gesprochenes, regional, sozial und temporal differenziertes Latein» (p. 41).

Representing the view of American structuralists is, above all, Leonard Bloomfield who equates Vulgar Latin with a reconstructed Primitive Romance (p. 302); more recently, Robert A. Hall, *Linguistics*, distinguishes between Proto-Italo-Western Romance (so-called «Vulgar Latin») (p. 86) and Proto-Romance, the latter term referring only to the ancestral language reconstructed by the comparative method, while the former to all the everyday language of the Latin speech-community, whether continued in the Romance languages or not» (p. 307).

Granting that the term «Vulgar Latin» indeed refers to the spoken language of the Latin speech-community there cannot, we realize, exist such a thing as a «Vulgar Latin document,» i.e. a text written in Vulgar Latin. The best we can hope for is to find hints as to the true nature of the spoken language through occasional inadvertences or unconscious mistakes of the writer since, as Palmer points out, «the chisel of the stonemason, the pen of the loquacious nun, and the chalk that scribbles on the wall, disregard the tongue and move self-willed in traditional patterns» (*loc. cit.*) and, as Einar Löfstedt reminds us, «even the most uneducated person, as soon as he begins to write, if it be only a letter or a few words on a plastered wall, is directly or indirectly influenced by innumerable literary precedents or reminiscences» (*Late Latin*, p. 15).

In our own study we shall retain the traditional term «Vulgar Latin» which, despite many objections, is nevertheless consecrated by usage and is, furthermore, used by most scholars to whom we shall have occasion to refer throughout this work.

³ Ever since Meyer-Lübke stated his neo-grammarian and reconstructionist stand in his article entitled «Die lateinische Sprache in den romanischen Ländern» in Gustav Gröber, *Grundriss der romanischen Philologie* (Strassburg, 1888), Band I, p. 359, giving documentary research and evidence but a very secondary role (for a full discussion, cf. Silva Neto, pp. 41/42), there has been a controversy between the reconstructionists and those who believe in the primacy of documentary evidence. (For a typical non-reconstructionist stand, cf. Niedermann, *Recueil*, pp. 29/30). For a summary of this controversy, cf. Mohrmann, *Latin vulgaire*, p. 7 ff. and Pei, *Voices*, p. 77 ff. In addition to the bibliographical references found in the works of these scholars, strong reconstructionist postulates have been advanced more recently by Hall, *Linguistics*, p. 307 ff. («The example of the Romance languages show that recon-

as dialectal differences are concerned, along the lines of the works of Sittl, *Die lokalen Verschiedenheiten der lateinischen Sprache,* Carnoy, *Le latin d'Espagne d'après les inscriptions,* Pirson, *La langue des inscriptions de Gaule,* Jeanneret, *La langue des tablettes d'exécration latines,* Väänänen, *Le latin vulgaire des inscriptions pompéiennes,* to name the best-known ones.

The question whether linguistic features that differentiate Romance languages and dialects correspond to dialectal differences already in existence in Vulgar Latin is still one of the most controversial ones that occupy Romance philologists. Many theories have been advanced in this connection, ranging all the way from the belief that dialectal differences in the Romance languages go back to an early stage of Vulgar Latin to that of a fundamental unity of language of the Roman world until well after the end of the Empire.[4]

Not since the work of Sittl on the local differences of the Latin language has, to the best of our knowledge, any comparative *étude d'ensemble* been made on the language of Roman Italy and its Provinces, based primarily on inscriptional material,[5] although comparative studies based exclusively on inscriptional material but restricted to a specific phenomenon have been published in the meantime.[6] Furthermore the studies referred to above generally deal with the Latin of one region only, even though Pirson does attempt to detect local peculiarities within the area of his study.[7] We felt, therefore, that a comparative study based on a given aspect of the language of inscriptions, the vocalism in this instance, may not be superfluous; however,

---

structed proto-languages can be accepted as valid representations of a reality that must have existed, even though we may have no written attestation for them» (p. 309)) and by Maurer, both in his *Gramática* («A fonte mais segura para o conhecimiento do latim vulgar é o conjunto das linguas românicas» (p. 6)) and his *O Problema,* p. 55 ff.

[4] For a discussion of this question and the two extreme views represented by Mohl, *Introduction à la chronologie du latin vulgaire* and Muller, *Chronology of Vulgar Latin,* cf. Vidos, pp. 209-214.

[5] It must be pointed out, however, that Sittl uses both inscriptional and literary sources and that his main objective is to prove the existence of an «African Latin.» In doing so, he bases himself primarily on lexical and syntactical phenomena. For the subsequent refutation of his own thesis and the criticism it aroused, cf. our conclusion, p. 292, footnote # 8.

[6] Diehl on final /m/ in inscriptions; Proskauer on final /s/; Prinz on the treatment of Lat. /ŏ/ and /u/; Cross on syncope.

[7] His conclusions, however, are not conclusive: «....nous sommes forcés d'avouer.... que les résultats obtenus en ce point ne sont pas importants» (p. 324).

in order to avoid any possible duplication with earlier studies and to go beyond a mere re-evaluation of the findings of these scholars, it was thought best to select some primary source that would be both manageable in size and appropriate for such a comparative investigation. Diehl's volumes entitled *Inscriptiones Latinae christianae veteres* seemed to fulfil our purpose particularly well, since, apart from being truly a *Corpus Inscriptionum Christianarum*, it contains inscriptions from all areas of Romania, whereas earlier collections concerned with Christian inscriptions are restricted to specific geographical areas. [8]

Diehl's collection, on which this study is primarily based, consists of three volumes, two of which containing inscriptional material from all regions of Romania where Christian inscriptions were found, numbering well over 5,000 items, [9] including 150 of Jewish origin. Excluding most metrical and official inscriptions on account of their literary nature, [10] we set up a *corpus* of about 4,000 prose inscriptions.

The inscriptional material is divided into two parts. The first, about one fourth of the *corpus*, is entitled *tituli christiani ad res romanas pertinentes* which includes inscriptions «qui christianitatis aliquod prae se ferebant,» to quote Diehl himself. Under fifteen separate headings inscriptions referring to emperors, kings, men of senatorial rank, patricians, members of the military, 'viri honesti, honestae feminae, virgines' and many others are given that show some kind of connection with Christian religion, such as the sign of the cross or any other Christian

---

[8] E. g. those of A. Hübner, *Inscriptiones Hispaniae Christianae* (Berlin, 1871), and *Supplementum* (Berlin, 1900), as well as his *Inscriptiones Britanniae Christianae* (Berlin, 1876); E. LeBlant, *Inscriptions chrétiennes de la Gaule antérieures au VIIIe siècle*, 3 volumes (Paris, 1856-65), and *Nouveau recueil d'inscriptions chrétiennes de la Gaule antérieures au VIIIe siècle* (Paris, 1892); G. B. De Rossi, *Inscriptiones christianae urbis Romae septimo saeculo antiquiores* (Rome, 1861-88).

Hübner's collection of Spanish inscriptions has been brought up-to-date and is now superseded by the Vives collection which is used as primary source for our study of the *Iberian Peninsula*.

[9] Diehl numbers the items from 1 to 5,000, but it must be pointed out that more often than not further inscriptions are given in his notes, which have also been used for this study. (These are given with an «N» after the number of the inscription which is preceded by the letter D for Diehl).

[10] Cf. Vossler-Schmeck, p. 61 and E. Lissberger, *Das Fortleben der römischen Elegiker in den Carmina Epigraphica* (Tübingen, 1934), p. 9.

Literary influences are sometimes also quite evident in prose inscriptions, as when we read 'quam abstulit nefanda dies et atra petitio sua funere mersit immeritam ante tempus' (D4273), strangely reminiscent of Vergil's 'abstulit atra dies, et funere mersit acerbo' (*Aeneid*, VI, 429).

mark (e. g. the Christ monogram ☧ in various forms), proper names, expressions and words used by the Christians, or were otherwise found in Christian cemeteries or affixed to Christian monuments.

The second and more extensive part deals with all *tituli christiani ad res christianas pertinentes*. As in the first part, the inscriptions are not organized topographically [11] but rather according to formulae illustrating «christianorum vita religiosa tam publica et privata quam monasterialis inde a nativitate et baptismate ad mortem sepulturamque christianam et vitam aeternam.» [12]

The third volume of the collection contains extensive indices.

The primary purpose of this study is, then, to investigate dialectal differences as they may be reflected in the vocalism of Latin Christian inscriptions, especially of the funeral type, [13] from those areas of the Western Roman world where Romance speech developed. In addition, since a goodly portion of these inscriptions are dated, [14] an attempt will also be made to establish a chronology of some linguistic changes, to the extent that our material permits it.

2. *Method of Analysis*

Even a cursory reading of inscriptional material from various areas will show a rather striking orthographic unity, also observed in connection with other late Latin documents [15] and forcefully underlined by H. F. Muller in his *Chronology*. Furthermore, since deviations are seldom limited to a particular area, it would seem that the only way in which a meaningful analysis could be made is by determining the frequency of occurrence of certain «mistakes» in one region as against another. Hence, it seemed to us that the most reliable method of analyzing our inscriptional material would be to count all occurrences of each

---

[11] Thus, for instance, in the *Corpus Inscriptionum Latinarum*.
[12] All Latin quotations from Diehl's *Praefatio*, ICLV, Vol. I, p. VIII.
[13] Cf. Vives who states in the Introduction to his collection: «Inscripciones sepulcrales.... son las que mejor manifiestan diferencias locales, esto debido sin duda a su carácter más bien popular» (p. 6).
[14] Dated material represents anywhere from 32 % to 89 % of the total material from a given area. In this material we also include inscriptions that are approximately dated, i.e. which either Diehl or a previous editor have placed in a given century.
[15] Cf. B. Löfstedt, p. 207.

individual phenomenon we propose to study according to classical Latin standards and deviations therefrom. This count is made for vowels and diphthongs in both stressed and unstressed positions and the extent of deviations is then compared among the various areas, together with percentage figures, whenever the number of examples seems to justify the application of such procedure. For the sake of chronology, the numerical analysis is based only on dated material, and, for the convenience of the reader, a tabulation of frequencies is given. Examples implying a deviation from the classical Latin norm also include non-dated inscriptions, both to illustrate further a particular phenomenon observed in dated material and to supplement it. Restored passages and abbreviations are excluded from the count but, otherwise, Diehl's reading (and Vives' for the *Iberian* area) has been accepted throughout.

It must be kept in mind that inscriptional material does not lend itself to numerical analysis as well as a running text of a few hundred or thousand lines, dealing with a particular subject matter, using largely the same type of vocabulary and phraseology, such as a legal or historical document. A statistical evaluation of inscriptional material would seem to pose quite a problem because of the generally stereotyped and formulaic nature of inscriptions, so that in a given area at a given time we may find a score or so inscriptions with the same formula and the frequent occurrence of the same phonemes, while a century later, in the very same area, we may not come upon this formula at all and, hence, find but a few sporadic occurrences of these same phonemes.[16] This is, no doubt, the reason why the validity of evidence of inscriptional studies on a statistical basis has been questioned;[17] nevertheless, we believe that such a method, unsatisfactory as it may seem in relation to its appplication to documentary studies, does have some validity and it is hoped that the present study will have given some demonstration thereof.

Since our study, for the most part, is a factual analysis of inscriptional material, we are not particularly concerned with the reasons that

---

[16] A case in point are the 70 inscriptions from the military cemetery at Concordia (No. Italy) from the IV/V centuries, most of which contain a standard penalty formula: *si quis eam arcam aperire voluerit*, or *molestaverit*, so that we find that in this particular material stressed Latin /ŭ/ in hiatus occurs 101 times and the penult /ĕ/ 26 times, while in our sixth century material, where this formula is not found (there being no inscriptions from Concordia), the same phonemes occur twice and three times, respectively.

[17] Cf. Frieda Politzer in *Romance Trends*, p. 35, where she discusses (and questions) the evidence presented by Proskauer and Cross.

may have led stonecutters to make errors but merely wish to show which are the areas in which they occur most frequently and consistently, with a view to deducing from them regional differences that may have existed in Latin during the period covered by our material, i.e. roughly the fourth, fifth and sixth centuries.

3. *Areas*

In our treatment of the individual areas covered by our study we follow the topographical classification of the *Corpus*. These areas, together with the volume reference of this collection, are the following:

A. *Iberian Peninsula* (CIL II), further subdivided into:
(a) *Baetica,* (b) *Lusitania,* and (c) *Tarraconensis*
B. *Gaul,* comprising
(a) *Gallia Narbonensis* (CIL XII) and (b) *Gallia Lugdunensis* (CIL XIII), in which we include the remaining territory
C. *Italy,* divided into
(a) *Northern* (CIL V), (b) *Central* (CIL XI) and (c) *Southern Italy* (CIL IX, X, XIV)
D. *Rome* (CIL VI)

Here is a more detailed description of individual areas, together with maps showing roughly the boundaries between specific regions within larger areas. (Place-names plotted on the maps are merely given as a *point de repère* and should not be interpreted as locations in which most inscriptions were found. The maps are taken from William R. Shepherd's *Historical Atlas* (9th ed.; New York, 1964), pp. 38/39.

A. *Iberian Peninsula*

1. Lucus Augusti
2. Emerita
3. Corduba
4. Hispalis
5. Nova Carthago
6. Tarraco
7. Caesaraugusta

For our analysis of inscriptional material from this area we have used as primary source the Vives collection of Christian inscriptions from Roman and Visigothic Spain, since it includes about 60 inscriptions not found in Diehl, having been discovered only in 1924 in the Roman-Christian necropolis at Tarragona. [18]

Diehl, as stated earlier, adopts a subject matter criterion for the organization of inscriptional material, whereas Vives orders it both along topographical lines and according to subject matter. Thus, all funeral inscriptions in prose are classified according to regions, whereas non-funeral inscriptions, such as church and monument dedications, are grouped in accordance with subject matter. As to funeral inscriptions in verse, he puts them into a special group because, as he says, they do not offer any local characteristics, either because of their learned nature or because, in many cases, they were not written in the same regions in which they were found. [19]

In connection with funeral inscriptions in prose, Vives divides the Spanish area into two major geographical zones, the Western and the Eastern, based largely on the use of the Spanish era as a dating device, [20] which was used exclusively in the Western zone, whereas in the East it does not appear before the year 800 A. D. In fact, the few specifically dated inscriptions that we find in the Eastern zone during the Roman and Visigothic periods are dated according to consular year. Another criterion for this division of the Spanish area is the use of the epithet *famulus* or *famula Dei* (or *Domini* or *Christi*) applied to the deceased in the Western zone, whereas in the Eastern zone it is not found.

These two zones are further subdivided into four regions, corresponding to the respective Roman provinces of *Lusitania*, *Baetica* and *Tarraconensis*, while *Gallaecia* is given a special place, despite the very small number of inscriptions found there, because of the dating by era and some of the formulae characteristic of the Western zone, even

---

[18] Cf. Vives, p. 5.

[19] Cf. Vives, p. 6.

[20] It is a characteristic feature of Spanish Christian epigraphy to date inscriptions with reference to a specific date, rather than with reference to consuls or emperors in office, as it was customary in Rome and other provinces of the Empire. The Spanish era refers back to the year 38 B.C., so that, for instance, *aera* (more commonly spelled *era*) DLIIII would mark the year 516 A.D., rather than 554 A.D. Cf. Vives, «Características hispanas de las inscripciones visigodas,» *Arbor*, II, (March-April 1944), p. 186 ff.

though it seems to partake of some of the features found in the *Tarraconensis* as well, particularly as regards the hesitation between *recessit, requievit in pace* and *hic requiescit*, the first one in use in *Baetica*, the second mostly in *Lusitania* and the third in *Tarraconensis*. [21]

We have adopted for our study the topological classification for both funeral and non-funeral inscriptions, except that we have included *Gallaecia* in our discussion of *Lusitania*, both because of the paucity of material from that area and the obvious influence of the Western zone.

Our *corpus* of inscriptions from this area, totalling 362 items, is broken down as follows:

		Dated	Non-dated	Percentage of dated material
(a)	Baetica	90	22	80.3 %
(b)	Lusitania	93	11	89.4 %
(c)	Tarraconensis	114	32	78.0 %

In view of the small number of dated inscriptions in the centuries preceding the sixth, in general, and the exceedingly small number of specifically dated inscriptions from *Tarraconensis*, in particular, we decided

(a) to treat all dated inscriptions of the fourth, fifth and sixth centuries as one group and reserve separate treatment only to inscriptions of the seventh century.

(b) to include in our dated material the funeral inscriptions (all in prose) found at *Tarragona* and presumed to originate from between the fourth and the early sixth centuries. [22]

Our material from this area also includes a special group of Visigothic coin inscriptions. [23] Generally speaking, these are very short and

---

[21] Cf. Vives, pp. 8/9.
[22] Cf. Vives, pp. 59/60. This scholar further notes that the majority of Christian epitaphs from the Tarraconensis area come from the *Tarragona* cemetery (p. 6).
[23] The selection of about 40 Visigothic coin inscriptions in the Vives collection was made by F. Mateu y Llopis, from both his own *Catálogo* and the work by A. Heiss, *Description générale des monnaies des rois visigoths d'Espagne*, Paris, 1872.
The most recent work on the coinage of the Visigoths of Spain is that of George C. Miles (cf. Bibliography).

merely give the name of the king under whom the coin was minted, the place where this was done (but not always) and an epithet such as *pius, inclitus* or *iustus* applied to the king.

B. *Gaul*

1. Colonia Agrippina
2. Mogontiacum
3. Augusta Treverorum
4. Lutetia
5. Vesontio
6. Lugdunum
7. Vienna
8. Massilia
9. Tolosa
10. Burdigalia
11. Augustonemetum

The *Corpus* devotes two volumes to the area of *Gaul*. CIL XII comprises the *Narbonensis,* while CIL XIII includes the *Lugdunensis, Aquitania, Belgica* and *Germania Superior* and *Inferior*. For the sake of convenience, we have designated this region simply as *Lugdunensis*. Furthermore, since Christian inscriptions from the two *Germaniae* are quite few (at least as far as their inclusion in the Diehl collection is concerned) they were not included in our count, unless originating in a place where Romance speech developed.

The breakdown of the total of 480 inscriptions from this area is as follows:

Area	Dated	Non-Dated	Percentage of dated material
(a) *Narbonensis*	104	110	48.5 %
(b) *Lugdunensis*	84	182	31.3 %

Our material from this area is divided into IV/V and VI/VII centuries, although the bulk of dated material comes from the fifth and sixth centuries. Material from both the fourth and seventh centuries is very scanty.

C. *Italy*

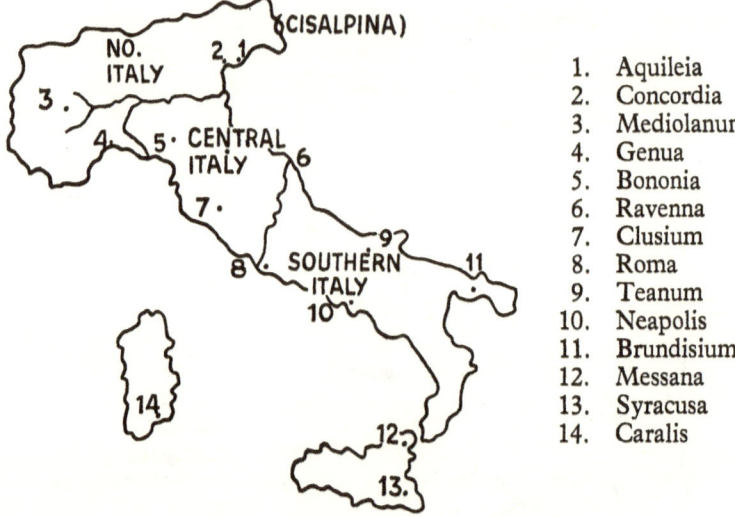

1. Aquileia
2. Concordia
3. Mediolanun
4. Genua
5. Bononia
6. Ravenna
7. Clusium
8. Roma
9. Teanum
10. Neapolis
11. Brundisium
12. Messana
13. Syracusa
14. Caralis

We have divided the Italian area into a *Northern, Central* and *Southern* region. (*Rome* is dealt with as a separate area, cf. *infra*). The *Northern* region, the *Cisalpina*, is included in CIL V and takes in *Liguria, Transpadana* and *Venetia*; the *Central* region with which CIL XI is concerned, includes *Aemilia, Etruria* and *Umbria*; finally, the *Southern* region includes inscriptions scattered over three volumes of the *Corpus*, CIL IX comprising *Calabria, Apulia, Samni* and *Picenum*, CIL X the regions of *Lucania, Campania, Sicilia* and *Sardinia*, and CIL XIV ancient *Latium*.

The grand total of 1183 inscriptions used from this general area is broken down as follows:

Area	Dated	Non-dated	Percentage of dated material
(a) Northern	190	228	45.4 %
(b) Central	127	153	45.3 %
(c) Southern	155	330	31.8 %

It will be noted from our tables that the inscriptional material from the *Northern* area is divided into IV/V and VI centuries, whereas inscriptions from the *Central* and *Southern* areas cover three periods, III/IV, V and VI/VII centuries.

INTRODUCTION 33

Actually, we do not have any specifically dated inscriptions from the *Northern* area before the fifth century, but we included in this material about 70 items from the military cemetery at *Concordia* (cf. # 2 on map), discovered in 1873 and said to date back to the end of the fourth and the first half of the fifth centuries, before it was taken and destroyed by the hordes of Attila in 452 A. D.[24] The few inscriptions from this necropolis that are specifically dated go back to the fifth century.

A somewhat similar situation obtains in the *Central* area where we did not find any specifically dated inscriptions from the third century but 18 inscriptions from the *St. Catherine* cemetery at *Clusium* (# 7 on the map), the modern *Chiusi*, are said to date back to the third century.[25] Our III/IV century material from this area also includes 9 epitaphs from the *S. Mustiola* cemetery at the same location, dating back to the fourth century.[26]

In the *Southern* area we found one dated item from the third century. Inscriptions from the seventh century from both the *Central* and *Southern* areas total about half a dozen.

D. *Rome*

If for no other reason, the supply of inscriptional material from this area would seem to justify its separate treatment. Of a total of 1818 inscriptions that we studied, 744 are dated, i.e. 42.0 % dated material. As will be seen from our tables, the third and fourth centuries have been treated as one group, since only 20 inscriptions were found in the former. The sixth and seventh centuries are also taken together, since we found only three inscriptions attributed to the latter century.

It may be of interest to note that in this particular area the bulk of dated inscriptions come from the fourth century with 393 epitaphs, decreasing to 229 and 99 in the fifth and sixth centuries, respectively,

---

[24] Cf. Pauly-Wissowa, IV, p. 831.
[25] Cf. *ibid.*, p. 118.
[26] On the importance of *Clusium* as one of the oldest cities in *Etruria*, Pauly-Wissowa makes the following statements which are of interest: «Zeugnis von der Bedeutung und Grösse der Stadt gibt aber vor allem die ausgedehten Nekropole.... (es sind) gegen 3000 etruskische Inschriften bekannt.... Das Christentum fand früh in C. Eingang.... Von den zwei unterirdischen Coemeterien die in der Nähe von C. gefunden sind, geht das Coem. S. Mustiolae ins 4. das von S. Caterina sogar ins 3. Jhd. zurück» (*loc. cit.*).

while in the other areas the bulk of dated material is found in either the fifth or sixth centuries. Furthermore, except for the *Iberian Peninsula,* the number of dated or even approximately dated inscriptions from the seventh century is so small as to be practically negligible.

It is, of course, outside the scope of this study to investigate the possible causes for this sharp decline in inscriptional material at about the end of the sixth century, but it would seem that the Germanic invasions of *Gaul* and *Italy* and the concomitant decline of Latin culture may have had something to do with it,[27] while in the *Iberian Peninsula,* due to the strong Roman-Visigothic monarchy, Latin tradition and culture survived until the early eighth century.

4. *The Value of Inscriptional Material in General and Christian Inscriptions in Particular*

At the head of the preface to his *magnum opus,* his *Handbuch der altkristlichen Epigraphik,* C. M. Kaufmann quotes the great German historian, Theodor Mommsen, as follows:

> Die Inschriften gehoren mit geringen Ausnahmen nicht der Literatur an, sondern dem Leben.

Few scholars, we believe, will deny the value of inscriptions as the oldest extant evidence for ancient forms of the Latin language and as a source of information on Geography, History or Chronology serving to supplement the records supplied by Latin literature. In fact, many details on the daily life of the ancient world have come to our notice through inscriptions and we must remember that their language is more closely connected with that of ordinary life than with that of literature.[28]

---

[27] On the decline of Roman schools in *Gaul* in the sixth century, cf. Michel Glatigny, *Histoire de l'enseignement en France* (Paris, 1949), p. 9 ff.
On the barbaric conditions in Italy from the end of the sixth century on, as the result of the invasion of the Lombards, cf. H. I. Marrou, *A History of Education in Antiquity,* trans. George Lamb (New York, 1964), p. 461.

[28] Cf. Väänänen, *Inscriptions.* Speaking of the Pompeian *graffiti* he says that their number which exceeds 5,000 «constituent un monument unique de la vie ordinaire» (p. 17).
In the same vein also Pirson: «Depuis que l'on possède cette vaste collection de documents épigraphiques, mise à la disposition des érudits par le

INTRODUCTION   35

The merit of having recognized the importance of the analysis of the language of inscriptions for the study of spoken Latin of all periods belongs to Hugo Schuchardt who, speaking of inscriptions in connection with various direct sources of knowledge of Vulgar Latin, makes the following statement:

> Beiläufig sei gesagt, dass von allen Inschriften die christlichen für die Erforschung des Plebejerlateins die wichtigsten sind. Die Eigenthümlichkeiten desselben treten in ihnen stärker und häufiger, als in den heidnischen, hervor. (*Vokalismus*, I, p. 12).

Apart from recognizing the necessity of treating pagan and Christian inscriptional material separately,[29] he has opened the way to critical linguistic studies, of which Diehl's *De m-finali epigraphica* has been considered as a model.[30] Just how strongly this latter feels about inscriptional sources is well illustrated by the opening sentence of his *prooemium*

> Linguae latinae ad linguas romanenses paulatim progredientis fontem nec graviorem nec certiorem habemus quam inscriptiones (p. 5).

As regards the separate treatment of Latin pagan and Christian epigraphy and the tenor of both kinds of inscriptions, Pirson is most informative when he says

> On doit.... distinguer les inscriptions païennes des inscriptions chrétiennes. Les premières disparaissent généralement dès le IVe siècle, tandis que les dernières ne commencent à se répandre en Gaule qu'à partir de la même époque, se multiplient

---

Corpus Inscriptionum Latinarum, les inscriptions sont devenues pour l'histoire des institutions romaines une source abondante de renseignements précieux. Leur importance au point de vue de la langue et spécialement de la langue parlée, dont elles sont une source directe, a été de même généralement reconnue» (p. VII).

In his *Der kulturgeschichtliche Wert der römischen Inschriften* (Hamburg, 1887), A. Zimmermann states that tomb inscriptions are the best evidence for knowing something about the turn of mind of the people and sums up his views, as follows: «Das ganze Volk kommt bei ihnen zum Ausdruck (Armen, Ungebildeten, Sklaven mehr als Reiche)» (p. 4).

[29] Cf. also Bloch, p. 9.
[30] Cf. Väänänen, *Inscriptions*, p. 19.

surtout pendant les Ve et VIe siècles et se prolongent jusqu'au VIIe.... (p. IX). [31]

As to the difference in language, we may again quote Pirson:

> La langue des documents païens n'est certainement plus du latin classique, mais la langue des textes chrétiens est encore bien plus altérée.... Les inscriptions chrétiennes, comme tous les documents de l'époque mérovingienne, à cause de leur date relativement récente, doivent donc être étudiées principalement au point de vue de la transformation du latin en roman. Elles ont encore sur les marbres païens l'avantage d'être très fréquemment datées et de fournir ainsi des points de repère d'une certitude absolue. (p. X).

In the same vein, LeBlant tells us that

> Nulle part mieux que dans nos inscriptions chrétiennes ne se montrent les façons de dire, la prononciation de nos pères. (p. 79).

Nevertheless, from a philological point of view, inscriptions have not escaped the critic's eye and limitations on their value have been pointed out more than once. For one thing, the variety of language is quite restricted and, except for metric inscriptions which are influenced to a large extent by literary and poetic traditions, they very often are made up of little more than traditional formulae, proper names, abbreviations, etc. Yet, even the severest critics admit that with a sufficient body of material it is often possible to cull some interesting information as to the state of the spoken language. [32]

---

[31] Although this statement specifically refers to the situation in *Gaul*, it is, we believe, applicable to all areas where Christian inscriptions were found, the more so since social and ideological changes were not restricted to specific localities but were universal in the Christian world, bringing about the same or, at least, similar changes in textual content. Even in the city of the Catacombs, funeral inscriptions do not appear in great number until the fourth century. Further on this subject, P. L. Zovatto, *Antiche iscrizioni cristiane* (Firenze, 1949), p. 10.

[32] Representative of this critical view is that expressed by Kroll: «Auch von den Inschriften darf man nicht viel erwarten. Die Mehrzahl besteht aus Namen und typischen Formeln, welche eine Entfaltung von Dialekticismen keinen Spielraum bieten; die wenigen etwas gesprachigeren sind meist ebenso wenig unbefangen wie die Erzeugnisse der Literatur, schon deshalb nicht, weil sie gewöhlich metrisch sind, also sich an die vorhandene Dichtersprache an-

Another limitation placed upon the value of inscriptional material —which, incidentally, it shares with other documentary evidence— is that certain spellings may not at all represent actual pronunciation but may be rather due to stereotyped orthography, much like French *eau* represents the phoneme /o/ in the modern language, while reflecting a former state. Furthermore, the possibility of spelling mistakes due to negligence or ignorance on the part of the stonecutter must also be taken into account and there is always the danger that the meticulous researcher may read into them more than he is entitled to.

Lastly, we must be on our guard concerning inscriptions found in one locality but actually composed in another,[33] seeing that some stonecutters may have got around in the world.[34] In this case, of course, the linguistic phenomenon would not be characteristic of the locality where the inscription was found; however, it would be safe to assume that these are rather exceptional cases and, at any rate, would involve inscriptions of a more learned nature, so that when all the material concerning a particular locality has been gathered, the danger of ascribing too much importance to such isolated instances would be reduced to a minimum.

All things considered and placing in the balance the merits and limitations of inscriptional material, the conclusion reached by Cross in his apology entitled «The Value of the Evidence from Inscriptions» (in his *Syncope*) seems to be justified:

> With all their shortcomings, there is no denying that for a study of ordinary, spoken Latin, the inscriptions are the best foundation we have. (p. 97).

---

lehnen. Trotzdem bleibt ein ganz ansehnlicher Rest, der Abweichungen von der Schriftsprache bietet, aber von diesen ist ein Theil über das ganze Sprachgebiet verbreitet, d.h. allgemein romanisch, ein anderer auf ein oder einige Individuen beschränkt» (p. 573). For a similar view also cf. W. Meyer-Lübke, «Die lateinische Sprache in den romanischen Ländern,» p. 357.

[33] Cf. Vives: «....las inscripciones métricas.... en general tampoco ofrecen características locales determinadas, ya sea a causa de su carácter erudito, ya porque en no pocos casos la inscripción no fue escrita en la misma localidad o región en donde ha sido encontrada, o donde estaría colocada. Así, por ejemplo, sabemos que el epitafio del abad Victoriano, del monasterio de Asán, Huesca, fue escrito por Venancio Fortunato de las Galias» (p. 6).

[34] Cf. Schuchardt: «Die Schreiber und Steinmetzen mochten viel in der Welt herumkommen» (I, p. 92).

The fact that inscriptions can be of help to us in the study of the spoken language does not, of course, mean that the writer or stonecutter of a particular epitaph intentionally wishes to write the way he speaks. But there is no doubt either that a person with insufficient education and training in the written language will make mistakes that may reveal something about his spoken language. This is clearly pointed out by Silva Neto (p. 100) who tells the story of a tailor who placed a sign over his shop reading: «Alfaiataria e *ropas feitas*,» instead of the correct spelling *roupas*. His comment concerning this form is the following:

> Não sei se o escrevedor dessa frase tinha, sob as vistas, o vocábulo correto *roupas;* é, porém fora de duvida, que êle, não sendo muito instruído, deixou levar-se pela pronúncia comum do ditongo «ou» que é «ô» (*ibid.*).

It would not be difficult to gather a substantial body of such spelling errors. The sign in the window of the small restaurant-bar on Bloomfield Avenue announcing *roust-beef* sandwiches and that of the clothing shop advertising *bargins* would seem to follow pronunciation rather than traditional orthography and even the college student who writes *frigatives* reveals the sonorizing trend of intervocalic voiceless stops in some American dialects. [35]

An example or two will further illustrate this point. In its November 1962 issue the French magazine *Réalités* reproduces (p. 59) a Cuban revolutionary poster on which forms like *puevlo* (= *pueblo*) and *venseremo* (= *venceremos*) can be read. These forms give rather clear evidence not only of the universal Spanish phenomenon of a single voiced bilabial phoneme, in contrast with the majority of Romance languages and dialects which keep voiced bilabial and labio-dental phonemes apart, [36] but also of such regional features as a single voiceless sibilant where the Spanish of Central and Northern Spain has two phonemes: (a) a voiceless interdental fricative /θ/ and (b) an

---

[35] Cf. Charles F. Hockett, *A Course in Modern Linguistics* (New York, 1958), p. 65.

[36] Cf. Jungemann, p. 336 ff.

apico-alveolar voiceless sibilant /ṡ/,[37] as well as the fall of final /s/ which, among other areas, is particularly widespread in *Cuban* speech, although it is considered to be a vulgarism.[38]

In order, however, not to think that this is a particularly isolated case, may we be permitted to mention also a semi-official document issued at Camagüey to a Cuban refugee friend of ours shortly before he left his country, which contains such «linguistic gems» as *cacilla* (= *casilla*), *liberta* (= *libertad*) and *por los mimo motibo* (= *mismos motivos*). The first word would seem to illustrate an obvious reverse spelling due to the merger of the interdental fricative and voiceless sibilant in non-Castilian speech; the second one the fall of final /d/ in the speech of the uneducated.[39] In the phrase *por los mimo motibo,* the word *mimo* shows both the fall of final /s/, already referred to, as well as the fall of /s/ before a consonant (cf. our footnote # 38), while *motibo,* in addition to the fall of final /s/, gives further evidence of the orthographic confusion of *b* and *v,* both of which stand for the bilabial phoneme /b/. On the other hand, the influence of schooling is evident in *los mimo,* where the pre-consonantal /s/ is graphically represented, although not pronounced.

Granted that these *are* spelling mistakes, do they not reflect actual pronunciation and might we not assume that similar mistakes made by a semi-literate writer or stonecutter are acceptable evidence of popular speech habits?

Speaking of the evidence furnished by spelling in the study of Middle English pronunciation, G. L. Brook seems to afford a golden mean in the much debated question of the value of written documents when he states

> .... there is much difference of opinion about the value that can be attached to occasional variations of spelling. It is unsafe to draw conclusions about pronunciation from single occasional spellings, but when a particular spelling occurs in several independent documents it is reasonable to use it as evidence.[40]

---

[37] Regarding the phenomenon in Spanish America and Southern Spain, cf. Jungemann, p. 96 ff.
[38] Cf. Navarro Tomás, p. 110, for the fall of syllable-final /s/ before a consonant and in final position.
[39] *Ibid.,* p. 103.
[40] *A History of the English Language* (New York, 1964), p. 57.

It is in the light of this good advice that we have attempted to learn something about the vocalism of Latin Christian inscriptions, in the hope that this modest undertaking may be a further contribution to our knowledge of this «Protean phenomenon» called Vulgar Latin.

Part II

ORTHOGRAPHY AND PHONOLOGY

Chapter I: The Accented Vowels

1. *Latin /ā/ and /ă/, represented by the letter a*

Grandgent states that «*A* regularly remained unchanged in the greater part of the Empire.... But in Gaul, especially in the North, it probably had a forward pronunciation tending somewhat toward ę» (p. 82). This palatal articulation of Latin /ă/ in Gaul is also mentioned by Vossler-Schmeck (p. 89), but neither of these scholars notes any other change in the pronunciation to the effect that Latin /ă/ may have had a pronunciation in the late Vulgar Latin period different from that in the so-called classical period.

Our inscriptional material gives no evidence of any change of Latin /ă/ in both open and closed syllables.[1]

2. *Latin /ĕ/, represented by the letter e*

Pei, *Texts*, finds that in his eighth century documents from Northern France «short *e*, which gave rise to the Romance open *e* and to

---

[1] The form *quem* for *quam*, i.e. the masculine form of the relative pronoun used with a feminine antecedent, which we find in all areas under investigation, would appear to be a morpho-syntactic substitution rather than a phonological change of /a/ to /e/. Cf. Diphthong /aj/, p. 246.

In an inscription from *Northern Italy* we read *Ehuderico* (D2740) for what we would expect to be *Eutharico*, i.e. the ablative case of *Eutharicus*, the *nomen* of the consul *Fl. Euthāricus Cillica* (a. 519). This name, which appears to be of Germanic origin, variously appears as *Eutaricus*, *Eutericus* and *Ehudericus* in both inscriptions and documents, according to Schönfeld (p. 82).

the diphthong *ie*, does not undergo any appreciable change» (p. 18) but notes some sporadic changes of Latin /ĕ/ to /i/ in other texts of the Vulgar Latin period. Grandgent holds that «short *e*, which was pronounced ę remained unchanged» (p. 84), while both Schuchardt and Nyrop (quoted in Pei, *Texts*, p. 19) point out the exceptional and sporadic nature of the change of Latin /ĕ/. Vossler-Schmeck merely state that «ę bleibt» (p. 89), while both Väänänen and Battisti make no mention of any change that Latin /ĕ/ may have undergone in the Vulgar Latin period. In fact, the latter expressly states that «il dittongo neolatino *ie*... non è documentato nel periodo latino» (p. 100).

The evidence from our inscriptional material is as follows:

2.1 Open Syllable

A. Iberian Peninsula

Area	Century	/ĕ/>e	/ĕ/>i
Baetica	IV-VI	5	0
	VII	8	0
Lusitania	IV-VI	10	0
	VII	2	0
Tarraconensis	IV-VI	9	0
	VII	2	0

An *ae* spelling for *e* was found in the form *quaeritur* (V276 a. 550) for *queritur* (from *queror*), which would seem to be indicative of the merger of the Latin diphthong /aj/, spelled *ae*, and Latin /ĕ/. Cf. Diphthongs, p. 240 ff. The fact that in the same inscription we also find *querunt* for *quaerunt* (from *quaero*), would seem to strengthen this hypothesis.

B. Gaul

Area	Century	/ĕ/>e	/ĕ/>i
Narbonensis	IV-V	6	0
	VI-VII	25	0
Lugdunensis	IV-V	2	0
	VI-VII	10	0

THE ACCENTED VOWELS   43

In non-dated material from this latter area, we read *braevis* (D3489) for *brevis*, an apparent reverse spelling.

C. *Italy*

Area	Century	/ĕ/>e	/ĕ/>i
Northern	IV-V	23	1
	VI	12	0
Central	III-IV	5	0
	V	9	0
	VI-VII	14	0
Southern	III-IV	16	0
	V	8	0
	VI-VII	17	0

The deviation in the *Northern* area occurs in the form *muniribus* (D3454 a. 488) for *muneribus*.

In non-dated material from this area we also find a form *baenae* (D439) for *bene*.

D. *Rome*

Century	/ĕ/>e	/ĕ/>i
III-IV	71	0
V	33	0
VI-VII	18	0

In non-dated material we find a few instances of reverse spelling, e. g. *aeques* (D278), *aequitum* (D525, attributed to the Diocletian era) and *praetium* (D3813).

2.2 Closed Syllable

A. *Iberian Peninsula*

Area	Century	/ĕ/>e	/ĕ/>i	/ĕ/>ie
Baetica	IV-VI	48	0	0
	VII	32	0	1 ?

Area	Century	/ĕ/>e	/ĕ/>i	/ĕ/>ie
Lusitania	IV-VI	51	0	0
	VII	6	0	0
Tarraconensis	IV-VI	18	0	0
	VII	7	0	0

The spelling *ie* for *e* appears in the form *era.... curriente* (V163 a. 682) in Vives' reading of this inscription. However, this form may not be conclusive as to the diphthongization of Latin /ĕ/, seeing that the facsimile of the original stone [2] reads CURRENTE, with the downstroke of the first letter R slightly lengthened at the top, which this scholar interprets as an attempt to show a letter *i* in hiatus.[3] Two other instances of this same formula, i. e. *era.... currente* (V172 a. 649, *Baetica* and V315 a. 737, *Tarraconensis*), give no evidence of any diphthongization.

B. *Gaul*

Area	Century	/ĕ/>e	/ĕ/>i	/ĕ/>ie
Narbonensis	IV-V	16	1	0
	VI-VII	46	0	0
Lugdunensis	IV-V	19	0	0
	VI-VII	29	1	0

---

[2] Reproduced in Hübner, IHC 378.

[3] Vives states in effect: «con el palo vertical de la primera R expresamente alargado, sin duda para indicar una I en nexo» (p. 51). Hübner transcribes this form as *cuirrente*, with the following comment: «I et R coniunctis, videtur error lapicidae esse pro currente; nisi significare voluit qui sculpsit currente, Hispanum corriendo.» We found a similar case of an extended down-stroke in HOMNES (IHC 490) which would seem to be a graphic device to save space and in which the «palo alargado,» to borrow Vives' phrase, would indicate that between the letters *m* and *n*, there is to be read a letter *i*. Inscriptions abound in abbreviations and ligatures but there is lack of evidence of other instances where hiatus *i* is represented in a similar fashion. Furthermore, one may wonder why the down-stroke of the first letter R should have been lengthened, rather than that of the second one, assuming that the stonecutter was indeed attempting to show a diphthong. Seeing that this particular inscription is not included in the Diehl collection, we, unfortunately, do not have the benefit of this eminent scholar's interpretation of his phenomenon.

The only deviation in the *Narbonensis* area occurs in the form *Fisto* (D2454 a. 472), the ablative case of the proper name *Festus*, while in the *Lugdunensis* we found the form *violintia* (D1676 a. 552) for *violentia*.

Noting that Latin /ĕ/ is occasionally rendered by the letter *i* in inscriptions from Gaul, Pirson states the following:

> ....il importe de remarquer que la permutation se produit dans des conditions spéciales, sous l'influence des phénomènes environnants. Ainsi l'*e* ouvert devient *i* dans les mots où il est suivi d'un *jod* qui, selon les lois de l'*umlaut* ou *inflexion*, peut élever d'un degré la qualité de cet *e* ouvert et en faire une voyelle fermée. D'où les graphies en *i*.... Un phénomène analogue se produit lorsque l'*e* ouvert est suivi de *n* ou de *m*, surtout quand ces consonnes sont elles mêmes suivies d'une autre.... (p. 6).

C. *Italy*

Area	Century	/ĕ/>e	/ĕ/>i	/ĕ/>ie
Northern	IV-V	76	0	0
	VI	30	0	0
	III-IV	35	0	0
Central	V	17	0	0
	VI-VII	30	0	0
	III-IV	32	0	0
Southern	V	20	0	0
	VI-VII	49	0	0

In non-dated material from the *Northern* area we found one in which Latin /ĕ/ is rendered by the letter *i*, namely *recisit* (D4398A) for *recessit*. In one instance it is rendered by *a*, in *kalandas September* (D1361A) for *kalendas*. The form *calandae* is mentioned by Lindsay as being «the Vulgar Latin form of *calendae*,» stating that, «it may be a I Conj. Gerundive form» (p. 23).

In our non-dated material from the *Southern* area, the form *kalendas* once appears as *kalindas* (D2812).

D. *Rome*

Century	/ĕ/>e	/ĕ/>i	%	/ĕ/>ie
III-IV	264	4	(1.4)	0
V	92	1	(1.0)	0
VI-VII	33	0		0

The four deviations in third/fourth century material area *siptim* (D645N a. 386), *decissit* (D2816 a. 341), *Valinte* (D4219 a. 376) and *siptimu* (D4379 a. 386).

In fifth century material we read [*bene*] *mirinti* (D2631C a. 405) for *benemerenti* and *praesbiter* (D1131 a. 405) for *presbyter*.

In non-dated material, there are a few instances of Latin /ĕ/ represented by *i*, namely *innocintem* (D2378), *benemerinti* (D2611C), *parinti* (D2614B), *merinti* (D414) and *Oristis* (D2825).

Concerning the change of Latin /ĕ/ to /i/ before the consonant combination /nt/, cf. Lindsay, p. 23, where he also states that «other consonant combinations may have influenced *e* towards the close e-sound or the i-sound. [4]

Our evidence concerning the sporadic change of Latin /ĕ/ to /i/ would indicate that it is most likely to occur in closed syllable, especially before the consonant combination /nt/. As to the single example of this change in open syllable (*muniribus*), it may be due to analogy with other third declension dative/ablative forms, e.g. *martiribus*. (For Greek epsilon rendered by /i/, cf. Appendix Probi «*cyrus* non *cirus*» (28) and Väänänen, p. 38).

Regarding the matter of diphthongization, there is no clear-cut evidence of this phenomenon in our inscriptional material.

2.3 Latin /ĕ/ in Monosyllables (Including Prepositions and Conjunctions)

Sporadic changes of Latin /ĕ/ to /i/ may be observed in a few instances, especially in connection with the conjunction *et*.

---

[4] For a different view, cf. Pisani, *Testi*, p. 128, where, in connection with the form *merinti*, he states: «*e*>*i* avanti *n* e caso rarissimo; si trattera piuttosto di scrittura inversa per *en* da *in*, p. es. in *Corintus* Dv. 92 (=Diehl, *Vulgärlateinische Inschriften* #92 — parenthesis is ours), *Corento* Dv. 1268, *Perento* Dv. 1392 e cfr. it. *venta* (Guittone d'Arezzo) < *vincta*, *lengua* (Bonvesin) < *lingua*, *enfençe* (Ugoccione da Lodi) < *-fingit* ecc.»

A. *Iberian Peninsula*

Throughout our material, both dated and non-dated, Latin /ĕ/ in monosyllabic words always appears represented by *e*.

B. *Gaul*

Area	Century	et /ĕ/>e	et /ĕ/>i	other /ĕ/>e	other /ĕ/ i
Narbonensis	IV-V	15	0	5	0
	VI-VII	28	1	3	1
Lugdunensis	IV-V	17	0	2	0
	VI-VII	10	0	2	0

Deviations in the *Narbonensis* area are the following:

> *vices* (= *vicies*) *it ter* (D3279 a. 564) *quim rapuit mors* (D4729 a. 577)

C. *Italy*

We found no deviation in dated material in any of the three areas under study.

In non-dated material, we found in the *Northern* area the forms *aet* (D4451A), *quaen* (= *quem*) (D4283) and *it* (D4586), while in the *Southern* area *it* for *et* appeared once, side by side with *et*, in *bixsit annos cinque et meses set. it diebus dece* (D4580).

D. *Rome*

Century	et /ĕ/>e	et /ĕ/>i	%	other /ĕ/>e	other /ĕ/>i
III-IV	197	5	1.9	16	0
V	87	0		6	0
VI-VII	27	0		7	0

In non-dated material we found the following forms:

> *ist* (D314), *it* (3663A), *cuin* (= *quem*) (D4277A) *cun quin* (but also *cun quen* in the same inscriptions) (D4322), *quaem* (D3727F), *aet* (D3728)

The instances in which Latin /ĕ/ is represented by *ae*, would appear to be obvious reverse spellings. For the spelling *it* for *et*, cf. Pisani, *Testi*, p. 165, where the suggestion is put forward that the change of /ĕ/ to /i/ may be due to proclitic position, in accordance with the general confusion of these vowels in unstressed syllable. This hypothesis, it would seem, might also be extended to such forms as *quin* and *ist*, which, for reasons of sentence stress, could be considered as being in unstressed position, e.g.

> *rebus ist humanis subtracta* (D314), *cun quin vixit ann* (D4322), etc....

2.4 Latin /ĕ/ in hiatus

In our whole material, we found a single instance in which Latin /ĕ/ in hiatus is rendered by the letter *i*. This occurs in a plural neuter nominative form *ia* for *ea*, in the phrase *qi ia* (i.e. *arcuselia*) *aperire voluei* (= *voluerit*) (D716), in fourth/fifth century material from the *Northern Italian* area. There are 48 correct occurrences of this vowel in the same material and we also find the form *ea* (= *eam*) in the same inscription.

There are a few instances of apparent reverse spelling in non-dated material from *Rome*, e.g. *daeo* (3366B), *Laea* (D3890E), etc.

3. Latin /ē/, represented by the letter e

«Long *e* —Grandgent informs us— which was pronounced *ẹ*, probably remained unchanged in Vulgar Latin, at least in most regions» (p. 83). He further notes, however, that «*I* is very often used for *ē* in inscriptions and late writings» (*ibid.*) and gives a number of examples, among others the form *ficet* from a third century inscription from *Spain*, adding that «these spellings are due in the main to the identity of *ē* and *ĭ* in late pronunciation» (*ibid.*) The «close relation between ĭ and *e* (close *e*)» is also mentioned by Lindsay (p. 29) and summed up by Pirson, as follows:

THE ACCENTED VOWELS 49

> Le vocalisme des documents latins des derniers siècles se caractérise surtout par l'assimilation des sons *e* et *i* et surtout de l'*ē* fermé avec l'*ĭ* bref, dont la parenté est déjà attestée par les grammairiens du IVe siècle. La tendance de l'*ē* à passer à *ĭ* s'est accentuée toujours davantage et c'est ce qui explique la richesse des graphies, où ce phénomène apparaît, dans le domaine des inscriptions de la Gaule (p. 2).

Väänänen reports the form *filix* for *felix* as being already attested in Pompeian inscriptions, but adds that «les graphies *i* pour *ē* .... sont rares avant l'époque tardive» (p. 36) whithout, however, specifying what he means by «époque tardive.» Pei, *Texts*, finds that the «change of accented long *e* to *i* in the spelling of the Eighth Century Documents.... is one of the most noteworthy characteristics of these texts» (p. 20) where, in one group of his documents, he finds a 46 % deviation, while finding only a few cases of the opposite change, i.e. Latin /ĭ/ represented by *e* (p. 25), and he concludes that «the pronunciation of the two vowels, coalescing at an uncertain, but undoubtedly much earlier period, resulted in a very closed *e*, whose timbre approached that of *i* rather than that of *e*, and probably closely resembled that of modern Italian closed *e*» (p. 27).

For the beginnings of the orthographic confusion of *e* and *i*, which he places in the second century A.D., cf. Battisti, p. 98.

Our own evidence shows the following:

3.1 Open Syllable

A. *Iberian Peninsula*

Area	Century	/ē/>e	/ē/>i	%	-erunt	-irunt
Baetica	IV-VI	16	1		0	0
	VII	11	0		0	0
Lusitania	IV-VI	53	2	3.6	2	0
	III	10	0		0	0
Tarraconensis	IV-VI	28	1	(3.1)	1	0
	VII	12	1	(7.6)	0	0

Examples of deviations are the following:

> *Filex* (= *Felix*) (V105, V cent., *Baetica*), *aeclisiae* (= *ecclesiae*) (V93 a. 525, *Lusitania*), *aera DLX trisis* (= *tresis?*)[5] (same inscription), *requivit* (= *requievit*) (V210 and V259 a. 622, *Tarraconensis*)

In non-dated material we found the forms *eclisie* (V378, *Baetica*) and *Aurilius* (V40, *Lusitania*).

B. *Gaul*

Area	Century	/ē/>e	/ē/>i	%	-erunt	-irunt
Narbonensis	IV-V	12	0		2	0
	VI-VII	13	3	12.5	1	0
Lugdunensis	IV-V	11	2	15.3	0	0
	VI-VII	16	6	27.2	0	0

The following examples will illustrate the deviations:

> *eclisiae* (D1554N a. 557), *Asclipi* (= gen. sing. of *Asclepius*) (D1808 a. 530),
> *riges* (= *regis*) (D2910 a. 518/533), from the *Narbonensis* area,
>
> *requibit* (=*requievit*) (D3559 a. 492), *Calipius* D1551 a. 447), *primicirius* (D1287 a. 552),
> *ficit* (D2352, VII cent.; D2456, VII cent.; D4423N, VI cent.), *ecli[sie]* (D4733A, VII cent.),
> *requiivit* (D3129, VI cent.), from the *Lugdunensis* area.

Deviations found in non-dated material include such forms as *ficit* (*passim*), *fedilis* (D1372), *ticum* (D2253, D2254b), *recensites* (= *re-*

---

[5] Editors do not seem to be in agreement concerning this form. Vives interprets it as *tres*, while Diehl believes that the stonecutter meant to write *ter* (cf. D1300). Díaz y Díaz, p. 135, accepts the interpretation of *tres* but also suggests the possibility of *tribus*, apparently taking the form *trisis* as an ablative form with a second declension ending. Another possibility would be to interpret this form as an alternate of *tres*, formed on the analogy of the neuter indeclinable noun *sexis*, used in the meaning of 'the number six' (cf. Lewis & Short, p. 1687); as a matter of fact, we do find this noun used in this sense in an inscription from this area, *era DL sexsis* (V29 a. 518).

censetis) (D3489) from the *Lugdunensis* area, while the only instance in the *Narbonensis* is the form *elegir*. (D3580) for *elegerunt*.

C. *Italy*

Area	Century	/ē/>e	/ē/>i	%	-erunt	-irunt
Northern	IV-V	39	1		11	0
	VI	8	0		1	0
Central	III-IV	14	0		7	0
	V	10	2	16.6	0	0
	VI-VII	6	0		3	0
Southern	III-IV	16	0		7	1
	V	12	0		1	0
	VI-VII	18	1		0	1

Examples of deviations:

Aurilius (D836), from the *Northern* area, *ficit* (D1028 a. 465), *aeclisiae* (D1315),[6] from the *Central* and *vixirunt* (D1491 a. 392), *recide* (D884 a. 565), *conparabirum* (= *comparaverunt* (D3860 a. 612) from the *Southern* area.

In non-dated material we found the following forms in which Latin /ē/ is represented by *i*:

havite (= *habete*) (D3349), *ficet* (D3401), from the *Northern;* *duodinos* (D1685), *quibit* (= *quievit*) (D3103C) from the *Southern* area.

In all three areas there are a few instances of apparent reverse spelling, e.g. *faecit* (D3577), *posuaerunt* (D4199) in the *Northern*, *faecit* (D2698A) in the *Central* and *fecaerunt* (D4170N) in the *Southern* areas.

---

[6] This particular inscription is dated by Diehl between a. 386 and 422. Since we made a break between the fourth and fifth centuries, it was arbitrarily assigned to this latter.

D. *Rome*

Century	/ē/>e	/ē/>i	%	-erunt	-irunt
III-IV	109	3	1.4	15	0
V	42	1	(2.3)	6	1
VI-VII	32	1	(3.0)	4	0

Deviations are illustrated by the following forms:

percipet (=*percepit*) (D1539 a. 338), *dibus* (=*diebus*) (D2772 a. 379), *dibitum* (D3302 a. 352), *fecirunt* (D3502N a. 405), *Acnite* (=*Agnete*, abl. of *Agnes*) (D3727D a. 490), *biro* (=*vero*) (D841 a. 584).

In non-dated material, we found a number of instances where Latin /ē/ is represented by *i*, of which we offer a few examples:

ficet (D766A), *Gisus* (=*Iesus*) (D2360B), *micum* (D4264HN), *himi* (=*emi*) (D3758), *fecirum* (=*fecerunt*) (D411A), *requiibit* (D3137N), *iius* (=*eius*) (D3898D), etc.

Apparent reverse spellings are represented by the following:

diaebus (D1404), *maecum* (D2265), *faecit* (D3253) *aeius* (D4125), *aemet* (=*emit*) (D3739GN), etc.

How many of the above *i* spellings to represent Latin /ē/ may be due to the umlaut,[7] a shift of accent,[8] dialectal pronunciation,[9]

---

[7] Discussing the form *Aurilius*, which occurs already on an inscription of 200 B.C. (CIL XIV 4268, *Ancient Latium*), Lindsay states that this form «proves the affinity of Latin *ē* with an *i* sound before a syllable with *i* (y) in hiatus» (pp. 22 & 225). Carnoy (p. 23) explains the form *eclisia* in the Spanish area as a closing of Latin /e/ to /i/, due to the influence of the *yod* in the following syllable, which has generally determined the *umlaut* in Spanish. Cf. Krepinsky, p. 128, who states that the *umlaut* of accented vowels before a consonant plus *yod* combination was an accomplished fact by the seventh century. Cf. Menéndez-Pidal, *Gramática*, p. 48, and the Old Spanish forms *eglisa, egrija* quoted by this scholar on p. 59. For a similar *umlaut* phenomenon in the inscriptions from Gaul, cf. *supra*, p. 45, our quote from Pirson (p. 6), although he postulates this process for Latin /ĕ/ only, e.g. *Antimius* (*Anthemius*), but not for *eclisia, primicirius, Asclipius*, etc. Why only Latin /ĕ/

or simply to misspelling is, of course, difficult to say. All that we feel authorized to state is that, on the basis of our evidence, the highest percentage of *i* spellings for Latin /ē/ in open syllable occurs in *Gaul,* especially in the *Lugdunensis* area, with 15.3 % and 27.2 % as against 0 % and 12.5 % in the *Narbonensis,* and that, as Grandgent puts it, «it must signify something» (p. 83), «a very real phenomenon of popular pronunciation, a narrowing of the *e*-sound into practically an *i* sound which greatly facilitated the combination of Latin long *e* and short *i* into the single sound postulated by the Romance languages,» concludes Pei, *Texts,* p. 25.

---

should be subject to this *umlauting* process and not Latin /ē/ is not clear. Bourciez, *Éléments,* p. 150, states that this particular *umlaut* phenomenon, which raises Latin /e/ and /o/ to /i/ and /u/, respectively, before a consonant plus *yod* combination is «spéciale (i.e. l'inflexion) à la péninsule ibérique.» Since the form *aeclisiae* was also found in Central Italy, where this *umlaut* does not seem to have been operative, it would appear that we would have to look for another explanation for the change of Latin /ē/ to /i/ before a consonant plus *yod* combination, at least outside of the Spanish area, or consider such forms as simply «spellings due in the main to the identity of *ē* and *ĭ* in late pronunciation» (Grandgent, p. 83).

Another *umlaut* process is illustrated by the form *ficit,* by which stressed Latin /ē/ shifts to /i/ in some perfect forms, under influence of a final /ī/ in the first person singular. Thus, French *fis,* Provençal *fis,* Spanish *hice,* Portuguese *fiz,* Milanese *fise* and Neapolitan *fice* (but note standard Italian *feci!*) postulate a form **fici* (cf. Bourciez, *Phonétique,* p. 58, Menéndez-Pidal, *Gramática,* p. 59, Meyer-Lübke, *Grammaire,* I, p. 103), rather than *feci,* which was then extended to the third person singular, cf. Pirson, p. 5. «Old French *fist* goes back to *ficit,* not to *fecit»* states Pei, *Texts,* p. 25.

⁸ In the main, the accent in Vulgar Latin remained on the same syllable as in classical Latin, cf. Battisti, p. 92 ff. Among the exceptions, this scholar notes the shift in the third person plural perfect form of strong verbs from the stem to the root vowel, e.g. *fécerunt, díxerunt, fúerunt,* Old French *fistrent, distrent, furent;* Italian *fecero, dissero, furono* (as against Spanish *hicieron, dijeron, fueron,* which go back to the classical form). It is very likely, therefore, that the spelling *-irunt* for *-erunt* in our material reflects this accent shift and that Latin /ē/ is not to be considered as being in stressed, but rather in unstressed position. The *i* spelling would then reflect the general merger of Latin /ĕ/ and /ĭ/ in unstressed syllable, cf. Grandgent «*e* and *i* came to be used almost indiscriminately» (p. 103).

⁹ Speaking of the change of Latin /ē/ to /i/ in Southern Italy, Grandgent states: «In Sicily, Calabria, and southern Apulia *e* has become *i»* (p. 83) and considers the possibility of an Oscan influence, although he finds no proof of historical connection between the phenomena.

3.2 Closed Syllable

A. Iberian Peninsula

Area	Century	/ē/>e	/ē/>i
Baetica	IV-VI	9	0
	VII	7	0
Lusitania	IV-VI	10	1
	VII	1	0
Tarraconensis	IV-VI	6	0
	VII	3	0

The only deviation is represented by the form *lictor* (V97 a. 566). We found no *i* spelling for Latin /ē/ in non-dated material.

B. Gaul

Area	Century	/ē/>e	/ē/>i	%
Narbonensis	IV-V	7	6	46.1
	VI-VII	50	10	10.6
Lugdunensis	IV-VI	11	5	31.6
	VI-VII	28	27	49.0

Deviations in both areas, in dated and non-dated material, may be classified under three headings, in which Latin /ē/ is represented by *i* namely

    (a) before the consonant group spelled *ct*:

        rictu (=*recto*) (D1075 about a. 630), *prelictus* (D1076 a. 622/3), from the *Lugdunensis* area.

    (b) before the group *ns*:

        minsis (D2765 about a. 485; D3488 a. 498; D47 a. 527; D2779 a. 516, *et passim*), occurring in both areas; *A[c]animsium* (=*Acaunensium*) (D2021 a. 521, *Narbonensis*), *Lugduninsi* (D1287 a. 552, *Lugdunensis*).

(c) before the group *sc*:

requiiscet (D1216 a. 496), *requiscet* (D2891 a. 527), *requiiscit* (3327 a. 454), *requicunt* (D1076 a. 622/3), *et passim, adoliscens* (D2747 a. 524), *aduliscens* (D2783B a. 438), *criscit* (D1076 a. 622/3), in *both* areas.

The above forms occur in non-dated material with some frequency also.

The only deviation that does not fit into the above categories is the form *rigno* (D1076 a. 622/3), *rigni* (D1218 a. 548 or 621), as well as the abbreviated form *rig.*, *passim*, which occurs with some frequency in the *Lugdunensis* area.[10]

By far the most frequent form in which Latin /ē/ is represented by *i* is *requiiscit*, but it is by no means «la forme normale des inscriptions chrétiennes,» as Pirson leads us to believe (p. 3) and there are plenty of instances where this verb form appears correctly spelled, especially in the *Narbonensis* area; as a matter of fact, it is because of the rather frequent occurrence of *requiescit* that we find in sixth/seventh century material from this area a 50:10 (10.6 %) ratio of deviations, as against a 7:6 (46.1 %) ratio in the previous centuries.

Pirson, p. 4, holds that the *i* spellings for Latin /ē/ have only an orthographic value in general and do not represent actual pronunciation,[11] merely proving that it was a very close [e]. Nevertheless, he concedes that «dans certains cas déterminés» (*ibid.*), people pronounced an /i/ when Latin /ē/ was followed by a nasal. For the closing influence («l' action fermante») of *n* plus consonant and *sc* group, cf. Väänänen, p. 36.

A single instance of an apparent reverse spelling occurs in *requiaescit* (D31216, *Narbonensis*).

---

[10] Referring to the work of Jeanne Vieillard, *La langue des diplômes royaux et chartes privées de l'époque mérovingienne* (Paris, 1927), Pei, *Texts*, p. 23, quotes this scholar who states that the formula *quod ficit minsis.... rigni* appears everywhere in the Merovingian Charters with *i* for *e*, except for the earliest ones dating back to a. 625.

[11] Pirson states in effect: «On n'a pu prononcer *i* à l'époque mérovingienne, puisque la majeure partie des langues romanes, notamment le français et le provençal, ont conservé le son *e* ou un son derivé de *e*.» (*ibid.*)

C. *Italy*

Area	Century	/ē/>e	/ē/>i	%
Northern	IV-V	37	2	5.1
	VI	44	5	10.2
Central	III-IV	11	0	
	V	12	0	
	VI-VII	21	5	19.2
Southern	III-IV	8	0	
	V	20	0	
	VI-VII	56	4	6.6

Except for the forms *lictur* (D1278 a. 537) in the *Northern*, *lictor* (D3869 a. 558) and *minses* (D31101E), both from the *Southern* area, all deviations are represented by one or the other incorrect spelling of *requiescit*, of which we offer a few examples:

> *requiiscit* (D2828 a. 435), *requiscit* (D2829 a. 447), *requiiscet* (D2827A a 529), *requixcit* (D1204 a. 551), and *passim*,

in non-dated material as well.

The hypercorrect form *caesquent* (= *quiescent*) (D3442) was found in the *Northern* area.

D. *Rome*

Century	/ē/>e	/ē/>i	%
III-IV	76	2	2.5
V	60	6	9.0
VI-VII	46	4	8.0

We find in this area, also that, except for *minses* (D3797 a 344) and *lictor* (D1272 a. 528/9), all deviations are represented by some misspelled form of *requiescit* or *quiescit*, as follows:

> *quiiscit* (D3108 a. 394/5), *requiiscunt* (D485a a. 476). *qiscet* (D4177 a. 404), *requiscet* (D318N a. 531), etc.

In non-dated material we find similar forms also, together with forms like *minsis* (D608), *misis* (D3656B) and *lictor* (D1273).

An apparent reverse spelling is represented by the form *quaescit* (D3113) in non-dated material.

Our evidence would seem to lend support to Väänänen's suggestion, whereby Latin /ē/ seems to have closed to /i/ through the influence of certain consonant groups, cf. *supra,* p. 55, especially since this phenomenon seems to be spread over wide areas. Might we not add to the consonant groups mentioned by this scholar (*n* plus consonant; *sc*), as exerting an «influence fermante» on the preceding Latin /ē/, the *ct* group (cf. *lictor, rictu, prelictu*) before which we find *i* spellings in widely separated areas also?

Just as in the case of Latin /ē/ in open syllable, the greatest number of deviations from the classical norm are found in Gaul, particularly in the *Lugdunensis* area.

3.3 Latin /ē/ in Monosyllables (Including Prepositions)

Occasionally we find Latin /ē/ in monosyllabic words represented by *i.*

A. *Iberian Peninsula*

In the few occurrences in this area, Latin /ē/ in monosyllabic words is always spelled with *e.*

B. *Gaul*

We have no deviation to report from the *Narbonensis* area.

In the *Lugdunensis* area, in sixth/seventh century material, the only occurrence of the word *tres* appears spelled *tris* (D2912 a. 526/7), which form we also find in non-dated material, *tris* (D4010).

C. *Italy*

No deviation to report from the *Northern* and *Central* areas, where there are very few occurrences of monosyllabic words, except for the preposition *de,* which is always correctly spelled.

In the *Southern* area, there is no deviation in dated material, in about half a dozen occurrences. In non-dated material, we found one occurrence of the form *tris* (D3120).

D. *Rome*

The most noteworthy deviation in this area being the form *si* for *se*, we made a separate count of the occurrence of this pronominal form.

Century	/ē/>e	/ē/>i	%	se	si	%	other
III-IV	4	0		8	0		1 [12]
V	7	0		12	0		0
VI-VII	2	1	(33.3)	4	3	42.8	0

Apart from the form *si*, in the expression *si vivos comparaberunt* (D694 a. 522), *si vivo conparavit* (D3783b a. 500), *si viva conparavit* (D3727G a. 542/65), and *passim* in non-dated material, the only deviation is the form *tris* (D4145N a. 522).

For *tris* and *treis* as attested alternative forms of *tres*, cf. Lewis & Short, p. 1896.

As to the form *si* for *se*, it would appear that, in view of the context in which this form appears exclusively, the closing of Latin /ē/ to /i/ is due to proclitic position, cf. Väänänen, p. 37.

4. *Latin /ĭ/, represented by the letter i.*

It is the consensus of scholars that Latin /ē/ and /ĭ/ had merged at a relatively early date during the Vulgar Latin period. Cf. conclusions presented by Pei, *Texts*, pp. 26 ff., Pirson, quoted *supra*, p. 49, as well as his statement to the effect that the merger of Latin /ē/ and /ĭ/ is abundantly proven by the spellings *e* for *i* and *i* for *e* (p. 8).

The evidence from our inscriptional material is the following:

---

[12] In D3501 a. 390 we read *sie viva.... fecit*, with the following comment by Diehl: «sie ortum ex sibi et se, vix si(v)e = sibi.»

4.1 Open Syllable

A. *Iberian Peninsula*

Area	Century	/ĭ/>i	/ĭ/>e	%
Baetica	IV-VI	20	0	
	VII	19	2	9.5
Lusitania	IV-VI	14	1	
	VII	4	0	
Tarraconensis	IV-VI	8	2	20.0
	VII	0	0	

The *e* spelling for Latin /ĭ/ is shown in the following forms:

baselica (V 308 a. 660 and V157), occurring twice in *Baetica*, *menus* (V4884b a. 504, *Lusitania*), *meserum* (=*miserum*, i.e. *miserorum*)[13] (V276 a. 550) and *tetulum* (V239), both from the *Tarraconensis* area.

In non-dated material from *Tarraconensis*, we found two more occurrences of *baselica* (V318 and V319).[14]

B. *Gaul*

Area	Century	/ĭ/>i	/ĭ/>e	%
Narbonensis	IV-V	7	1	(12.5)
	VI-VII	35	24	40.6
Lugdunensis	IV-V	9	3	25.0
	VI-VII	10	6	37.5

A few examples of deviations are the following:

---

[13] For *miserum* as being a poetic form of *miserorum* (our inscription being in verse), cf. Allen & Greenough, p. 22.

[14] For the survival of this form, cf. Engadine *baselgia*, Old Venetian *baselega* 'church,' as well as *baselga* 'belly' in the dialect of *Algarve* (*So. Portugal*), cf. Meyer-Lübke, REW, #972. The form also survives in the Portuguese place-name *Baselgas*, cf. Entwistle, p. 278.

baselicam (D1807 a. 455), *menus* (D1421 a. 571) *et passim*, *eterum* (D1213 a. 536), *veri* (D2256, a. 509), *fede* (4728 a. 563), *adsedua* (=*assidua*) (D1687 a. 527).

from the *Narbonensis* area,

temens (D1340 a. 486), *vigelia* (D1551 a. 447) *egetur* (=*igitur*) (D1075 a. ca. 630), *sene* (D1075), *vero* (D1616a a. 501), *adsedue* (D2483 a. 601).

from the *Lugdunensis* area.

In non-dated material from both areas, we find some of the above forms also, and such others as

tetol(um) (D3580), *Domenecus* (D2024), *lecit* (D3489), *tetulum* (D3584), *nemis* (D4824), *Princepius* (D3094A), and, *passim*, *menus* and *menos*.

C. *Italian Peninsula*

Area	Century	/ĭ/>i	/ĭ/>e	%	other	
Northern	IV-V	62	7	10.1	0	
	VI	10	0		0	
Central	III-IV	19	0		0	
	V	15	0		0	
	VI-VII	25	1		0	
Southern	III-IV	10	0		0	
	V	10	1		0	
	VI-VII	59	1		1	(/ĭ/>u)

Some examples illustrating deviations are the following:

menus (D1500a/b a. 409, occurring twice), *eterum* (D339 a. 491), *vero* (D674 a. 440), *Prencepia* (D1500a), etc.

in the *Northern* area, while the few deviations in the *Central* and *Southern* areas are limited to *menus* (D253 a. 570 and D3185 a. 461/82) and *univera* (D4302 a. 570).

In a garbled inscription (D3162 a. 542/567) from *Beneventum* (*Apulia*) we read [*p*]*lus munus* (the formula *vixit annos plus minus* followed by a round number to give the age of the deceased being widespread in inscriptions from all areas (cf. Lattimore, p. 16), which, seeing that this is an isolated case, would seem to be due to a stonecutter's error.

In non-dated material, we find the form *menus* (*passim*), *semul* (D1933) (possibly by confusion with *semel*, but cf. Lewis & Short, p. 1702, for *semul* used by Plautus), and *sene* (D1331).

D. *Rome*

Century	/ĭ/>i	/ĭ/>e	other	
III-IV	84	1	1	(/ĭ/>y)
V	55	1	0	
VI-VII	43	1	0	

Deviation occur in the following three forms:

Calleroe (=*Callirhoe*) (D4219 a. 376) *sebi* (D3206b a. 449/94), *menus* (D3000A a. 530).

In non-dated material we find forms like

sene (D161), *fede* (D1601), *agneglus* (=*agniculus*) (D2481), *virgenium* (D2788A), *sebi* (D3818A) and *menus* (2687A).

The *y* spelling for Latin /ĭ/, in *vyris* (D3821 a. 391) would appear to be a reverse spelling, a «pura notazione di *i*» as Pisani, *Testi*, p. 147 B 152, puts it, evidencing, it would seem, that the Greek *upsilon* had merged with Latin /i/. For the possibility of the existence of a «prononciation précieuse,» based on his interpretation of «*vir non vyr*,» «*virgo non vyrgo*» of the Appendix Probi, cf. Väänänen, p. 38.

In non-dated material we find such forms as *byro* (=*viro*) (D1537) and *virgynia* (D2308A). Two apparent reverse spellings occur in non-dated material in the *Southern Italian* area also, namely *univyria* (D4723) and *Fyrmi* (=gen. sing. of *Firmius*) (D898A). [15]

---

[15] That the *y* spelling may indeed stand for an [y] sound after a labial consonant is clearly stated by Kieckers when he says: «Nach dem Zeugnis

4.2 Closed Syllable

A. *Iberian Peninsula*

Area	Century	/ĭ/>i	/ĭ/>e	%
Baetica	IV-VI	8	0	
	VII	13	0	
Lusitania	IV-VI	9	0	
	VII	6	0	
Tarraconensis	IV-VI	13	2	13.3
	VII	6	0	

The two deviations in this latter area are illustrated by the following form:

antestis (=*antistes*) (V276 a. 550), *vigenti* (V203 IV/VI cent.)

Regarding the first form, Carnoy (p. 20) states that both *antistes* and *antestis* existed side by side in Christian inscriptions of all regions (cf. the alternative forms *antesto* and *antisto* 'to stand before, to excel,' Lewis & Short, p. 131). For *vigenti* surviving in the Aragonese form *vient*, cf. Zamora Vicente, p. 191.[16]

B. *Gaul*

Area	Century	/ĭ/>i	/ĭ/>e	%
Narbonensis	IV-V	4	1	(20.0)
	VI-VII	9	4	30.7
Lugdunensis	IV-V	5	0	
	VI-VII	16	3	15.8

---

der antiken Grammatiker...., erscheint für anlautendes *vi* häufig *vy* (= vü; *i* nach *v* labialisiert, wie nhd. schles. *würklich* = *wirklich* .... Die Appendix Probi verwirft die schlechte Aussprache in *vyr* 'Mann,' *vyrgo* 'Jungfrau.' Auf jüngeren Inschr. auch *fyrmus* = *firmus*, *fydes* = *fides*, *myser* = *miser*» (p. 48). Also cf. Sommer, p. 63.

[16] The normal outcome of *viginti* in Old Spanish is *veínte*, in which Latin /i/ was prevented from shifting to /e/ under the influence of a final /i/, cf. our footnote #7. The Aragonese forms *vient* and *veyent* are attested in the XIVth century and the modern popular form is *vente*.

THE ACCENTED VOWELS

Some examples of deviations are the following:

> *minester* (D1303, V cent.), *semplix* (D180 a. 525) *ancella, quinquagenta* (D1670 a. 557/602), *enox* (=*innox*) (D3551 a. 560).[17]

from the *Narbonensis* area.

> *septuagenta* (D1463 a. 643), *vigenti, sexagenta* (D1674 a. 520).

from the *Lugdunensis* area.
In non-dated material from both areas, we find such forms as

> *antestis* (but *antistes* in the same inscription also, cf. Carnoy, supra, p. 62) (D1062), *ennocens* (D1280), *insegnem* (D1512), *trienta* (D3126), *octogenta* (D3468A), *Vector, claresimus* (D202), *dulcesime* (D353), etc.[18]

C. Italy

Area	Century	/ĭ/>i	/ĭ/>e	%	other	
Northern	IV-V	28	1		0	
	VI	11	0		0	
Central	III-IV	9	1		1	(/ĭ/>ei)
	V	5	0		0	
	VI-VII	7	0		0	
Southern	III-IV	13	0		0	
	V	6	1	(13.2)	0	
	VI-VII	25	2	7.4	0	

Forms illustrating the few deviations are the following:

> *vergo* (D1500a a. 409), in the *Northern* area; *minestrum* (D2169 a. 348), *eille* (=*ille*) (D3916, III cent.),[19] from the

---

[17] For the popular form *innox*, corresponding to the learned form *innocens*, cf. Pirson, p. 247.

[18] For the development of the numerals in French, postulating an -*enti*, -*enta* stage, cf. Pope, *From Latin to Modern French* (Manchester, 1934), p. 318. For the survival in Old French of some synthetic superlatives in -*esmes* from Vulgar Latin -*esimus*, cf. Ewert, p. 136.

[19] For an occasional *ei* spelling for Latin /ĭ/, cf. Sommer, p. 74.

Central area; *Ellu* (=dat./abl. of proper name Illus) (D1029A a. 478) *dulcessima* (248 a. 508), *aepescopus* (D1026, VII cent.) from the *Southern* area.

In non-dated inscriptions from the *Northern* area we find the forms *vigenti* (D1445) and *beatessema* (D1445); no deviations were found in non-dated material from the other two areas.

D. *Rome*

Century	/ĭ/>i	/ĭ/>e	%
III-IV	105	2	1.8
V	47	2	4.5
VI-VII	19	1	5.0

Deviations occur mainly in proper names, some of which may be due to suffix substitution, e.g. *Nebeta* (=*Nevitta*) (D2967 a. 362) and *Petronella* (D1995B). Others, like *Arenteo* (D2795BN a. 373), *Plentae* (D2635 a. 419) and *Yacentus* (=*Hyacinthus*) (D4531) would seem to contradict the hypothesis advanced by Lindsay (p. 23) that the consonant group /nt/ may have had a closing infuence on the preceding vowel, cf. *innocintem, benemerinti, parinti*, unless we assume that in certain dialects the sound which resulted from the merger of Latin /ē/ and /ĭ/ was more open than in others.[20] The forms *Vitelessema* (D4394B a. 425) and *piessimo* (25a a. 553) complete the examples of deviations in the *Roman* area.[21]

4.3 Latin /ĭ/ in Monosyllables (Including Prepositions)

In monosyllabic words, Latin /ĭ/ generally appears as *i* in orthography, with the following exceptions:

---

[20] In connection with the close relationship between Latin /ē/ and /ĭ/ («i.... näherte sich dem *e*-Laut und findet sich daher in älterer wie in späterer Zeit öfters durch *e* dargestellt....» (p. 62)), Sommer states: «Nach antikem Zeugnis ist die offene Aussprache des *i* besonders auf dem Lande üblich gewesen, wo man z.B. *ve(h)a* für *via* sagte....» (*ibid.*)

[21] The superlative ending *-essimus*, is already attested in a Pompeian inscription of the first century A.D., cf. Väänänen, *Inscriptions*, p. 33.

B. *Gaul*

Area	Century	/ĭ/>i	/ĭ/>e	in	en
Narbonensis	IV-V	2	0	20	0
	VI-VII	1	0	50	1
Lugdunensis	IV-V	3	0	18	0
	VI-VII	1	1	39	0

The deviation in this latter area occurs in the word *ver* (D1076 a. 622/3), the correct form *vir* appearing once also.

With regard to the form *en* for *in*, which occurs in the formula *hic en pace requiescet.... Eulogios* (D2889A a. 524), in which all *e*-s, standing for both Latin /ĕ/ and /ē/ are transcribed by Greek *epsilon*, it is probably a hypercorrect form, influenced by the Greek ἐν.

The preposition *in* appears spelled *en* in a few inscriptions from various other areas, as follows:

> *flecte genu en signu....* (V340, *Lusitania*), *recyiescet en pace* (D3170A, *No. Italy*) *benemerenti en pace* (D2597N, D2614, *Rome*)

where the apparent shift of Latin /ĭ/ to /e/ may also be due to the merger of these phonemes in unstressed syllable, due to the proclitic use of this preposition.

In a few instances *en* also appears in connection with the expression *en irene* (*erene*), the apparent Latin transliteration of Greek ἐν ἠιρήνῃ (corresponding to Latin *in pace*, cf. Lattimore, p. 307), e.g. *en* ἠρήνε (D2716A), *en irene* (D2717N) (but *in irene* D2718), all from *Rome*.

4.4 Latin /ĭ/ in hiatus

The merger of Latin /ē/ and /ĭ/ can also be seen in a few forms in which Latin /ĭ/ occurs in hiatus. Here are the few examples that we found:

perfecit atrea trea (V359, *Lusitania*), *dabit fisco auri pondo trea* (D813/D514, V cent., *No. Italy*),[22] and *corpora trea* (D3800, *Rome*).

To these examples, we must add the forms *dees* (=*dies*) (D1216 a. 496), from *Narbonensis* (of a total of 9 occurrences in this material) and *des* (D4389 occurring twice) from *Rome*, showing also a merger of the stressed vowel and the ending. While the form *trea* might possibly be explained by analogy of *tres*, the spelling *e* for Latin /ĭ/ in hiatus in the word *dies* is most unusual.

Summarizing the relationship between Latin /ē/ and /ĭ/, in both open and closed syllables, taking the total occurrences of these vowels and the total orthographic deviations, we find the following percentage figures for each of the areas under study:

---

[22] The form *trea* is, of course, incorrectly used in this penalty formula that we find on numerous inscriptions from the military cemetery at *Concordia*. The word *libras* is to be understood but the use of the neuter plural of *tres* is not clear, especially since *pondo* is used here as an adverb, rather than as a neuter noun. Might there have been a confusion in the writer's mind between *tres libras* and *tria pondera*?

THE ACCENTED VOWELS

Area	Century	Free /ē/	Free /ĭ/	Checked /ē/	Checked /ĭ/	Total Correct	Total Dev.	% of Deviations
Baetica	IV-VI	16	20	9	8	53	1	1.8
	VII	11	19	7	13	50	2	3.8
Lusitania	IV-VI	55	14	10	9	88	4	4.3
	VII	10	4	1	6	21	0	0.0
Tarraconensis	IV-VI	29	8	6	13	56	5	8.2
	VII	12	0	3	6	21	1	4.7
Narbonensis	IV-V	14	7	7	4	32	8	20.0
	VI-VII	14	35	50	9	118	41	25.9
Lugdunensis	IV-V	11	9	11	5	36	10	21.7
	VI-VII	16	10	28	16	70	42	37.5
No. Italy	IV-V	50	62	37	28	147	15	9.2
	VI	9	10	44	11	74	5	6.3
Ce. Italy	III-IV	21	19	11	9	60	1	1.6
	V	10	15	12	5	42	2	4.6
	VI-VII	9	25	21	7	62	6	8.6
So. Italy	III-IV	23	10	8	13	54	1	1.8
	V	13	10	20	6	49	2	3.9
	VI-VII	18	59	56	25	158	9	5.4
Rome	III-IV	124	84	76	105	389	8	2.0
	V	48	55	60	47	210	11	4.9
	VI-VII	36	43	46	19	144	7	4.6

The formulaic nature of inscriptional material in general, which would seem to cause the rather haphazard occurrence of Latin /ē/ and /ĭ/ in our material, as well as the unequal number of inscriptions for a given period, makes it difficult in some cases to interpret the percentage figures given in this table. How are we to interpret, for instance, such decreasing figures as those we obtain for *Lusitania* or *Tarraconensis?* Shall we conclude that there has been a sudden conservative influence in these areas, or that we are faced with a particularly carefully written group of inscriptions in our seventh century material? Clearly, the fact that our sampling in both areas in this particular period is reduced to one fourth and one third, respectively, has to be taken into account, so that this decrease in deviations may be just coincidental. All we would seem to be able to state is that in the area of the *Iberian Peninsula* the percentage difference of deviations in the *Tarraconensis* area, —more especially in the Eastern region of this area, since the bulk of the inscriptions come from here—, are important enough, with respect to *Baetica* and *Lusitania*, to point to a merger of Latin /ē/ and /ĭ/. Of course, this does not necessarily mean that the same merger may not have taken place in these areas also and that it is merely masked by a greater orthographic conservatism on the part of well-trained scribes.

The complete merger of Latin /ē/ and /ĭ/ in both areas of *Gaul* seems to be rather clearly established by the fourth/fifth centuries.

The almost 10 % deviation in *No. Italy*, i.e. a 5 % or so differential with respect to the other Italian areas during a comparable period, would point, it would seem, to a somewhat earlier merger of these two Latin vowel phonemes in this region. The approx. 3 % drop in sixth century material, on the other hand, may again be due to the considerably smaller sampling that we have for this period, rather than to a sudden spurt of conservatism reflected in more careful language.

Except for *Ce. Italy*, where the 5 % jump in sixth/seventh century material with respect to the fifth century would seem to be significant in the direction of a merger of Latin /ē/ and /ĭ/ by, at least, the sixth century, there is but a gradual increase in both *Rome* and *So. Italy* where, as in the case of *Baetica* and *Lusitania*, a seemingly conservative orthographic tradition may conceal the true state of affairs regarding the merger of these phonemes, so that it is difficult to say when it may have taken place.

5. *Latin /ī/, represented by the letter i.*

According to the description of Latin grammarians, the sound of Latin /ī/ was fuller (*plenior*) than that of /ĭ/, which, they say, was «a sound between *e* and *i*» (quoted in Lindsay, p. 24). This vowel, Meyer-Lübke, *Grammaire*, I, p. 57, informs us is «la plus résistante de toutes les voyelles» and his views are confirmed by the consensus of Romance scholars, cf. Pei, *Texts*, pp. 28/29, for a summary of opinions.

Both Kieckers (p. 24) and Sommer (p. 63) mention the fact that Latin /ī/ occasionally appears represented by *e* on some «vulgar» inscriptions [23] and refer to the grammarian Consentius who remarks on the pronunciation of this vowel as tending towards the [e] sound in the Latin of Gaul. [24]

Our inscriptional material offers the following evidence:

5.1 Open Syllable

A. *Iberian Peninsula*

Area	Century	/ī/>i	/ī/>e
Baetica	IV-VI	20	0
	VII	23	0
Lusitania	IV-VI	21	0
	VII	6	1
Tarraconensis	IV-VI	31	0
	VII	5	0

---

[23] Sommer mentions such forms as *oreginem*, *peregreno* and *felius*.

[24] Pirson (pp. 11/12) doubts the validity of Consentius' testimony for forms like *benegnus* and *vexit* (the former occurring twice and the latter once in both his and our material) in which Latin /ī/ appears spelled with *e* and which might be considered as last vestiges of a Gaulish pronunciation, seeing that in this language the diphthong /ej/ had been reduced to /ē/ and not /ī/ as in Latin. This is, in effect, what he says: «....il est peu probable qu'à l'époque de Consentius même, cette voyelle (i.e. /ē/) jouit encore d'une grande extension et à plus forte raison aux VIe et VIIe siècles, auxquelles nous reportons les inscriptions mentionnées. L'ī latin a dû le supplanter de bonne heure dans la majeure partie de la Gaule puisqu'il a seul survécu et pour ainsi dire sans altération dans tous les parlers de cette contrée, à l'exception de quelques dialectes du Nord-Est. La date relativement récente de ces graphies rend toute influence celtique fort sujette à caution et il serait dangereux de les citer à l'appui d'une différenciation locale du latin de la Gaule.»

The only deviation occurs in the word *ed(us) Ian.* (V79 a. 679) for *idus* which, as has been suggested in connection with similar spelling of this word, is an archaic spelling or the reflection of a dialectal pronunciation.[25]

B. *Gaul*

Area	Century	/ī/>i	/ī/>e
Narbonensis	IV-V	11	0
	VI-VII	26	0
Lugdunensis	IV-V	15	0
	VI-VII	17	1

The only deviation in dated material is represented by the form *Lupecenos* (D3563 a. 523) for *Lupicinus,* in which the substitution of suffix would seem to be a reasonable assumption. Pirson (p. 5) mentions the interchange of *-enus* and *-inus* «dans les textes vulgaires» and the objection of the Appendix Probi to *Bizacinus,* rather than *Byzacenus,* would point to this confusion.

In non-dated material from this latter area we read *eds Aguas* (D4374 for *idus Augustas.*

C. *Italy*

Area	Century	/ī/>i	/ī/>e	%	Other
Northern	IV-V	111	1		0
	VI	35	0		1 (/ī/>ei)
Central	III-IV	43	0		0
	V	13	0		0
	VI-VII	28	0		0
Southern	III-IV	31	0		0
	V	22	0		0
	VI-VII	44	0		0

---

[25] Cf. Väänänen, *Inscriptions,* pp. 35/36, where he gives a number of examples of this word spelled *eidus* and *edus.* Because, this scholar holds, the I.E. /ej/ diphthong had been reduced to /ī/ in the course of the second century B.C., passing through an intermediate /ē/ stage, thus merging with

In the *Northern* area we find the form *aperere* (D816b, IV/V cent.) for *aperire*. [26]

In sixth century material from this area we find the form *eid. Ianuarii* (D1668 a. 513), while in a non-dated inscription we read *felia* (D2168) for *filia*. [27]

In non-dated material from the *Southern* area, we find the spelling *edus Apriles* (D568N) and *eid(ibus)* (D1291A).

D. Rome

Century	/ī/>i	/ī/>e
III-IV	251	0
V	116	0
VI-VII	48	0

There is no deviation to report from non-dated inscriptions either.

5.2 Closed Syllable

A. *Iberian Peninsula*

Area	Century	/ī/>i	/ī/>e
Baetica	IV-VI	38	0
	VII	13	0
Lusitania	IV-VI	56	0
	VII	6	0
Tarraconensis	IV-VI	31	0
	VII	3	0

---

original Latin /ī/, the above spelling cannot be but «une notation archaisante» or, possibly, a dialectal pronunciation, seeing that «les dialectes italiques ont tendu à rapprocher la dipthongue *ei* du son *e*.» (p. 35). For similar interpretations of the spelling *e* for Latin /ī/, cf. Sommer, p. 73; Kieckers, p. 24; Carnoy, p. 44; Lindsay, pp. 29/30.

[26] This form appears in the context of the penalty formula which is so characteristic of the inscriptions from the Concordia military cemetery (cf. our note #22). *Mutatis mutandis*, it reads as follows: *si quis eam (i.e. arcam) aperire voluerit, dabit fisco auri pondo....* In D515 we read the form *apere* for *aperire*, which Diehl interprets as «*voluit aperere*,» but might it not also be an abbreviation? In all other instances, at least two score, this verb form appears correctly spelled.

[27] Cf. Sommer, p. 64, who cites the form *felius* on an inscription from Latium (CIL XIV 1011), not included in Diehl's collection.

Latin /ī/ in non-dated material also consistently appears spelled with *i*.

B. *Gaul*

Area	Century	/ī/>i	/ī/>e
Narbonensis	IV-V	12	0
	VI-VII	47	0
Lugdunensis	IV-V	17	0
	VI-VII	26	1

The deviation in this latter area occurs in the word *benegnus* (D1075 ca. a. 630) for *benignus*.[28]

Deviations in non-dated material occur in the *Narbonensis* area, where we find *vexit* (D1467A) and *benegnus* (D1167).[29]

C. *Italy*

Area	Century	/ī/>i	/ī/>e	other
Northern	IV-V	116	1	1 (/ī/>ei)
	VI	111	0	0
	III-IV	21	0	0
Central	V	17	0	0
	VI-VII	37	0	0
	III-IV	28	0	0
Southern	V	17	0	0
	VI-VII	59	0	0

---

[28] For Latin /ī/ in *benignus*, cf. Lindsay, p. 138; Sommer, p. 121; Battisti, p. 97; Pirson, p. 12; however, as this latter scholar points out, in those words in which Latin /ī/ was followed by the consonant group /gn/, the quantity of the vowel seems to have been uncertain, as proven by such forms as It. *degno*, Fr. *dédain*, Prov. *denh*, which postulate a Latin etymon *dignus* with Latin /ĭ/. It is, therefore, possible that, by analogy, there may have existed a form *benignus* with Latin /ĭ/. For a slightly different interpretation, cf. Battisti, p. 97, who, instead of postulating two concurrent forms, would rather postulate a form *benignus* with an open /ī/, i.e. a change of quality rather than of quantity. The form *benegnus* found in our material, which this scholar cites also, would go back to *benīgnus*, giving also rise to the Northern Italian, Marchigiano and Neapolitan forms *belegno* and the toponyms *S. Belegno* in Italy and *S. Broing* in France. Of course, the etymon with /ī/ is postulated for It. *benigno* and Fr. *bénin, benigne*.

[29] For the interpretation of *vexit*, cf. our footnote #24. We might add —and Pirson also points out this fact (p. 13)— that this form, in which

Deviations in the *Northern* area are represented by the forms *fesco* (D545) and *feisco* (D500) for *fisco,* both appearing on inscriptions from Concordia.

In a non-dated inscription from this area we also find the form *fescu* (D811b) for *fisco*.[30]

D. Rome

Century	/ī/>i	/ī/>e
III-IV	154	0
V	98	0
VI-VII	49	0

In non-dated material we find the following deviations, all of them occurring in the verb form *vixit*

> *vexe* (D2572), *bexit* (D2825) (but also *vixit* in same), *vexse* (D2952B), and *vexxit* (D4265F).[31]

5.3 Latin /ī/ in Monosyllables.

Monosyllabic words with Latin /ī/ are represented by the adverb *hic*, the relative pronoun *qui* and by the conjunction *si*.

On a dated verse inscription from the *Lugdunensis* area, which is particularly badly written, we find the following:

> *ordene que rictu vita comentante beata gesisti sacrum prbr officio* (D1075 ca. a. 630)

This particular passage and the form *que* are discussed by Pirson at some length, who suggests that there may have been confusion in

---

Latin /ī/ is represented by *e*, is an isolated occurrence in the face of the very frequent appearance of *vixit* or *vixet*.

[30] For Latin /ī/ in *Fisco* cf. Pisani, *Testi*, p. 124. The form *feisco* may even suggest that the source of this Latin /ī/ could be I.E. /ej/, and that the *e* spelling may be an archaic spelling or a dialectal pronunciation, cf. our footnote #25.

[31] Despite the fact that in dated inscriptions we never find *vexit* for *vixit*, these few instances showing an *e* spelling for *i* may be more than either archaic or incorrect spellings, pointing to the kind of rustic pronunciation that the grammarian Varro mentions in *speca* for *spīca* and *vella* for *vīlla*. Cf. Sommer, p. 63; Lindsay, p. 29.

the mind of the stonecutter between the pronoun and the enclitic *-que* since, it seems that on the original stone *que* and *ordene* were written together. [32]

The adverb *hic* appears written with *e* in *hec requiescit* (V114, *Lusitania*) and *ec bene pausa*[*nti*....] (D3242AN, *Lugdunensis*), in which the proclitic use of the word may possibly account for the change of Latin /ī/; however, in these very areas we found also other forms in which Latin /ī/ is spelled with *e*, so that other interpretations may also be taken into account, cf. our footnote #25.

On the basis of the evidence offered by our inscriptional material, it would seem that Latin /ī/, spelled almost universally *i*, was pronounced throughout the Vulgar Latin period as /i/.

6. *Latin /ŏ/, represented by the letter o.*

Grandgent states that «short *o*, pronounced *o*, remained unchanged» (p. 86). He mentions, however, that in inscriptions we find an occasional *u* spelling for Latin /ŏ/, e.g. a form like *lucus* for *locus*. Pirson notes that the apparent change of Latin /ŏ/ to /u/, as reflected in the spelling *u* for *o*, may be due to the influence of a *yod* or a nasal, just as in the case of the apparent change of Latin /ĕ/ to /i/ (cf. *supra*, p. 42), e.g. in the forms *Pannunia* and *cenubium*. This scholar admits, however, that an occasional *u* spelling for Latin /ŏ/ appears in forms in which such an influence is not at work, as in *pupulus* for *populus* and *pus* for *post*, and he feels that these misspellings are due to the analogical influence of the merger of Latin /ō/ and /ŭ/ in Vulgar Latin (p. 15). [33]

Other works dealing with Vulgar Latin texts show Latin /ŏ/ represented by *u* only very exceptionally and none of the scholars finds any trace of the diphthongization of this vowel which characterizes some of the major Romance languages, particularly French, Spanish and Italian. Cf. Pei, *Texts*, pp. 29/30 and Lausberg, I, pp. 109 ff.

---

[32] Pirson states: «....le lapicide ne paraît pas avoir compris le passage qui renferme le *que* (= *qui*) en question; car, alors qu'il sépare soigneusement chaque mot, il a rattaché ce *que* à *ordene* en le confondant probablement avec la conjonction enclitique.... On pourrait d'ailleurs traduire en considérant *que* comme enclitique....» (pp. 12/13).

[33] On the whole question of the interchange of Latin /ŏ/, /ō/, /ŭ/ and /ū/, cf. Prinz.

THE ACCENTED VOWELS

Our inscriptions show the following:

6.1 Open Syllable

A. *Iberian Peninsula*

Area	Century	/ŏ/>o	/ŏ/>u
Baetica	IV-VI	9	0
	VII	17	0
Lusitania	IV-VI	18	0
	VII	5	0
Tarraconensis	IV-VI	15	0
	VII	4	0

B. *Gaul*

Area	Century	/ŏ/>o	/ŏ/>u
Narbonensis	IV-V	31	0
	VI-VII	121	0
Lugdunensis	IV-V	28	0
	VI-VII	60	0

In non-dated material from this latter area, we found the form *pupulo* (D444) for *populo*.[34]

C. *Italy*

Area	Century	/ŏ/>o	/ŏ/>u
Northern	IV-V	79	0
	VI	21	0
	III-IV	22	0
Central	V	17	0
	VI-VII	30	0
	III-IV	29	0
Southern	V	22	0
	VI-VII	50	0

---

[34] Under the heading *de assimilatione*, where Prinz attempts to account for the spelling *u* for Latin /ŏ/ in various forms as a result of assimilation,

D. *Rome*

Century	/ŏ/>o	/ŏ/>u
III-IV	196	0
V	157	0
VI-VII	59	0

6.2 Closed Syllable

A. *Iberian Peninsula*

Area	Century	/ŏ/>o	/ŏ/>u
Baetica	IV-VI	5	1
	VII	9	0
Lusitania	IV-VI	4	0
	VII	4	0
Tarraconensis	IV-VI	8	0
	VII	1	0

The single deviation occurs in the word *cupari* (V143) for *compari*, which, however, would appear to be an etymological reconstruction with *cum*, rather than a possible confusion of Latin /o/ and /u/.[35]

B. *Gaul*

Area	Century	/ŏ/>o	/ŏ/>u
Narbonensis	IV-V	4	0
	VI-VII	14	4
Lugdunensis	IV-V	8	0
	VI-VII	10	0

---

we read, in connection with *pupulo*: «ad vocalis mutationem etiam «pūpulus» vox atribuisse potest» (p. 81).

[35] Cf. Prinz, p. 82.

The four deviations are represented by the name of the consul *Mavortius* (a. 527), which appears variously spelled as

Mavurtio (D47 a. 527), *Mavurti* (D2891A a. 529; D3542 a. 528/29) and *Maurti* (D3550A a. 528) [36]

In non-dated material from the *Lugdunensis* area we found the form *curpure* (D4827) for *corpore*. For the apparent change of Latin /ŏ/ to /u/, as evidenced by the *u* spelling, the influence of a following /r/ has been postulated. [37]

C. *Italy*

Area	Century	/ŏ/>o	/ŏ/>u
Northern	IV-V	51	1
	VI	8	1
	III-IV	14	0
Central	V	3	0
	VI-VII	7	0
	III-IV	13	0
Southern	V	8	0
	VI-VII	28	2

---

[36] There seems to be some disagreement as to the quantity of Latin /o/ in this name, since Pirson (p. 14) treats it as /ō/, whereas Prinz (p. 86) treats it as /ŏ/. The name *Mavortius* is given in Lewis & Short (p. 1121) as containing a short /o/, so that in our treatment of this vowel we have followed both their authority and that of Prinz. In connection with the spelling of this name, which appears spelled with *u* more frequently than with *o* in our inscriptional material (only once in Gaul in the form of *Mafortio* (D2891 a. 527)), Prinz states: «Saepe nomen Mavortii, consulis anni 527, U exhibet in titulis christianis Italiae et Galliae Cisalpinae et Galliae Transalpinae. Factum esse potest, ut V praecedens ad vocalis mutationem attulerit» (p. 86). The loss of the intervocalic *v* before *u* in Vulgar Latin, cf. Lindsay, p. 52, and *rivus non rius* of the Appendix Probi, as evidenced by the spelling *Maurti*, may strengthen the hypothesis that, at least in the area of Gaul, this name was pronounced with /u/ rather than with /o/.

[37] Cf. Prinz, p. 80; Sommer, p. 65. For a contrary opinion cf. B. Löfstedt, p. 73, who holds that the consonant /r/ has an opening, rather than a closing effect on the preceding vowel. This scholar concedes, however, that there was a tendency (Tendenz) in ancient and vulgar Latin to close both /e/ and /o/ before /r/ plus consonant and sees in this phenomenon a dialectal feature (p. 82).

Deviations in the *Northern* area are represented by the forms *pudo* (D819 IV/V cent.) for *pondo* and *Mavurtio* (D2829AN a. 527). In non-dated material there are a few deviations shown in the forms *cuntra votu* (DD3401), *gurpus* (D811b) for *corpus* and *cum cumpare* (D1933), this latter being a rather obvious etymological reconstruction with *cum*.[38]

The change that we observe in *pudo* and *cuntra* would seem to bear out Pirson's statement concerning the change of Latin /ŏ/ to /u/ before a nasal. Cf. Prinz, p. 88, who states that the interchange of Latin /ŏ/ and /u/ before *n* plus dental consonant is not infrequent in pagan inscriptions from all over the Roman Empire and makes reference to Priscian's remark that «in sermone rustico» /u/ was pronounced for /ŏ/ before the consonant /n/ followed by a dental, e.g. *funtes pro fontes* (quoted in Lindsay, p. 33).

From the *Central Italian* area we have two deviations to report, both occurring in the word *compar*, namely *cunpari* (DD4714B) and *cum cumparem* (D4231).

The two deviations found in our dated material from the *Southern* area occur in the name *Mavortius*, which appears as *Maburti(us)* (D3030 a. 527; D4677 a. 529). In non-dated material we read *cuiugi* (D4299) for *coniugi*, for which both the possibility of etymological reconstruction with *cum* and assimilation of the stressed to the unstressed vowel have been postulated.[39]

D. *Rome*

Century	/ŏ/>o	/ŏ/>u
III-IV	72	3
V	18	0
VI-VII	13	3

The three deviations in III/IV century material occur in the word *compar*, which appears written as *cum cupare* (D968, a. 366/384; D3797B a. 368) and *cum[pari]* (D4330 ca. a. 312) (cf. *supra* for other examples of etymological reconstruction in this form). In VI/VII cen-

---

[38] In connection with the form *cumpare* (*No. Italy*), *cunpari* (*Ce. Italy*), *cupare* (*Rome*), note that *cunpari* is the universal form in present southern Italian dialects. For Latin stressed /ŏ/ and /ō/ turning into /u/ before a nasal consonant in some southern Italian dialects, cf. Rohlfs, I, p. 210.

[39] Cf. Prinz, p. 84.

tury material, the three deviations occur in the name *Mavortius*, which appears as *Maburti* (D119 a. 528), *Maburtio* (D344 a. 527) and *Mamburtii* (D3157 a. 527) (cf. our footnote #36).

In non-dated material we found a few instances in which Latin /ŏ/ is represented by *u* before a nasal consonant, as shown in the following forms:

> *nuno* (D2584) for *nonno*, *Laeuntis* (D2999F) for *Leontis*, and *nunum* (D4602) for *nonnum*

6.3 Latin /ŏ/ in Monosyllables.

The only form in which Latin /ŏ/ appears spelled with *u* is the preposition *post*. In our whole material we found only two instances of this phenomenon, namely

> *pus con(sulatum)* (D270 a. 562) from the *Narbonensis* area, of a total of 15 occurrences, and *pus con.* (D324 a. 488) from the *Central Italian* area, where this is the only occurrence of *post*.

It would seem reasonable to assume that the apparent shift of Latin /ŏ/ to /u/ in this preposition is due to its proclitic position, so that the vowel may be considered as being in unaccented syllable where, as Muller-Taylor put it, «confusion between *i* and *e* and *u* and *o* is frequent and due to the shifting condition of the vowel system at this period» (p. 33).

Our material would seem to indicate that in open syllable Latin /ŏ/ remained stable throughout the centuries covered by our inscriptions. In closed syllable, on the other hand, Latin /ŏ/, as we have seen, occasionally appears transcribed with *u*, possibly indicating, with due allowances made for cases where etymological reconstruction may have been at work, that the checked position favored the merger of /ŏ/ and /u/, especially before a nasal consonant. (Cf. Latin /ĕ/ in closed syllable, p. 43).

7. *Latin /ō/, represented by the letter o.*

Grandgent states that «Long *o*, pronounced *ǫ*, remained unchanged in Vulgar Latin, at least in most regions....» (p. 85). He goes on to say, however, that «the spelling *u* for *o* is very common in Gaul.... (and) probably represents a very close sound, which later, in northern Gaul, became *ou* or *u̯*: *cōrtem*>Old Fr. *court*» (p. 86). Lindsay, on the other hand, finds that «In Late Latin inscriptions the expression of *o* by *u* is very common» (p. 33/34) and cites Probus' censure of *sobrius non suber* (*ibid.*). Sommer (p. 68) believes that the frequent spelling of *u* for Latin /ō/—just as the spelling *i* for Latin /ē/—is due to the close quality of this vowel, and offers such examples as *octubris, punere* and *uxure* from inscriptional material to illustrate his point.

The parallelism of the relationship between Latin /ē/ and /ĭ/, on the one hand, and Latin /ō/ and /ŭ/, on the other, is pointed out by Väänänen (p. 36), who finds, however, that the spelling *i* for Latin /ē/ and *u* for Latin /ō/ are not frequent before the late Vulgar Latin period (just how late this «époque tardive,» as he calls it, is, he does not say) but that the orthographic confusion between *i* and *e* and *o* and *u* is especially widespread in Merovingian Latin. Supporting Grandgent's statement to the effect that the spelling *u* for Latin /ō/ is very common in Gaul, Pirson finds that the inscriptions from Gaul, especially the Christian inscriptions, are characterized by

> la permutation fréquente de l'*ō* et de l'*ŭ toniques*, qui se produit dans des conditions tout à fait analogues à celles de l'*ē* et de l'*ĭ* (p. 13).

Our own material reveals the following situation:

7.1 Open Syllable

A. *Iberian Peninsula*

Area	Century	/ō/>o	/ō/>u
Baetica	IV-VI	7	0
	VII	12	1
Lusitania	IV-VI	18	1?
	VII	2	0
Tarraconensis	IV-V	15	0
	VII	1	0

Deviations in our dated material are shown in the forms *Octubres* (V287 a. 642) for *Octobres,* from *Baetica,* and *Victura* (V54) for *Victoria* (?), from *Lusitania*.[40]

Regarding the form *Octubres,* the earliest example of which is attested in a Spanish inscription from *Pamplona,* dated 119 A.D. (cf. Carnoy, p. 63), it is found in other areas also (cf. *infra* and Prinz, p. 69) but it is interesting to note that, except for the Neapolitan form *attufre,* which is said to go back to the Oscan form *octufri* (cf. Meyer-Lübke, REW, #6036), the stressed /u/ is characteristic of the Iberian Romance forms, i.e. Old Sp. *otubre,* mod. Sp. *octubre* (*ochubre*), Port. *outubro* and Catalan *uytubre,* which leads Prinz to advance the possibility that «U pro O longa in voce 'October' iam primis p. Ch. n. saeculis vulgo pronuntiata sit» (p. 69).[41]

In non-dated material from the *Tarraconensis,* we found the form *Muses* (V374) for *Moses.*

B. *Gaul*

Area	Century	/ō/>o	/ō/>u	%
Narbonensis	IV-V	23	0	
	VI-VII	37	2	5.1
Lugdunensis	IV-V	28	1	(3.4)
	VI-VII	35	6	14.4

The following forms are illustrative of deviations:

indicciune (D2910 a. 515/533) for *indictione*
Petrunia (D3550A a. 528), from *Narbonensis*
Octubris (D3488 a. 498), *nuvelis* (D1075 ca. a. 630) for *nobilis, ex mure* (D1075; D1076 a. 623), for *more, amure, dulure* (D1076), *Octubrs* (D1674 a. 520), from the *Lugdunensis* area.

---

[40] Vives reads *Victura,* while Diehl has *Victuria* (D1725). It is, of course, possible that the former represents the feminine form of *Victurus,* a name which is occasionally found in our inscriptions, cf. Diehl, ICLV, Vol. III (Index), p. 169. Therefore, *Victura* may not be indicative of the *u* spelling for Latin /ō/.

[41] In his *Gramática,* the eminent Spanish scholar Menéndez-Pidal states the following: «....en España se decía.... *octūber,* acaso siguiendo la pronunciación de colonos de la Italia meridional, pues en osco la ō es la ū, por lo cual el español dice.... *ochubre, octubre,* el portugués *outubro....* y el catalán *uytubre,* contra los demás casos en que se conserva la ō clásica....» (p. 6).

In non-dated material we find forms like

> *subrius* (D1648) from *Narbonensis*
> *matrune* (D353), *sermune* (D1613AN), *amure*, *dulure*, *eurum* (D4827), from *Lugdunensis*.

For a systematic treatment of all instances (not only in the area of Gaul) in which the spelling *u* appears for Latin /ō/ and an interpretation thereof, cf. Prinz, pp. 60-75.

C. *Italy*

Area	Century	/ō/>o	/ō/>u	%
Northern	IV-V	52	2	3.7
	VI	25	2	7.4
	III-IV	21	1	(4.5)
Central	V	14	2	12.5
	VI-VII	28	4	12.5
	III-IV	22	0	
Southern	V	25	0	
	VI-VII	32	1	

The following forms will illustrate deviations:

> *Herulurum* (D494 (but *seniorum!*), *Octubris* (D2737a a. 466), *labure* (D799 a. 556), *October* (D1254 ca. a. 540), from the *Northern* area,
> *October* (D2169 a. 384), *Lumenusa* (D324 a. 488) for *Luminosa* (?),[42] *Octubris* (D1308 ca. a. 435) (occurring also in D325 a. 507/528 and D2962N a. 544), *cum uxure* (D846 a. 493/526), *in numine Dni* (D1029 VI/VII cent.)[43] from the *Central* area,
> *Deusduna* (D3549 a. 560)[44] is the only form in dated material from the *Southern* area in which a deviation occurs.

---

[42] In connection with this spelling and the form *Luminusus* attested in an inscription from Rome (D3159A a. 556), Prinz states: «In nominibus propriis in OSUS, OSA exeuntibus interdum U pro O occurrit in inscriptionibus christianis» (p. 72). Cf. *formosus non formunsus* of the Appendix Probi.

[43] For an analogical influence of *numen* 'divine will, authority' upon *nomen* (cf. *in numine dni*), cf. Prinz, p. 61.

[44] The name *Deusdona* is attested in the same area, cf. D141b a. 570.

In non-dated material we also find an occasional deviation, but it is interesting to note that the apparent conservatism in the *Southern* area, as reflected in our dated material, is evidenced by the fact that the spelling *Victuria* (D3163B) is the only deviation. In the *Northern* area we find forms like

> *uxure* (D1445), *numen* and *nuvet* (=*novit*) (D2496) and *custude* (D3863),

while deviations in the *Central* area are represented by

> *puniri* (=*ponere*) (D824) and *in numine* (D2450A)

D. Rome

Century	/ō/>o	/ō/>u	%
III-IV	160	2	1.2
V	117	4	3.3
VI-VII	40	4	9.0

Examples of deviations are the following:

> *Promuto* (D2945B a. 389) (=abl. of *Promotus*, the name of a Roman consul), *numine* (D4460 a. 385), *sulvit* (D1905, V cent.) (occurring twice), *fossure* (D3782 a. 465), *patrunus* (D622N a. 520), *Petrunia* (D694 a. 522), *oxure* (D840 a. 522), etc....

In non-dated material we find *pisturis* (D132; D621), *fosure* (D3756), and *Rumulus* (D4006CN).

It will be recalled that, on the basis of our evidence, the highest percentage of deviations with respect to Latin /ē/ in open syllable was found in the area of *Gaul*, particularly the *Lugdunensis* (cf. *supra*, p. 53. This absolute «lead» does not seem to obtain for Latin /ō/ in open syllable. As a matter of fact, our figures show that significant deviations, i.e. *u* spelling for Lat. /ō/, do not occur here before the sixth century, while in our fifth century material from *Central Italy* we find a 12.5 % deviation from the classical norm. This fact is of considerable interest, since it would suggest that in this particular area the Latin back vowels /ō/ and /ŭ/ may have merged earlier than in other areas.

84 AN INQUIRY INTO LOCAL VARIATIONS IN VULGAR LATIN

The implication of this evidence is important; it means that our inscriptional material may have shown that the widely accepted theory to the effect that front vowels universally merged before back vowels in Vulgar Latin may not be altogether accurate. (For further discussion, cf. comparison of relationship between Latin /ē/ and /ĭ/ and Latin /ō/ and /ŭ/, pp. 97-99).

7.2 Closed Syllable

The occurrence of Latin /ō/ in this position is very infrequent in our inscriptional material.

A. *Iberian Peninsula*

Area	Century	/ō/>o	/ō/>u
Baetica	IV-VI	0	0
	VII	2	0
Lusitania	IV-VI	1	0
	VII	0	0
Tarraconensis	IV-VI	0	0
	VII	0	0

No deviation in non-dated material.

B. *Gaul*

Area	Century	/ō/>o	/ō/>u
Narbonensis	IV-V	0	0
	VI-VII	3	0
Lugdunensis	IV-V	2	0
	VI-VII	4	0

In a non-dated inscription from the *Narbonensis* area we read *prumta* (D1652) for *prompta* and the same form *prum*[*ptus*...] (D1717) also occurs in a garbled verse inscription from *Lugdunensis*.

C. *Italy*

Area	Century	/ō/>o	/ō/>u
Northern	IV-V	46	0
	VI	4	0
	III-IV	0	0
Central	V	5	0
	VI-VII	3	1
	III-IV	2	0
Southern	V	3	0
	VI-VII	3	0

The only deviation in the *Central* area occurs in the word *cunsule* (D2827A a. 529) for *consule*.

On a non-dated and very garbled verse inscription from the *Northern* area we read.... *p]rumptus* (D269). [45]

D. *Rome*

Century	/ō/>o	/ō/>u
III-IV	4	0
V	8	0
VI-VII	2	0

In a non-dated inscription we read the form *tussor* (D604) for *tonsor*. [46]

7.3 Latin /ō/ in Monosyllables.

Monosyllabic words, for the most part, are restricted to the ablative singular form of the demonstrative, *hōc*, appearing in the frequent

---

[45] In connection with this form, Prinz states: «factum esse potest, ut U ad analogiam vocabuli «sumptus» orta sit» (p. 67).

[46] For the *u* spelling for *o* before the consonant group *ns* in late Latin texts (parallelling the orthography *ins* for *ens*), cf. Väänänen, p. 36. The possibility of the closing of /ō/ to /u/ (also /ē/ to /i/ before an /s/, e.g. *nus* for *nos*, or the second declension plural accusative ending -*us* for -*os*, is discussed by B. Löfstedt, p. 76, with reference to a theory first advanced by Sepulcri and supported by Grandgent, cf. Pei, *Texts*, p. 33.

formula *in hoc tumulo/loco requiescit....* Some monosyllables are represented by the pronouns *nos, vos,* the adverb *non* and the preposition *pro.*

With the single exception of the form *vus* (*vus adiuro*) (D3862) found on a non-dated inscription in the *Northern Italian* area, the orthography of *u* for *o* is limited to the area of *Gaul,* as follows:

Area	Century	/ō/>o	/ō/>u	%
Narbonensis	IV-V	0	1	
	VI-VII	16	0	
Lugdunensis	IV-V	3	2	40.0
	VI-VII	21	2	8.6

The deviation in the *Narbonensis* area occurs in the formula *in huc loc[u requiescunt]* (D2454 a. 472). On a non-dated inscription from this area we read *in huc to[molo]* (D2455N).[47]

Turning to the *Lugdunensis* area, we find the deviations in IV/V century material represented by two occurrences of *huc* (D1340 a. 486; D1703 a. 431), while in VI/VII century material we find two occurrences of *nus* (*ora pro nus*) (D2352; D2352A, both VII cent.).[48]

The extremely scarce sampling of Latin /ō/ in closed syllable makes it impossible to draw any conclusions in connection with the merger of Latin /ō/ and /ŭ/ in this position and we must turn to the discussion of Latin /ŭ/ first, in order to determine on an overall basis the percentage of the merger of these two vowels in the various areas under study.

---

[47] It may be of interest to note that in VI/VII century material from this area, all 16 occurrences of Latin /ō/ are found in *hoc.*

It must be pointed out, however, that in the case of the form *huc,* appearing in the formula *in hoc tumulo* and other similar ones, there is also the possibility of the use of the accusative form *hunc* in which the stonecutter omitted the /n/ before the velar consonant, pointing to a morphological confusion of the classical accusative and ablative forms. As a matter of fact, the use of *hoc* for *hunc,* or a phrase like *in hunc tumulo* are attested more than once in our material.

[48] For the frequent occurrence of *nus* and *vus* in Merovingian documents, cf. Pei, *Texts,* p. 32.

8. Latin /ŭ/, represented by the letter u.

Lindsay states that «the coincidence of Latin ō and ŭ in the Romance languages makes it natural that we shoul find o written for u on late inscriptions, and in plebeian forms.» (p. 37). As to the chronology of the merger of Latin /ŭ/ and /ō/, Grandgent believes that «short u, pronounced ų, became, probably by the fourth century or earlier, o in most of the Empire» (p. 87), drawing attention to the censured forms *colomna* for *columna* and *torma* for *turma* in the Appendix Probi.

Väänänen, on the other hand, states that «le changement ŭ>o, sauf à la finale, est très peu attesté même à l'époque tardive» (p. 37) and holds that the merger of Latin /ĭ/ and /ē/ is prior to that of Latin /ŭ/ and /ō/, which is quite in line with later Romance developments, seeing that in Sardinian, Roumanian and some Southern Italian dialects this merger has not taken place, while the merger of Latin /ĭ/ and /ē/ has had a greater extension and, in particular, has reached the area of Roumania (p. 30).

The situation, as reflected in our inscriptional material, is the following:

8.1 Open Syllable

Area	Century	/ŭ/>u	/ŭ/>o	%
Baetica	IV-VI	1	0	
	VII	6	0	
Lusitania	IV-VI	0	0	
	VII	2	0	
Tarraconensis	IV-VI	2	4	(66.6)
	VII	0	0	

Deviations in this latter area are represented by the following:

tomolo (=*tumulo*) and *sobitus* (V276 a. 550)
Martoria (V189 a. 393 and V223) for *Marturia*.[49]

---

[49] The masculine form *Marturius* occurs also several times. Diehl seems to think that the correct spelling is *Martyrius* and *Martyria* (cf. Index to ICLV,

It may be interesting to note that in V189 we find both the spelling *Martoria* and *Marturia*.

B. *Gaul*

Area	Century	/ŭ/>u	/ŭ/>o	%
Narbonensis	IV-V	1	1	(50.0)
	VI-VII	10	11	52.4
Lugdunensis	IV-V	6	1	(14.3)
	VI-VII	20	10	33.3

By far the most frequent example showing an *o* spelling for Latin /ŭ/ is *tomulus, tomolus, tomolo,* etc. In fact, all deviations from VI/VII century material from both areas occur in this word exclusively, although the correct form *tumulus* is not infrequent. Thus, we find *in hoc tomolum* (D3550 a. 560) but *in hoc tumolo* (D3550A a. 528) in the very same area (*Vienne, Narbonensis*), as well as *tumulo* (D3559 a. 492) alternating with *tomolo* (D3563E) (both from *Lugudunum, Lugdunensis*) (cf. Diehl, ICLV, Part II, Chapter XXIIII, pp. 235-238).

Other deviations occur in *Gerosale* (D1303, V cent.) for *Hierusalem*[50] and *Lopa* (D3472) for the proper name *Lupa*, both in the *Narbonensis* area, while *Astorio* (= abl. sing. of *Asturius*) (D1422 a. 449) and *Lopolus* (D3584) occur in the *Lugdudensis*. In this area was also found the form *iovenim* (= *iuvenem*) (D1218 a. 548/612), for which an open [o] has been postulated to account for Old Fr. *juene*, due to the influence of the following labial, cf. Bourciez, *Phonétique*, p. 75; M. K. Pope, *From Latin to Modern French* (Manchester, 1934), p. 185.

In non-dated inscriptions, we find the same hesitation in the spelling of *tumulus* that we observe in dated material.

Vol. III, p. 108), although *Marturius, Marturus* and *Marturia* are attested throughout his whole corpus as well. There seems to be little doubt that the name ultimately goes back to *martyr*, which is spelled either *martir* or, more frequently, *martur* throughout the Christian inscriptions (cf. Diehl's Index, p. 365). The proper names are not attested in the classical dictionary and our assumption of Latin /ŭ/ in *Marturia* and *Marturius* is based on the analogy of other names in *-urius*, e.g. *Mercurius*.

[50] Lewis & Short (p. 854) give the form *Hierusalem* with both a short and a long *u*. It is also conceivable that *Gerosale* represents a crossing between *Hierusalem* and *Hierosolyma*, the Latin transcription of the Greek name of *Jerusalem*.

C. Italy

Area	Century	/ŭ/>u	/ŭ/>o
Northern	IV-V	24	0
	VI	1	1
Central	III-IV	1	1
	V	2	0
	VI-VII	1	0
Southern	III-IV	4	0
	V	2	0
	VI-VII	8	0

The only deviation in the *Northern* area occurs in *nom(eri)* (D550 a. 589), while in the *Central* area we find the form *norui* (= dat. sg. of *nurus*) (D365 a. 376).[51]

No deviations were found in non-dated material.

D. Rome

Century	/ŭ/>u	/ŭ/>o
III-IV	19	0
V	15	0
VI-VII	4	0

Two deviations were found in non-dated material, namely *soboli* (= dat. sg. of *suboles*) (D102) and *iovina defuncta* (= *iuvenis*) (D3535). This latter form is all the more interesting since it would seem to show a shift from a third declension to a first/second declension adjective, cf. *pauper mulier non paupera mulier* in the Appendix Probi.

---

[51] From the evidence of the later development of this word in Italian, the [o] must have been open, possibly by analogy of *socrus*, cf. Italian *nuora* and *suocera/suocero*. C. Grandgent, *From Latin to Italian* (2nd ed.; Cambridge-Mass., 1933), p. 29, gives *soror* and *nova* as having influenced the vowel quality in *norus*. (For the declensional shift in *nora* for *norus*, cf. Appendix Probi: *nurus non nura*).

8.2 Closed Syllable

A. *Iberian Peninsula*

Area	Century	/ŭ/>u	/ŭ/>o
Baetica	IV-VI	6	0
	VII	8	0
Lusitania	IV-VI	8	0
	VII	7	0
Tarraconensis	IV-VI	3	1
	VII	3	0

The deviation in this latter area occurs in the proper name *Cesaracosta* (V436) for *Caesaraugusta*, which we find on a Visigothic coin inscription.[52]

B. *Gaul*

Area	Century	/ŭ/>u	/ŭ/>o
Narbonensis	IV-V	5	0
	VI-VII	7	0
Lugdunensis	IV-V	6	0
	VI-VII	10	1

The only deviation in this dated material occurs in the verb form *occort* (= *occurrit*) (D1075 ca. a. 630).

In non-dated material we find a few deviations as follows:

> *resorge (in Cristo!)* (D3472, *oxsur* (D3580)[53] and *Teodemodos* (=*Teudemundus*) (D4426), from *Narbonensis;* *volontas* (D4827), from the *Lugdunensis* area.

---

[52] It may be of interest to note that in the Mateu y Llopis collection of Visigothic coins, the name of this city appears five times as *Cesaracosta* and twice as *Cesaracusta*.

[53] Cf. Old Fr. *oissor* (Grandsaignes-d'Hauterive, *Dictionnaire d'ancien français* (Paris, 1947), p. 439).

C. *Italy*

Area	Century	/ŭ/>u	/ŭ/>o
Northern	IV-V	30	0
	VI	15	0
Central	III-IV	12	0
	V	4	0
	VI-VII	17	0
Southern	III-IV	6	0
	V	7	0
	VI-VII	10	0

In non-dated material from the *Northern* area we find one instance of *o* spelling for Latin /ŭ/ in *ocsor sua* (D4179B).

D. *Rome*

Century	/ŭ/>u	/ŭ/>o
III-IV	59	1
V	41	1
VI-VII	16	0

Deviations appear in the following words:

alom(no) (D760N a. 340) and *colomna* (D701 a. 452).[54]

In non-dated material we found *o* spellings for Latin /ŭ/ in the following forms:

alomna (D762), *oxor* (D293; D4135H).

8.3 Latin /ŭ/ in Monosyllables (Including Prepositions and Conjunctions)

Except for a single occurrence of *sob* (D2889A ca. a. 524) for *sub* found in the *Narbonensis* area (out of a total of 10 instances of this

---

[54] Cf. *columna non colomna* in the Appendix Probi.

preposition), the *o* spelling for Latin /ŭ/ is found in connection with the preposition *cum,* appearing variously spelled *com* or *con.*

A. *Iberian Peninsula*

> Baetica: ⎫ About half a dozen occurrences of this preposition,
> Lusitania: ⎬ always appearing as *cum.*
> Tarraconensis: One occurrence of *com* (V262, VII cent.) to four instances of *cum* (all of them in fourth/sixth cent. material).

B. *Gaul*

A total of three occurrences throughout this area, always spelled *cum.*

C. *Italy*

It is in this area (as well as in *Rome*) that we find the greatest number of instances of *com/con* for *cum,* in the following ratio:

Area:	Northern		Central			Southern		
Century:	IV-V	VI	III-IV	V	VI-VII	III-IV	V	VI-VII
CUM	4	0	4	2	2	6	3	1
COM(CON)	2	0	1	0	0	0	0	1

The following will serve as a few illustrative examples:

> *com patre* (D208 a. 470), *con ipsa* (D844),
> *con conpare* (D4206), *con nept. sua* (D847)

from the *Northern* area,

> *con filiis* (D3918, III cent.), *con coiuge* (D3902B)

from the *Central* area, and

> *con patre suo* (D141b a. 570), *con tua sorore* (D2533) (but *cun Silbina* in the same inscription), *con quen* (D4278B)

from the *Southern* area.

D. *Rome*

Century:	III-IV	V	VI-VII
CUM	33	8	5
COM(CON)	1	1	1

A few examples in both dated and non-dated material:

con coiuge (D3501 a. 390), *con filiis* (D3727CN a. 481), *con filio* (D3115D a. 550), *com pace* (D3701A), *con conpare sua* (D4231B), *et passim*.

The form *com* is already attested in an inscription from Pompei [55] and has been explained by analogy with compound verbs,[56] but it would seem that because of the constant proclitic use of this preposition a merger of Latin /ŭ/ and /ō/ in unstressed position might also be postulated. In any event, the absence of the forms *com* and *con* in the area of Gaul may be insofar interesting to note, as this preposition in the form of *con* has survived in Spanish and Italian only.[57]

8.4 Latin /ŭ/ in Hiatus

We find an occasional *o* spelling for Latin /ŭ/ in this position, but the instances are so few that no special count was made to establish a ratio of correct versus incorrect occurrences.

In *Gaul* we found a single example: *filius sous* (D1373A) from the *Lugdunensis* area.

In the *Italian* area (including *Rome*), the only examples were found in the North, e.g. *doas* (D516) and *doa* (D545) in the fourth/fifth century material from the same area (*Concordia* cemetery) as well as *voloeret* (= *voluerit*) (D811b).

---

[55] Cf. Väänänen, *Inscriptions*, p. 45.
[56] Cf. Prinz, p. 30, where he argues in favor of an analogical interference as follows: «'com, con' e verbis compositis sumpta esset inde cognoscitur, quod plerumque.... M et N finales eodem modo quo in vocalibus compositis adhibitae sunt et vicissim 'cum' in vocalibus compositis invenitur (velut 'cumparare').»
[57] Neither Pirson, pp. 15-17, nor Pei, *Texts*, p. 34, give any instance of *com* or *con* for *cum*.

Looking back over our evidence pointing to a merger of Latin /ŭ/ and /ō/, we find, first of all, that the occurrence of Latin /ŭ/ especially in open syllable, is quite infrequent and the question arises whether the figures showing deviations in some areas can be taken at face value. Thus, we find in fourth/sixth century material from the *Tarraconensis* area that this vowel in free position is represented by *o* four times out of a total of six occurrences. Would it be legitimate, therefore, to conclude that in this particular area the merger of Latin /ŭ/ and /ō/ is an accomplished fact? Possibly so, but it must be borne in mind that

a) our sampling is too small to draw a positive conclusion

b) two *o* spellings for Latin /ŭ/ occur in the very same inscription (Southeastern *Tarraconensis*) and may simply represent the spelling of a single individual

c) two more *o* spellings occurring in the proper name *Marturia* are found on two inscriptions from the very same area (*Tarragona* cemetery) and may also represent a localism only.

Nevertheless, and bearing these reservations in mind, we do not believe that the figure representing deviations can be entirely discarded since, given a larger sampling, *o* spellings for Latin /ŭ/ may well have occurred over a larger area.

The same reservation must be made, of course, in connection with other areas, especially the *Northern* and *Central Italian* areas where we find one deviation out of a total of two occurrences. The danger of attaching too much importance to a single example is obvious.

We shall now summarize the relationship between Latin /ō/ and /ŭ/ in both open and closed syllables (cf. Latin /ē/ and /ĭ/, p. 67) to determine overall percentage figures that might indicate the trend of the merger of these vowels in the various areas under study.

THE ACCENTED VOWELS

Area	Century	Free /ō/	Free /ŭ/	Checked /ō/	Checked /ŭ/	Total Correct	Total Dev.	% of Deviations
Baetica	IV-VI	7	1	0	6	14	0	0.0
	VII	12	6	2	8	28	1	3.5
Lusitania	IV-VI	18	0	1	8	27	1	3.5
	VII	2	2	0	7	11	0	0.0
Tarraconensis	IV-VI	15	2	0	3	20	5	20.0
	VII	1	0	0	3	4	0	0.0
Narbonensis	IV-V	23	1	0	5	29	1	3.4
	VI-VII	37	10	3	7	57	13	18.5
Lugdunensis	IV-V	28	6	2	6	42	2	4.3
	VI-VII	35	20	4	10	71	17	19.3
No. Italy	IV-V	52	24	46	30	152	2	1.3
	VI	25	1	4	15	45	3	6.6
Ce. Italy	III-IV	21	1	0	12	34	2	5.5
	V	14	2	5	4	25	2	7.4
	VI-VII	28	1	3	17	49	5	9.3
So. Italy	III-IV	22	4	2	6	34	0	0.0
	V	25	2	3	7	37	0	0.0
	VI-VII	32	8	3	10	53	1	1.8
Rome	III-IV	160	19	4	59	242	3	1.2
	V	117	15	8	41	181	5	2.6
	VI-VII	40	4	2	16	62	4	6.0

This table calls for the following comments:

The 20 % figure in the *Tarraconensis* area is rather misleading since, as stated above, it includes two deviations, i.e. two *o* spellings for Latin /ŭ/, in the same inscription and, hence, may represent the mistake of a single individual only. Even if we leave this particular item out of our count, we get a 13 % deviation which includes two inscriptions from the same restricted area (cf. *supra*, p. 87). But, while the evidence may not be conclusive as to the merger of Latin /ō/ and /ŭ/ in this whole area, due to the small sampling of the occurrence of these vowels, there would seem to be little doubt that of the three Spanish areas this one is the least conservative (cf. summary table of Latin /ē/ and /ĭ/, p. 67). As to the decrease in the percentage of deviations in seventh century material to zero, the fact that we have a total of only four occurrences of these vowels, i.e. one fifth of the material with respect to the previous centuries, may be offered as an explanation.

The single deviations in *Baetica* and *Lusitania,* respectively, are also subject to reservations, seeing that one occurs in a proper name and may not at all be indicative of a merger of Latin /ō/ and /ŭ/ and the other may be a dialectal form (cf. *supra* our footnotes Nos. 40 and 41. p. 81).

There seems to be little doubt that the merger of Latin /ō/ and /ŭ/ is an accomplished fact in *Gaul* by the sixth century, as indicated by the considerable jump in percentage figures as against the previous century.

In the *Italian* area, it would seem that the *Northern, Central* and *Roman* areas show a very definite trend towards a merger of these two Latin vowel phonemes, while the *South* is most conservative. This conservatism would seem to be in line with later developments in this particular area, seeing that the merger of Latin /ō/ and /ŭ/ has not taken place in *Sardinia* and a few *Southern Italian* dialects (cf. Väänänen, p. 30). [58] Furthermore, it would also seem that this trend may

---

[58] *Sardinia* is included in our *Southern Italian* material, in accordance with the divisions of the *Corpus Inscriptionum Latinarum* which we are following.

Dacia, i.e. grosso modo present-day *Rumania,* which does not partake in the merger of Latin /ō/ and /ŭ/ either, is represented in the Diehl collection by only three inscriptions (D434, D1610, D3314), much too insignificant a sampling to be useful. However, it may be of interest to note a reference by B. Löfstedt (addenda to p. 211) to a study of inscriptional material from the

have started in the *Central Italian* area considerably earlier than in other areas (excepting the inconclusive evidence in *Tarraconensis*), as shown by the consistently increasing pattern of our percentage figures.

Comparing the percentage figures obtained for the relationship between Latin /ē/ and /ĭ/, on the one hand, and Latin /ō/ and /ŭ/, on the other hand, we find the following situation:

Area	Century	/ē/ and /ĭ/	/ō/ and /ŭ/
Baetica	IV-VI	1.8	0.0
	VII	3.8	3.5
Lusitania	IV-VI	4.3	3.5
	VII	0.0	0.0
Tarraconensis	IV-VI	8.2	20.0
	VII	4.7	0.0
Narbonensis	IV-V	20.0	3.4
	VI-VII	25.9	18.5
Lugdunensis	IV-V	21.7	4.3
	VI-VII	37.5	19.3
No. Italy	IV-V	9.2	1.3
	VI	6.3	6.6
	III-IV	1.6	5.5
Ce. Italy	V	4.6	7.4
	VI-VII	8.6	9.3
	III-IV	1.8	0.0
So. Italy	V	3.9	0.0
	VI-VII	5.4	1.8
	III-IV	2.0	1.2
Rome	V	4.9	2.6
	VI-VII	4.6	6.0

Danubian provinces (i.e. Pannonia, Dacia and Moesia) by the Rumanian scholar Mihǎescu (*Recueil d'études romanes*, Bucarest, 1950, p. 150), in which he notes several instances of *o* spelling for Latin /ŭ/. In his study of Pannanian inscriptions, the Hungarian scholar V. Luzsénszky, «A pannónai latin feliratok nyelvtana» in *Egyetemes Philologiai Közlöny*, LVII (May-July 1933), gives a number of *o* spellings for Latin /ŭ/, which might very well point to the fact that there was an incipient merger in the Danubian provinces also, as evidenced by the Rumanian forms *toamnǎ*<*autumnus*, *roib*<*rubeus* and *coif*<*cufea*, cf. Vidos, p. 195.

Some Romance scholars hold that the merger of Latin /ē/ and /ĭ/ preceded that of Latin /ō/ and /ŭ/, thereby also accounting for the fact that the merger of the latter occurred at such a late date as not to reach the East after communications had broken down in the Empire.[59]

While this may be true for some areas, for instance the areas of *Gaul* and *Northern Italy*, on the basis of our figures it would seem that in other areas either the contrary took place, i.e. the merger of Latin /ō/ and /ŭ/ preceding that of /ē/ and /ĭ/ (cf. our figures for *Central Italy*) or the mergers of Latin /ē/ and /ĭ/, on the one hand, and Latin /ō/ and /ŭ/, on the other hand, proceeded more or less *pari passu* (cf. our figures for *Rome*).

Regarding the question of chronology of the merger of these Latin vowel phonemes, Bourciez, *Éléments*, pp. 42/43, places it in the course of the third or fourth centuries. On the basis of our evidence, the merger of Latin /ē/ and /ĭ/ may very well have taken place in the area of *Gaul*, and possibly also *Northern Italy*, by the time indicated by this scholar, while the merger of Latin /ō/ and /ŭ/, in these very same areas, may have occurred only a century or so later. On the other hand, Latin /ō/ and /ŭ/ in the area of *Central Italy* and possibly also the *Eastern Tarraconensis*[60] may also have merged by the time specified by Bourciez, whereas the merger of Latin /ē/ and /ĭ/, in these very areas, would have taken place at a subsequent time, the reverse phenomenon of what we observe in *Gaul* and *Northern Italy*. There is, indeed, nothing in the nature of things that says that Latin /ē/ and /ĭ/ must have merged before /ō/ and /ŭ/ and there would seem to be no reason not to assume that the merger of the back vowels may have preceded that of the front vowels,[61] at least in some areas.

Prinz (p. 74) believes that in the area of *Gaul* the merger of Latin /ō/ and /ŭ/ was an accomplished fact by about the fifth century, while inscriptions from *Italy* and *Spain* do not offer enough examples, so this scholar says, to draw any specific conclusions. He suggests that the apparent conservatism in these areas may be due to the fact that

---

[59] Vidos, p. 194; B. Löfstedt, p. 90; Bourciez, *Éléments*, p. 43; Väänänen, p. 30.

[60] Be it said, in passing, that the *Eastern Tarraconensis* is precisely the area where the *Catalan* language developed and that our material may point to an early dialectal separation of this area from the rest of the Spanish Peninsula. Cf. Entwistle, p. 82 ff.

[61] Cf. Martinet, p. 99.

> in iis regionibus, quae non tantopere bellis exagitatae erant quantopere Gallia Transalpina in universum homines orthographiae magis periti erant (p. 75),

but concludes

> Immo vero in omnibus his terris eodem fere tempore vocalium O et U confusionem factam esse opinor (*ibid.*).

Our analysis by regions would indicate that, on the whole, the conclusions arrived at by Prinz are tenable, although it must be kept in mind that this scholar takes the areas of *Gaul, Italy,* and *Spain* as a whole, rather than breaking them up into more restricted regions. Whatever the situation in seemingly conservative *Baetica* and *Lusitania* may be (the 0 % in seventh century material from the *Tarraconensis* would seem to be due to the fact that there is a total of only four occurrences of Latin /ō/ and /ŭ/ and no deviation), the conclusions of Prinz would certainly not be applicable to *Southern Italy* where, as shown by our figures, there can be hardly any question of a merger of Latin /ō/ and /ŭ/.

Summing up the question of the merger of Latin /ē/ and /ĭ/ and /ō/ and /ŭ/, respectively, it would seem, on the basis of our analysis, that it is not accurate to state that in those areas of Romania in which these mergers did take place, the front vowels universally merged first; rather, the situation might be summed up as follows:

> (a) the merger of Latin /ē/ and /ĭ/ preceded that of Latin /ō/ and /ŭ/ in the areas of *Gaul* and *Northern Italy,*
>
> (b) the merger of Latin /ō/ and /ŭ/ preceded that of /ē/ and /ĭ/ in the area of *Central Italy* and, possibly, the *Eastern Tarraconensis*, essentially the area of what is *Catalonia* today,
>
> (c) the merger of Latin /ē/ and /ĭ/ and /ō/ and /ŭ/ proceeded more or less *pari passu* in the areas of *Baetica, Lusitania* and *Rome,*
>
> (d) the merger of Latin /ē/ and /ĭ/ alone seems to have taken place in the *Southern Italian* area.

9. Latin /ū/, represented by the letter u.

Latin /ū/, which differed in quality from Latin /ŭ/ (cf. Lindsay, p. 14), remained unchanged in Vulgar Latin, thus Grandgent (p. 86) informs us, and this scholar adds that «in Gaul, a large part of Northern Italy and Western Rhaetia it was probably formed a little forward of its normal position» (*ibid.*), approaching the [y] sound it has assumed in these areas today. For this palatal articulation of Latin /ū/ some scholars have attempted to seek an explanation in the Celtic substratum, cf. Pei, *Texts*, p. 36, for a discussion of these theories.

Sommer states that Latin /ū/ «bleibt durchweg unverändert» (p. 70), but notes an occasional *o* spelling for this vowel in both stressed and unstressed positions, e.g. *fortona, futuro, omane* (= *humanae*) and *iocunda*, although in the last two cases there may have been analogical interference with *homo* and *iocus*, respectively.

An occasional *o* spelling for Latin /ū/ appears in our material also but these instances are very rare.

We found three occurrences of *orna* for *urna*, as follows:

(a) V285 a. 630, verse inscription from *León* (*Tarraconensis*)
(b) D3778a a. 577, verse inscription from *Rome*
(c) D1809, verse fragment from *Arles* (*Narbonensis*)

Seeing that this form appears in widely separated areas, it is likely that Latin /ū/ in this word had become /o/ in Vulgar Latin, as suggested by Pirson,[62] although the possibility of an analogical influence of the verb *ornare* has also been advanced.[63]

An isolated instance of an *o* spelling for Latin /ū/ was found on an inscription from *Aquileia* (*Northern Italy*) which, in part, reads as follows:

videas in die iudicii inmones ... ebadas[64]
(VI or VII cent. ?)

---

[62] Dans *orna* au lieu de *ūrna*.... l'*u* a subi la même altération que l'*ū* de *ūrina, ūrsus, ūrtica*, dont la voyelle tonique est devenue *o* en latin vulgaire, comme l'attestent les formes romanes correspondantes (p. 16). Cf. It., Sp. *orina*, It. *orso*, Sp. *oso*, Fr. *ours* and It. *ortica*, Sp. *ortiga*, Fr. *ortie*.

[63] Cf. Prinz, p. 94.

[64] For the *b* spelling for Latin /v/, reflecting a spirantization of the labio-velar phoneme, cf. Sturtevant, p. 43; Pei, *Texts*, pp. 95/96 (summary

for *inmunis*. It may be of interest to note that in this very area we also find the form *froniti* (D4694) for *fruniti* (p.p. of *fruniscor*), one of the very rare occurrences of an *o* spelling for Latin /ū/ in *unstressed* position. Both forms are interpreted by Prinz as a reflection of an [o] pronunciation of Latin /ū/ before a nasal, a regional feature which is still found in some Northern Italian dialects.[65]

In view of the evidence of our inscriptional material, in which Latin /ū/ appears generally represented by *u*, it would seem fair to state that, with the exception just noted, this vowel is quite stable in our corpus, in both open and closed syllables.

---

of opinions); Battisti, p. 154 (concerning the graphic distribution of *b* and *v*); Jungemann, p. 336 ff. (particularly with reference to the Iberian Peninsula); Pei, *Italian Language*, p. 60 (advancing his own theory regarding the confusion of *b* and *v*).

[65] Cf. p. 97. Meyer-Lübke, *Grammaire*, I, p. 80, mentions this phenomenon in the dialect of Emilia.

Chapter II: The Unaccented Vowels

Introductory

Grandgent (p. 91 ff.) treats the unaccented vowels from the point of view of whether they are (a) in hiatus, (b) initial, (c) intertonic (i.e. the syllable which follows the secondary and precedes the primary stress), (d) penult and (e) final positions. It is our intention to follow this classification.

In connection with the treatment of the unaccented vowels, i.e. vowels that do not bear the primary stress,[1] this scholar makes the following comments:

> Among the unstressed vowels, those of the first syllable had most resistance, possibly through a lingering influence of the Old Latin accent. The vowels of the final syllable lost much of their distinctness, but did not fall, except sporadically, until long after the Vulgar Latin period, and then only in part of the Empire. Grammarians testify to the confusion of *o* and *u*.... *Quase, sibe* are found in place of *quasi, sibi*.... According to Quintilian I, IV, 7, «in *here* [for *heri*] neque *e* plane neque *i* auditur.» Weakest were medial vowels immediately following the secondary or the primary stress.... (pp. 91/92)[2]

---

[1] For a discussion of secondary stress in Vulgar Latin, cf. Grandgent, p. 67.

[2] For a similar classification of unstressed vowels, cf. Vossler-Schmeck, pp. 91 ff. «Es sind nämlich mindestens zwei Arten von nichthochtonigen Vokalen zu unterscheiden: *schwachtonige* and *unbetonte*. Dabei gilt im groben die Regel, dass hinter dem Akzent vorzugsweise die Unbetonheit, vor dem Akzent vorzugsweise die Schwachbetonheit ihre Stelle haben, dass also in den Anlautsilben der Ton meist stärker ist als in den Auslautsilben....»

It is the consensus of Romance scholars that the quantitative difference of the so-called classical Latin vowel system was reduced to a qualitative system of seven vowels in the greatest part of Romania, in stressed position,[3] while in unstressed position this system was reduced to a five vowel system, i.e. apart from the merger of Latin /ē/ and /ĭ/, on the one hand, and Latin /ō/ and /ŭ/, on the other hand, Latin /ĕ/ and /ŏ/ were qualitatively not different from their long counterparts.[4]

The evidence that our inscriptional material offers in regard to unstressed vowels is the following:

1. *Latin /ā/ and /ă/, represented by the letter a*

Lindsay (p. 17) notes that on inscriptions the spellings *je-* and *jej-* appear for *ja-* and *jaj-* and that «the Vulgar Latin name of the month was Jenuarius.» Sommer (pp. 55/56) also points out this «Wandel von *i̯a-* zu *i̯e-*» which appears in *ieiunus* for *iaiunus* but states that this change is limited to the initial syllable.[5]

In several areas we find Latin /ă/ spelled *e* when preceded, in the initial syllable, by the semivowel /j/, particularly in the forms *Ienuarius* and *Ienuaria*, i.e. not only in the meaning of «the month of January» but also in the proper names.

Here are a few examples:

(a) Gaul (both *Narbonensis* and *Lugdunensis*):

Ienoarii (D2222A, V/VI cent.)
Genoarias (D2891A a. 529); *Genarius* (D2803B)
Ienuarias (D4426,)

---

[3] Cf. Lausberg I, pp. 96-101. For a recent discussion, cf. N.C.W. Spence, «Quantity and Quality in the Vowel System of Vulgar Latin,» *Word*, 21.1 (April 1965), 1-18.

[4] Cf. Maurer, *Gramática*, p. 15, where the following statement is made: «Distinguem-se, em geral, apenas cinco vogais, pois que, em conseqüência do desenvolvimento do acento intensivo, estas se enfraqueceram, de modo que não se conservou a distinção entre ẹ e ę e ọ e ọ». Cf. also Battisti who states: ....delle vocali lat. volg. si mantennero generalmente i tipi (*a, e, i, o, u*) ma non le differenze di qualità o di timbro» (p. 108).

[5] Also cf. Väänänen, p. 36; Battisti, p. 110; Grandgent, p. 96; Kieckers, p. 89; Niedermann, *Phonétique*, p. 53.

(b) *Italy* (exclusive of the *Southern* area):

Ienuarius (D1060 a. 490); *Genuarias* (D4451A)
kal. *Ienuarias* (D1366); *Ge[n]uaarus* (D4601)

(c) *Rome*:

Ienuario (D287a a. 338); cal. *Ien*. (D2969AN a. 385)
Zenuarius (D1905, V cent.); *Genuara* (D3508N a. 530)
Zemnare (=*Ianuariae*) (D2698), *et passim*.

In the area of *Narbonensis* (*Gaul*) we even find a form *Ginnoarius* (D2890 a. 525) for *Ianuarius*, in connection with which Pirson (p. 29) comments that the /e/ from Latin initial /a/ in contact with a palatal sometimes became /i/ and offers the example of Prov. *getar* and *gitar* from *iectare* (cf. It. *gettare*, and occasionally, *gittare*, Fr. *jeter*) to illustrate his point. [6]

That the form *Ienuarius* must have been widespread throughout Romania seems to be shown by the subsequent development of the word for January in various Romance languages, cf. It. *gennaio*, Sic. *yinnaru*, Log. *bennardzu*, Friul. *dzenar*, Old Picard *jenvier*, Prov. *genvier*, Cat. *gener*, Sp. *enero*,[7] as against Fr. *janvier*, Pg. *janeiro*, while Rum. *ghenar* seems to be a borrowing from mod. Greek. [8]

In the area of Rome we also found a single occurrence of *treiecit* (D4462) for *traiecit*. Battisti (p. 110) quotes several examples of comparable forms (the earliest attested form *reliquiae treiectae* going back to 130 A.D.) and brings this change in line with the one we observe in words where initial /ă/ is preceded, rather than followed by a palatal semivowel.

The only apparent change of Latin /ă/ in penult position occurs in the forms *monuchus* (D1655) and *monicus* (D1657), both from the *Lugdunensis* (*Gaul*) area. [9] Discussing these forms, Pirson states:

---

[6] For the attested form *iectare*, cf. Battisti, p. 110.

[7] There seems to be no example of Ienuarius in Spanish inscriptions. Brüch, in his article «Der Wandel iā - iē im Latein,» *Glotta*, XXV (1936), 35-42, believes that this may be due to a greater conservatism on the part of scribes and stonecutters in the Spanish area who consistently wrote *Ianuarius* under the influence of the school.

[8] Cf. Meyer-Lübke, REW, #4576, p. 336; Meyer-Lübke, *Einführung*, p. 157; Diehl, ILCV, Vol. III, p. 292; Grandgent, p. 96; Väänänen, p. 36; Sommer, p. 55; Kieckers, p. 89.

[9] Battisti (p. 112) states that *monicus* for *monachus* is attested in the fifth century but fails to give information as to where it was found.

Conformément aux lois qui régissent le développement de la voyelle atone, l'*a* s'affaiblit en *i* et cet *i* est rendu tantôt par *e* et tantôt par le son *ü*, intermédiaire entre *ī* et *ū*. (p. 28)

Because *monachus* is a learned loan-word in which there seems to have been hesitation in the quality of the penult,[10] it is hardly possible to come to any conclusion regarding Latin /ă/ in this position, especially since in the few occurrences in other words this vowel appears written as *a*. In any event, it is the form *monicus* which is postulated as the etymon of Prov. *monge* and Fr. *moine*.[11]

Latin /ă/ in *final* syllable, in both morphological and non-morphological endings, occurs quite infrequently and appears as *a*, with the following exceptions:

In an inscription from the *Narbonensis* area we read
diem futuri iudicii... letus spectit (D3485, V/VI cent.)

for what we would expect to be *spectat* (in the sense of *expectat*?). Could this form indicate the weakening of Latin /ă/ in this position in the direction of a *schwa*, as it is said to have occurred in northern Gaul by the eighth century?[12] The total absence of other first conjugation third person singular present indicative forms in this area makes any kind of statement in this regard highly questionable and hypothetical.

In the sentence

cui sistint lacreme et cesint (= *cessent*) *suspiria fletus* (D1076 a. 632/3)

the form *sistint* for *sistant* (third conjugation present active subjunctive third person plural) would seem to be of a morphological nature, in that the third conjugation present subjunctive plural ending *ant* is replaced by the first conjugation *ent* ending.[13] The spelling *int*, which we also observe in *cesint*, would then be due to a confusion of Latin

---

[10] Cf. Meyer-Lübke, *Einführung*, p. 153.
[11] Cf. Meyer-Lübke, REW, #5654, p. 414; Pope, p. 181. Cf. also the Italian family name *Lomonico*.
[12] Cf. Grandgent, p. 103; Pei, *Texts*, p. 38.
[13] Cf. Pisani, *Grammatica*, where in connection with the conjugational system in Vulgar Latin, this scholar states: «...osserviamo del verbo latino a) La tendenza ad ampliare le coniugazioni I e, in minor misura, IV a scapito delle altre due che vengono in parte confuse fra loro....» (p. 229).

/ĕ/ and /ĭ/ in the final syllable.[14] The form *sistint*, for *sistent*, may also represent an etymological reconstruction with the first conjugation verb *stare*.

Except for the few deviations noted above, of which the change of Latin /ă/ in initial position when preceded by a palatal semivowel seems to be the most widespread, this vowel appears as *a* in unstressed position.

Preliminary Note on the Treatment of Latin /ĕ/ and /ē/, and Latin /ŏ/ and /ō/ in Unstressed Syllable

Pirson, in his study of Latin inscriptions from Gaul, treats Latin /ĕ/ and /ē/, as well as Latin /ŏ/ and /ō/ under the same heading, because, as he says

> le latin vulgaire avait déjà, comme plus tard les langues romanes, la tendance à fusionner l'ĕ et l'ē atones en un même son fermé, qui pouvait s'exprimer au moyen de *i* (p. 30).... l'ŏ et l'ō atones, parallèlement à l'ĕ et à l'ē, se sont unifiés dans un même son fermé représenté par *u* (p. 41)

as evidenced by such forms as *sinatus* for *sĕnatus* and *divota* for *dēvota*, as well as *furmica* for *fŏrmica* and *nubiscum* for *nōbiscum*.

More recently, Bengt Löfstedt, in his study of Longobard legal documents, states that because of the obliteration of quantitative differences between Latin /ĕ/ and /ē/ on the one hand, and Latin /ŏ/ and /ō/, on the other hand, in the unstressed syllable,

> brauchen die Belege für *i* statt klat. *e* mit dem Lautwert *ē* and die für *i* statt klat. *e* mit dem Lautwert *ĕ* nicht unterschieden zu werden.... (p. 37)

---

[14] Cf. the statement by Grandgent that in the final syllable «*e* and *i* came to be used almost indiscriminately» (p. 103). Muller-Taylor, pp. 35/36, mention the frequent interchange of *et* and *it* in morphological endings. For the «phonetic-morphological confusion that arises in the case of final vowels,» cf. Pei, *Texts*, pp. 37-60. This scholar is specifically concerned with unstressed vowels in the area of Northern Gaul, i.e. *grosso modo* the area of *Lugdunensis*.

For the /i/ endings in the singular and the third plural forms of the first conjugation present active subjunctive of Italian verbs, cf. Pei, *Italian Language*, pp. 104/105.

and he sees no objection

> die spätlat. Graphien *u* für klat. *o* mit dem Lautwert *ō* and *u* für klat. *o* mit dem Lautwert *ŏ* in unbetonter Silbe in einem Zusammenhang zu behandeln.... (p. 83)

None of these scholars, however, make any pronouncement on the possible chronology of the merger of Latin /ĕ/ and /ē/ and Latin /ŏ/ and /ō/ in unstressed syllable and merely follow the established theory of the reduction of the classical Latin vowel system to a five vowel pattern, as a result of the loss of vowel quantities which, according to one authority, has occurred in the course of the third and fourth centuries. [15]

It is not our intention to put in doubt an established theory concerning the loss of vowel quantities, on the one hand, and the merger of Latin /ĕ/ and /ē/ and /ŏ/ and /ō/ in the unstressed syllable; [16] however, we shall nevertheless attempt to re-examine the possible chronology of this latter phenomenon on the basis of our inscriptional material and shall, therefore, treat these vowels under separate headings, paralleling our discussion of stressed vowels.

Our methodology in dealing with unstressed vowels will consist in presenting tables showing occurrences and deviations in all positions, including morphological endings, together with percentage figures. [17] Separate tables, if necessary, comparing Latin /ĕ/ and /ē/ and /ŏ/ and /ō/ will also be offered in an attempt to determine whether there is any justification in treating these vowels separately, or whether such a separation is indeed unnecessary, as suggested by both Pirson and B. Löfstedt. Our criterion in this connection will be the percentage of *i* spellings for Latin /ĕ/ as against /ē/ and the percentage of *u* spellings for Latin /ŏ/ as against /ō/. If the percentage of *i* spellings for Latin /ē/ and *u* for Latin /ō/ should significantly exceed the same spellings for Latin /ĕ/ and /ŏ/, respectively, within a given period of time, we would seem to be safe in assuming that there was still enough of a qualitative difference between the originally short and long vowels to keep them apart.

---

[15] Cf. Bourciez, *Éléments*, p. 42. For the five vowel pattern in unstressed syllables, cf. our Note #4.
[16] Forcefully advanced already by Meyer-Lübke, *Grammaire*, I, pp. 55/56.
[17] Cf. *supra*, Preliminary Note, p. 12.

If, on the other hand, no substantial difference in the percentage of deviations, or none at all, should be found in a given area under consideration, it will either have to be assumed with B. Löfstedt, Pirson and others that the speakers were no longer aware of a qualitative difference between the originally short and long vowels and, hence, agree that they be treated under the same heading, or else admitted, however reluctantly, that the problem is difficult or even impossible of solution, at least as far as our inscriptional material is concerned.

2. *Latin /ĕ/, represented by the letter e*

2.1 Initial

Area	Century	/ĕ/>e	/ĕ/>i	%
Baetica	IV-VI	45	0	
	VII	36	1	
Lusitania	IV-VI	86	2	2.3
	VII	10	0	
Tarraconensis	IV-VI	48	0	
	VII	9	1	
Narbonensis	IV-V	45	0	
	VI-VII	97	2	2.0
Lugdunensis	IV-V	43	0	
	VI-VII	83	0	
No. Italy	IV-V	129	0	
	VI	69	0	
Ce. Italy	III-IV	33	0	
	V	32	0	
	VI-VII	54	0	
So. Italy	III-IV	28	1	(3.5)
	V	35	1	(2.9)
	VI-VII	99	2	2.0
Rome	III-IV	207	1	(0.4)
	V	131	1	(0.7)
	VI-VII	88	4	3.2

2.1 Initial

A. *Iberian Peninsula*

Examples of *i* spellings for Latin /ĕ/ are the following:

(a) *Baetica*.—We find the spelling *sissdenis... annis* (V113 a. 684) for an expected *sex denis*, where the cardinal and distributive numerals appear written as one word, so that the initial *i* would seem to have to be considered as being in unstressed position.

(b) *Lusitania*.—Two instances of *i* spelling occur in *era sisccens quattus* and *era siscens qattus* (V52 a/b IV/VI cent.), what would appear to be an abbreviation for the ordinal *sescentesimus...*

Since in these examples and the one given above the *i* appears in the same phonetic context (i.e. before an original /ks/ which seems to have lost its velar element and was already reduced to /s/) and we found no other example in which Latin /ĕ/ in this position is written as *i*, there would seem to be good reason to support Carnoy's explanation of this apparent phonological change being due to an umlaut phenomenon.[18]

(c) *Tarraconensis*.—Only one example found in *Dicembr*[19] (V336 VII cent.) for *December*. On the basis of this single deviation we do not feel justified to draw any conclusions as to a possible merger of Latin /ĕ/ and /i/ in this particular area.[20]

---

[18] Discussing the forms *sissdenis* and *siscens* at the end of a list of forms illustrating the change of Latin /ĕ/ to /i/ before /ks/, written *x*, this scholar states: «Les.... derniers exemples sont assez récents pour qu'il soit naturel de voir dans l'emploi de l'*i* un indice de la fermeture de l'*ĕ* entravé devant une palatale, processus qui s'est opéré régulièrement en espagnol» (p. 29).

[19] The dash over the «mbr» group is a conventional sign of abbreviation, cf. Diehl, AI, pp. 79-82, for the most common ones.

[20] In the modern Spanish form *diciembre*, the initial /i/ is said to be due to the palatal element in the following syllable brought about by the diphthongization of the stressed /ĕ/, cf. Menéndez-Pidal, *Gramática*, p. 69. Since we found no evidence of diphthongization of this vowel in our material, it would seem rather doubtful whether the *i* spelling indeed reflects this umlaut phenomenon.

B. Gaul

(a) *Narbonensis.*—The two deviations are shown in *Fibruarias* (D1673N a. 511) and *bonae mimo[riae]* (D3580, VI/VII cent.), while in non-dated material we found one instance in *risurrecturus* (D3469A).

(b) *Lugdunensis.*—No deviation in dated material.

The following forms were found in non-dated material:

riquiiscunt (D483); *riqiscit* (D3132A); *Fibruarias* (D4824)

Both our table and the few deviations in non-dated material would seem to indicate that Latin /ĕ/ in initial position was quite stable in this area.

C. Italy

No examples from both the *Northern* and *Central* areas.

Deviations in both dated and non-dated material from the *Southern* area occur in the following forms:

Ciminiae (D2883N a. 380) for *Geminiae* [21]
nipo(ti) (D2959 ca. V cent.) [22]
p.c. (i.e. *post consulatum*) *Bilisari* (D260 a. 538) [23]
riq[quiescit....] (D341b a. 553)
Mirurianete (D2948A) for *Mercurianeti* [24]

---

[21] It may be of interest to note that in the same inscription we also find the spellings *Ceminia, Ceminius* and *Geminius*, a name which would seem to be formed on the adjective *gĕmĭnus;* hence the treatment of the initial vowel as a short one.

[22] Cf. the modern Italian form *nipote*.

[23] The name of the *consul ordinarius orientis, Flavius Belisarius,* cf. Kaufmann, p. 488.

[24] For the change of Latin /ĕ/ to /i/ before /r/ plus consonant, as being a dialectal feature and the forms *Mircurius, commircium*, attested by Velius Longus and said to have been known to Varro, cf. Pisani, *Grammatica*, p. 14 and Sommer, p. 58. For the new declension type in *-etis, -eti* (e.g. *Mercuriane, Mercurianetis,* etc.), cf. Albert Hehl, *Die Formen der lateinischen Ersten Deklination in den Inschriften* (Tübingen), pp. 62-65.

THE UNACCENTED VOWELS 111

sipurco (D3539A) for *sepulcro* [25]
boni mimorie (D4170) for *bonae memoriae*

Even with deviations in proper names (where orthographic tradition may have been entirely lacking, cf. the Germanic name *Belisarius*), these are too few, it would seem, to speak of anything more than a possible trend towards the merger of Latin /ĕ/ and /i/ in this area, in relationship to the other Italian areas (except *Rome*), where not so much as a hint of this phenomenon was found.

D. *Rome*

The following examples were found in this area:

Viricunda (D3444 a. 397) for *Verecunda* [26]
Bilisarii (D4477 a. 537); *Vilisari* (D713 a. 536)
VVilisarii (D3764 a. 536) for *Belisarii*
imtores (D1137a a. 521) for *emptores*
mirinti (D2631C a. 408) for *merenti*
Cristeni (D2952E) for *Chresteni* [27]
Himerita (D3758) for *Emerita*
cum... Sibirinu (D3828) for *Severino*
bone mimorie (D1602A) for *memoriae*

It is worth noting that most deviations occur in proper names which generally lend themselves to more frequent misspellings than common words used in daily communication. Our figures show that deviations through the fifth century are quite negligible and that even in the subsequent period the jump in the percentage figure is due to deviations in the same Germanic proper name, so that it is questionable whether this figure reflects a true state of affairs.

The normal outcome of Latin /ĕ/ in initial position in standard Italian is generally /i/. [28] Our investigation would show that the merger

---

[25] Found on an inscription from Sicily. For rhotacism before labials and velars as a specific characteristic of most Sicilian dialectal varieties, cf. Pei, *Italian Language*, p. 158.

[26] Both this name and the masculine form *Verecundus* are quite frequent in Christian inscriptions, apparently formed on the adjective *vĕrēcundus*.

[27] The name *Chreste* appears especially in inscriptions from Rome and Central Italy. *Chresteni* is a new dative formation. Cf. our note #24 in re new declensional formations.

[28] Cf. Pei, *Italian Language*, p. 36.

of these vowels must have occurred at a late date, as evidenced by the very sporadic *i* spellings for Latin /ĕ/.

2.2 Intertonic

Area	Century	/ĕ/>e	/ĕ/>i	%
Baetica	IV-VI	0	1*	
	VII	15	2*	
Lusitania	IV-VI	8	0	
	VII	3	0	
Tarraconensis	IV-VI	10	1	
	VII	1	0	
Narbonensis	IV-V	5	0	
	VI-VII	16	1	(6.2)
Lugdunensis	IV-V	5	0	
	VI-VII	8	0	
No. Italy	IV-V	43	2	4.6
	VI	6	0	
Ce. Italy	III-IV	22	0	
	V	7	0	
	VI-VII	13	0	
So. Italy	III-IV	15	0	
	V	12	0	
	VI-VII	10	0	
Rome	III-IV	213	3	1.4
	V	73	1	1.3
	VI-VII	11	0	

* Germanic proper names.

2.2 Intertonic

There are few examples of deviations in our material and there are not enough of them to be able to establish a consistent pattern or trend. Furthermore, in some cases the *i* spelling appears in foreign proper names only in which misspellings are more likely to occur.

The following forms show *i* spelling for Latin /ĕ/:

A. *Iberian Peninsula*

(a) *Baetica*.—The Germanic proper names *Hermenegildus*[29] and *Reccesvinthus* appear as *Erminigildus* (V364 a. 573) and *Reccisvinthus* (V174 a. 643; V178 a. 650), respectively.[30]

(b) *Lusitania*.—No example.

(c) *Tarraconensis*.—The only deviation is found in *crede(s resur)rictionem* (V193 a. 471).

B. *Gaul*

(a) *Narbonensis*.—To the form *redimtionem* (D47 a. 527) there must be added the *i* spelling in *surrictura* (fut. part.) (D3475) in non-dated material.

(b) *Lugdunensis*.—No example found.

C. *Italy*

(a) *Northern*.—Two *i* spellings in *molistavirit* (D441) and *apirire* (D506)[31] both from inscriptions coming from the *Concordia* military cemetery, fourth/fifth centuries.

---

[29] Miles, p. 23, feels that *Ermenegildus* is doubtless the correct spelling and that the form with the initial letter *h* is merely «an orthographic tradition of medieval times.» For the same opinion, cf. Schönfeld, p. XXIII.

[30] The accepted spelling of this name seems to be *Reccesvinthus*, cf. Miles, p. 33. This is how it appears three times out of five in our material from this area.

[31] Cf. the standard *Italian* form *aprire*, evidencing subsequent syncope of the intertonic vowel, cf. Grandgent, p. 98. The *i* spelling could possibly indicate the weakening of Latin /ĕ/ in this position before its disappearance.

(b) *Central.*—No example found.

(c) *Southern.*—A single deviation was found in the form *comindavi* (D2302) for *commendavi* in non-dated material.

D. Rome

Sporadic *i* spellings occur in the following forms:

> *benivolentiae* (D4330Aa, ca. IV cent.), *itir* (i.e. *iterum*) (D4378 a. 378), *descindentibus* (D2128 a. 405) *benimerenti* (D2614B) and *benemirinti* (D2611C)

In summary, it would seem that, just as in the case of Latin /ĕ/ in initial position, sporadic cases of *i* spelling occur in virtually all areas; however, it would also seem that the evidence is far from sufficient (lack of consistency in the percentage figures!) to be able to draw any conclusions as to a possible merger of Latin /ĕ/ and /i/.

From the point of view of regional differences, it may be worth noting that there seems to be an absolute parallelism between the absence of *i* spellings for Latin /ĕ/ in both positions in the *Central Italian* area, a fact which may not be without significance.

2.3 Hiatus

Area	Century	/ĕ/>e	/ĕ/>i	%
Baetica	IV-VI	1	0	
	VII	0	0	
Lusitania	IV-VI	2	0	
	VII	0	0	
Tarraconensis	IV-VI	5	0	
	VII	0	0	
Narbonensis	IV-V	2	0	
	VI-VII	1	0	
Lugdunensis	IV-V	8	0	
	VI-VII	2	0	
No. Italy	IV-V	13	0	
	VI	3	0	

Ce. Italy	III-IV	9	1	
	V	5	0	
	VI-VII	5	0	
So. Italy	III-IV	4	1	
	V	10	0	
	VI-VII	11	0	
Rome	III-IV	40	3	6.5
	V	31	3	8.7
	VI-VII	12	0	

Grandgent states that «*e, i* and *u* in hiatus with following vowels lost their syllabic value probably by the first century of our era, and sporadically earlier» (p. 93). Väänänen (p. 46) notes frequent occurrences of *i* spelling for hiatus /ĕ/ (e.g. *peria* for *pereat, valiat* for *valeat,* etc.) and holds that the semi-vocalic pronunciation of this vowel is confirmed by inverse spellings, as in *Iuleas, moreor, pateor,* etc.[32]

Sporadic *i* spelling for Latin /ĕ/ in this position occurs in the *Central* and *Southern Italian* areas, as well as in the area of *Rome* only, so that it would seem that this general area was the focal point of this phenomenon, which later spread to the North and other areas of Romania. Unfortunately, the scant sampling of hiatus /ĕ/ in *Northern Italy, Gaul* and the *Iberian Peninsula* and the absence of any deviations does not enable us to establish a chronology regarding the yodization of this vowel in these areas, although Pirson (p. 48) gives a few examples of *i* spelling, e.g. in *diabus, oriaturam, viniae,* found on non-dated inscriptions, not included in our material.

---

[32] Cf. *calceus non calcius, lilium non lileum, puella non poella* in the Appendix Probi.

The consensus of Romance scholars regarding the yodization of hiatus /ĕ/ and /ĭ/ in Vulgar Latin is summed up by Pirson in the following sentence: «En syllabe atone et en hiatus, l'*i* and l'*ĕ* ont pris dans la langue parlée une valeur commune, celle de *jod*, et c'est en cette qualité qu'ils se sont transmis aux langues romanes» (p. 47).

Grandgent believes that the semivowels which developed from /ĕ/, /ĭ/ and /ŭ/ in hiatus «presumably developed into the fricative consonants *y* and *w*» (p. 94) by the third century and that, hence, in Late Latin spelling there arises a confusion of spelling, particularly between *i* and *e* before a vowel. cf. also Battisti, p. 118.

A few examples of deviations from our *Italian* material are the following:

> *niofitus* (D1494 a. 394/402); *Tiodoto* (D2138A); *Ceriali* (D3911 a. 358); *Cliarco* (D4159 a. 384) *Ariobindo*; (D843 a. 434); *oliaria* (D687)

2.4 Penult

Area	Century	/ĕ/>e	/ĕ/>i	%
Baetica	IV-VI	0	0	
	VII	1	0	
Lusitania	IV-VI	2	0	
	VII	1	0	
Tarraconensis	IV-VI	0	0	
	VII	0	0	
Narbonensis	IV-V	3	0	
	VI-VII	10	0	
Lugdunensis	IV-V	3	0	
	VI-VII	2	0	
No. Italy	IV-V	91	2	2.2
	VI	3	0	
	III-IV	4	0	
Ce. Italy	V	0	0	
	VI-VII	3	0	
	III-IV	2	0	
So. Italy	V	3	0	
	VI-VII	6	0	
	III-IV	22	1	
Rome	V	11	0	
	VI-VII	6	0	

Our sampling for Latin /ĕ/ in *penult* position is generally speaking quite small, except for the *Northern Italian* area where this vowel occurs in the numerous future perfect tense endings, due to the stereotyped penalty formula *si quis eam arcam aperire voluerit...., si quis.... molestaverit....,* (cf. our note #26 under stressed vowels, p. 71) which is so very characteristic of all inscriptions from the *Concordia* military cemetery, making up about two/thirds of our fourth/fifth century material from this area. As a matter of fact, the two deviations from this area come from one and the same inscription, namely *voluirit* and *molistavirit* (D441), which may merely reflect the ignorance of a single stonecutter in matters of spelling.

The single deviation in the area of *Rome* is represented by the form *catecumino* (D1508 a. 397), while in non-dated material we found the form *puniri* (D824) for *ponere* in the *Central Italian* area.

This evidence is obviously too scanty to permit any conclusion as to a merger of Latin /ĕ/ and /ĭ/ in this position.

2.5 Final

Area	*Century*	/ĕ/>e	/ĕ/>i	%
Baetica	IV-VI	4	0	
	VII	3	0	
Lusitania	IV-VI	4	0	
	VII	0	0	
Tarraconensis	IV-VI	10	0	
	VII	2	0	
Narbonensis	IV-V	1	0	
	VI-VII	7	0	
Lugdunensis	IV-V	1	0	
	VI-VII	7	0	
No. Italy	IV-V	26	0	
	VI	3	0	
	III-IV	7	0	
Ce. Italy	V	2	0	
	VI-VII	12	0	
	III-IV	4	0	
So. Italy	V	4	0	
	VI-VII	13	0	
	III-IV	49	0	
Rome	V	20	0	
	VI-VII	7	0	

Our table shows that in the *final* syllable, in non-morphological endings, Latin /ĕ/ is quite stable. Nevertheless, there are a number of examples in non-dated material where this vowel appears spelled with an *i*, especially from the *Lugdunensis* area, as follows:

decim (D438N); *septim* (D1574) (but also *novem*); *quinqui* (D2024); *sempir* (D4828)

A single deviation from the area of *Rome* appears in *anti* (D2930A).

Speaking of final vowels in general (without distinction as to vowels merely in the final syllable or in morphological endings), Grandgent states that «the changes in pronunciation led to a great confusion in spelling» (p. 103) and that *e* and *i* and *o* and *u* «came to be used almost indiscriminately» (*ibid.*). «It is likely —this scholar goes on to say— that final vowels were especially obscure in Gaul in the sixth and seventh centuries» (*ibid.*). Forms such as those listed above would tend to support Grandgent's claim, despite the lack of deviations in dated material. It would seem, however, that before reaching any conclusions in this regard, it is well to examine Latin /ĕ/ in morphological endings.

Romance scholars seem to treat the confusion in spelling of *e* and *i* and *o* and *u* in morphological endings as a reflection of a phonetic phenomenon, namely a trend to merge final vowels represented by these letters, cf. Grandgent quoted above. The phonetic rather than morphological nature of this interchange is implicit in the further statements by this scholar, namely that «*e* for *i* is frequent in the dative and ablative» (p. 103).... «*es* and *is* are continually interchanged» (p. 104).... «so *et* and *it*.... (and) *o* and *u*....» (*ibid.*), statements echoed more recently by Battisti (pp. 111-112). [33]

---

[33] This scholar also notes the frequent spelling of -*ex* for -*ix* (e.g. *felex*), taking into account also the possibility of an analogical extension of the numerous nominatives in -*ex*. But cf. forms like *semplix* and *milix* (=*miles*) from our material, pointing to a confusion in spelling going both ways.

For further opinions regarding the phonetic nature of the confusion of these vowels in morphological endings, cf. Pisani, *Grammatica*, p. 74; Vidos, p. 205; Väänänen, p. 37; B. Löfstedt, p. 52.

Pei, *Texts,* calls attention to the fact that in the case of unaccented vowels in the final syllable «the change is very frequently of a morphological rather than a phonetic character» (p. 42) and that forms like *abbati* for *abbate, ipsi* and *illi* for *ipse* and *ille* are cases «where the morphological factor of the development of a single oblique case looms large» (*ibid.*). In his tabulation of all cases of deviations versus all cases of correct occurrences, whether they be of a phonological or morphological nature, this scholar proceeds «on the theory that the phonetic change preceded and was the cause of the morphological change» (*ibid.*). As to forms like *gregim* (acc. sg. for *gregem*), *comis* (nom. sg. for *comes*), Pei seems to feel that the *i* spelling merely reflects the confusion of these vowels in the final syllable, without implying morphological consequences.

It would seem, therefore, that each case must be judged on its own merits and that in certain morphological endings the confusion in spelling may reflect a change due to some morphological factor, whereas in others this factor may be absent and the cause must be sought on the phonetic level.

Our inscriptional material shows a few instances of *i* spelling for Latin /ĕ/ in both noun-adjective and verb endings. We have thought it best to show these in detailed tabular forms also, so that the reader may see, at a glance, in which areas under study deviations are most frequent.

2.6 Noun and Adjective Endings

A. Nom. sg. second/third decl.
B. Nom. sg. third decl.
C. Acc. sg. third/fifth decl.
D. Abl. sg. third decl.

Area	Century	A er	ir	%	B es	is	%	ex	ix	%	C em	im	%	D e	i	%
Baetica	IV-VI	3	0		0	0		0	0		1	0		44	0	
	VII	3	0		0	0		0	0		0	0		26	0	
Lusitania	IV-VI	1	0		0	0		0	0		6	0		53	0	
	VII	1	0		1	0		1	0		0	0		8	0	
Tarraconensis	IV-VI	3	0		0	0		0	0		2	0		29	0	
	VII	1	0		0	0		0	0		0	0		4	0	
Narbonensis	IV-V	1	0		0	0		0	0		2	0		22	0	
	VI-VII	0	0		0	0		0	1		4	0		69	2	2.8
Lugdunensis	IV-V	1	0		0	0		0	0		1	0		23	0	
	VI-VII	1	0		0	0		-en 0	-in 1		3	2	40.0	46	1	

2.6 Noun and Adjective Endings (Continued)

Area	Century	A			B						C			D		
		er	ir	%	es	is	%	ex	ix	%	em	im	%	e	i	%
No. Italy	IV-V	7	0		3	0		0	0		2	0		59	0	
	VI	0	0		1	0		0	0		0	0		51	0	
Ce. Italy	III-IV	3	0		0	0		0	0		3	0		13	1	
	V	2	0		0	0		0	0		3	0		15	0	
	VI-VII	2	0		0	0		0	0		4	0		44	0	
So. Italy	III-IV	2	0		0	0		0	0		3	0		21	0	
	V	2	0		0	0		0	0		1	0		14	0	
	VI-VII	1	0		1	3*		1	0		2	0		47	0	
Rome	III-IV	19	0		0	0		0	0		6	0		199	9	4.5
	V	8	0		2	0		0	0		2	0		123	4	3.2
	VI-VII	2	0		0	0		0	0		4	0		74	0	

* Cf. infra. footnote # 37.

2.6 Noun and Adjective Endings

Examples of deviations:

A. *Iberian Peninsula*

A single instance of *ir* for *er* spelling in a second declension noun was found on a non-dated inscription from *Tarraconensis*, namely *puir* (V266) for *puer*. [34]

B. *Gaul*

(a) *Narbonensis*

1. Third decl. nom. sg.: *semplix* (D180 a. 525)
2. Third decl. abl. sg.: *indexioni* (D3279 a. 564)
    ini (= *indictioni*)
                    (D3552 a. 597)
    paci (D3289/D3473)

(b) *Lugdunensis*

1. Third decl. nom. sg.: *karmin* (=*carmen*) (D1075 a. 630)
2. Third decl. acc. sg.: *iovenim* (D1218 a. 548/621)
    requiim (D2478 ca. VI cent.)
3. Third decl. abl. sg.: *mensi* (D3129 ca. VI cent.)

C. *Italy*

(a) *Northern*

1. Third decl. nom. sg.: *milis* (D558)

---

[34] Carnoy (p. 30) sees in the change of /ĕ/ to /i/ before /r/ a dialectal influence on the Latin of Italy, this phenomenon being «une tendance générale des dialectes italiques.» The survival of this dialectal feature would be due to the postulated Italic influence in Northeastern *Spain* (the area covered by *Tarraconensis*), brought about by Oscan colonization, as reflected in certain toponymic correspondences, e.g. the name of *Huesca*, the ancient town of *Osca*, cf. Menéndez-Pidal, *Origenes*, pp. 304 ff.

(b) *Central*

 1. Third decl. abl. sg.: *Constanti* (D3226 a. 339) [35]
 2. Second decl. voc. sg.: *Reremti* (= *Redempte*) (D2297L) [36]

(c) *Southern*

 1. Third decl. nom. sg.: *comis* (D114 a. 549)
    Iohannis (D195 a. 557) [37]
    Iuhannis (1260 a. 511)
    Monsis (= *Moses*) (1150)
 2. Third decl. abl. sg.: *Bautoni* (D81 a. 385)
    in paci (D1148, D2812)

D. *Rome*

Except for the nominative singular forms *milix* (=*miles*) (D529/D414N) and *patir* (D2713AN) [38] of the second and third declensions, respectively, all deviations occur in the third declension ablative singular, of which we offer a few examples:

Dioni (D2305); *Valenti.... iuniori* (D1328 a. 376); [39] *Victori* (D1603 a. 369), *in paci* (D2115 a. 401) (and *passim* in non-dated inscriptions); *conli* (= *consuli* (D3333 a. 432); *virginitati* (D314); *nomeni* (D854) *cum coiugi* (D3697), etc.

---

[35] For the final /ĕ/ in the ablative singular of participles used as nouns, cf. Allen and Greenough, p. 53.

[36] There is a strong possibility of a morphological replacement under the influence of the vocative form of nouns in *ius*, such as *Concordius*, *Abundantius*, etc. As a matter of fact, *Reremti*, appears on the same inscription with *Abundanti* and *Concordi*.

[37] We placed an asterisk next to the figure indicating deviations in our table, because the form *Iohannis* may also represent an alternative spelling (cf. Lewis & Short, p. 1013).

[38] Cf. our note #34 on the possible Oscan influence for the change of /ĕ/ to /i/ before /r/. It may be argued, quite legitimately, it would seem, that the apparent confusion of *i* and *e* spelling in the forms *milix* and *patir* represents one and the same phenomenon, namely a merger of the vowels represented by these letters, or at least a trend towards such a merger, rather than two separate and unrelated phenomena.

[39] Regarding ablatives of comparative forms ending in *i*, Pirson states that, despite their having been censured by Latin grammarians, they are frequently used in postclassical literature and adds that the expressions *a priori*, *a fortiori*, etc... must be traced back to this postclassical usage (p. 121). cf. Kieckers, II, p. 57.

In connection with the ablatives of third declension nouns that appear spelled with an *i*, Pirson states

> L'*i* des ablatifs *paci* (*in paci dominica*).... *mensi*..... *capiti*.... *libertati*.... trouve naturellement sa raison d'être dans l'équivalence des sons *i* et *e* atones (p. 121)

implicitly rejecting any morphological factor involved in this change, contrary to Pei who believes that «the morphological factor of the development of a single oblique case looms large,» (*Texts*, p. 42) in these ablative forms.

It is early at this point to take sides with one or the other view, at least until we have examined the situation in connection with the ablative form of third declension adjectives, in order to determine whether these ablatives ending in /ī/ are just as likely to be spelled with *e* as those ending in /ĕ/ (and /ē/) with *i*.

2.7 Verb Endings

A. Second conj. pres. ind. third sg.
B. First conj. pres. subj. third sg.
C. First conj. pres. subj. third pl.
D. First/second/third/fourth conj. pres. inf.

Area	Century	A et	A it	%	B et	B it	%	C ent	C int	%	D re	D ri	%
Baetica	IV-VI	2	0		0	0		0	0		0	0	
	VII	3	1		0	0		0	0		0	0	
Lusitania	IV-VI	0	0		0	0		0	0		2	0	
	VII	1	0		0	0		0	0		0	0	
Tarraconensis	IV-VI	1	1		0	0		0	0		0	0	
	VII	3	0		0	0		0	0		0	0	
Narbonensis	IV-V	0	0		1	0		0	0		0	0	
	VI-VII	0	2		0	0		0	0		0	0	
Lugdunensis	IV-V	3	1		0	1		0	0		0	0	
	VI-VII	0	1		0	2		0	1		3	0	

2.7 Verb Endings (continued)

Area	Century	A et	A it	A %	B et	B it	B %	C ent	C int	C %	D re	D ri	D %
No. Italy	IV-V	4	1		3	0		0	0		39	0	
	VII	0	0		0	0		0	0		0	0	
Ce. Italy	III-IV	1	0		0	0		0	0		0	0	
	V	0	0		0	0		0	0		0	0	
	VI-VII	0	0		0	0		0	0		0	0	
So. Italy	III-IV	0	0		0	0		0	0		0	0	
	V	0	0		0	0		0	0		0	0	
	VI-VII	0	0		2	0		0	0		0	0	
Rome	III-IV	6	1		0	0		0	0		3	0	
	V	7	1		0	0		0	0		2	0	
	VI-VII	2	0		0	0		0	0		0	0	

2.7 Verb Endings

The most frequent occurrence of Latin /ĕ/ in verb endings is in the third person singular present active indicative of second conjugation verbs (shown under A in our table). The spelling *it* for *et* appears in most areas where this particular verb form occurs, as evidenced by the following examples. (Because of the scanty sampling of this particular second declension verb ending and the fact that even a single deviation may give a high percentage figure that may not accurately reflect a true state of affairs, we decided to omit percentage figures altogether).

A. *Iberian Peninsula*

(a) *Baetica.*—We read *lugit* (V287 a. 624) (but also *continet* in the same inscription).

(b) *Lusitania.*—No example.

(c) *Tarraconensis.*—A single deviation in *iacit* (V192 a 459).

B. *Gaul*

(a) *Narbonensis.*—The couple of occurrences in dated material appear spelled *it*:

tenit (D270 a. 562); *habit* (D3439, VI cent.)

In non-dated inscriptions we found several occurrences of *iacit* (D179; D1433; D2909; D3066A).

(b) *Lugdunensis.*—The form *iacit* occurs in both dated and non-dated inscriptions (D2783B a. 438; D554; D2916N; D3583) side by side with *iacet* (e.g. D3583A; D3583B; D3587). Other third singular present indicative forms in -*it* are *tenit* (D1237 ca. IV cent.) and *lecit* (D3489) for *licet*.

Deviations in first conjugation subjunctive forms are shown in *aiutit* (D2361, IV/V cent.), *dignit* (D2340 ca. VII cent.) (occurring twice) and *cesint* (D1076 a. 632/3) for *cessent*.

Pei, pp. 41/42, notes that *i* is exclusively used for *e* ...in verb endings of the -*et* type....» and interprets this phenomenon as «the forerunner of the total disappearance of the vowel in the termination -*et*. The *e* —this scholar goes on to say— is already so weakened that its true nature does not appear.» It would seem, therefore, that Pei sees in the confusion of *et* and *it* in these verb forms a reflection of a phonological phenomenon, rather than a morphological replacement of the second conjugation *et* ending by the third conjugation *it* ending, as one might be inclined to think at first glance. Cf. Grandgent's statement to the effect that final vowels were probably quite obscure in *Gaul* in the sixth and seventh centuries (quoted *supra*, p. 118). The fact that verbs of the *et* type appear spelled *it* in our sixth/seventh century material would seem to lend support to this statement.

In the Italian area a few instances of *it* spelling occur as follows:

C. *Italy*

(a) *Northern*.—In dated material there is one occurrence of *iacit* (D822, IV/V cent.), while in non-dated material we found the form *potis* (D4725, twice) (second sing. pres. ind. of *posse*).[40]

(b) *Central*.—There are two deviations in non-dated material only:

An *it* spelling appears in the fut. ind. *conferit* (D824). In the same inscription we also read *puniri* (= *ponere*). The third sing. pres. ind. is represented by *iacit* (D563).

(c) *Southern*.—No example.

D. *Rome*

Two occurrences of *iacit* (D3057AN a. 396; D1351 a. 404).

The third conjugation infinitive *re* ending appears as *ri* in *biolari* (= *violare*) (D3865).

Discussing the frequent *it* spelling of the second conjugation present active indicative *et* verb ending in his Lombardic legal texts, B. Löfstedt comments as follows:

> Es könnte nahe liegen, diese Belege für -*it* statt -*et* als Zeugnisse eines Konjugationswechsels aufzufassen (p. 52).

However, this scholar points out that the third person present active indicative of both the *i* and *e* conjugations of the Italian verb ends in

---

[40] For the question of the /i/ outcome of the second person singular of the Italian verb, cf. Pei, «Latin and Italian Front Vowels,» *Studies*, pp. 79-84.

/e/ —and we may add that the same thing holds true for the Spanish and Portuguese verb as well,[41] and concludes

> Ich halte es daher für wahrscheinlich, dass diese Endungen schon im 7. Jh. mehr oder weniger gleich waren und dass die Schreibungen -*it* statt -*et* mit den übrigen Belegen für orthographisches Schwanken zwischen -*it*, -*im*, -*i* und -*et*, -*em*, -*e* in der Schlussilbe auf eine Stufe zu stellen sind (*ibid.*)[42]

As to the *i* spelling for Latin /ĕ/ in the active infinitive *re* ending, the conclusions of this scholar are quite in line with the foregoing, when he says

> Belege für -*i* statt -*e* im Inf. Akt. dürften meistens mit den anderen Fällen von -*it* für -*et* etc. in der Schlussilbe in Zusammenhang zu bringen sein (p. 53).

To reach a definite conclusion regarding the problem of verb endings of the *et* type and to determine whether we are faced with primarily a phonological or a morphological phenomenon, it would appear indispensable to examine verb endings of the *it* type (i.e. third and fourth conjugation present active indicative) as well and see whether the stonecutter was as likely to spell *vincet* for *vincit* as *iacit* for *iacet*. Indeed, if we should find that the orthographic change is moving in the direction of *et* and *it* only and not vice versa, the case of a phonetic confusion will be considerably weakened and that of a morphological replacement of one ending by another clearly established. Cf. *infra*, p. 174.

3. *Latin /ē/, represented by the letter e*

3.1 Initial

Area	Century	/ē/>e	/ē/>i	%
Baetica	IV-VI	4	0	
	VII	17	0	

---

[41] Cf. Menéndez-Pidal, *Gramática*, p. 301; Pilar Vázquez Cuesta y Maria Albertina de Mendes Luz, *Gramática Portuguesa* (Madrid, 1961), pp. 365-366.
[42] For a similar view, cf. Politzer, *Study*, p. 102.

130   AN INQUIRY INTO LOCAL VARIATIONS IN VULGAR LATIN

Area	Century	/ē/>e	/ē/>i	%
Lusitania	IV-VI	9	0	
	VII	5	0	
Tarraconensis	IV-VI	8	0	
	VII	1	0	
Narbonensis	IV-V	3	0	
	VI-VII	8	1	(11.2)
Lugdunensis	IV-V	7	0	
	VI-VII	2	1	(33.3)
No. Italy	IV-V	29	1	
	VI	14	0	
Ce. Italy	III-IV	17	0	
	V	8	0	
	VI-VII	22	0	
So. Italy	III-IV	23	0	
	V	16	1	
	VI-VII	53	0	
Rome	III-IV	162	10	5.8
	V	95	10	9.4
	VI-VII	38	6	13.6

Examples of *i* spellings for Latin /ē/ in this position:

A. *Iberian Peninsula*

No deviation to be reported.

B. *Gaul*

Deviations occur in the following forms:

(a) *Narbonensis*

diposisio (D3038 a. 536) for *depositio Filicissimae* (D1467); *Hiraclius* (D1503)

(b) *Lugdunensis*

　　Disderio (D1255 a. 536) for *Desiderio*
　　divote (D1699)

It may be of interest to note that, at least as far as our dated inscriptions go (the only ones that permit us to establish some kind of chronology), we find no orthographic indication of a possible merger of Latin /ē/ and /ĭ/ before our sixth/seventh century material, whereas in stressed position our figures would indicate that this phenomenon had occurred at least by the fifth century (cf. *supra*, The Accented Vowels, p. 68).

C. *Italy*

Sporadic deviations are found in all three areas but most of them occur in non-dated material. It may be worth noting that, paralleling Latin /ĕ/ in this position, most deviations were found in the *Southern* area.

Examples of *i* spellings are as follows:

(a) *Northern*

　　Disiderius (D343, V cent.)
　　ficierunt (=*fecerunt* (D1366)

(b) *Central*

　　Filicis (D824); *dipossio* (D2261)

(c) *Southern*

　　dip (=*depositus*) (D2959, ca. V cent.)
　　diponitur (D1419); *dicessit* (D2820)
　　ficerun (D4169B); *Birissima* (=*Verissima*) (D4007)

The absence of a consistent pattern of deviations in dated inscriptions, as can be seen in our table, and percentage figures based on single deviations does not permit us to draw any specific conclusions regarding the merger of Latin /ē/ and /ĭ/ in this general area; however, the number of instances in whcih this vowel is represented by *i* in non-dated inscriptions in the latter of the three areas would seem to point in the direction of a development which, eventually, resulted in the merger of these vowels.[43]

D. *Rome*

The consistent pattern that we do not find in our figures from the rest of the general Italian area is very clear in the area of Rome. We would be justified in stating, it would seem, that the merger of Latin /ē/ and /ĭ/ is well underway by the third/fourth centuries and that this area can, indeed, be considered the focal point of this phenomenon.

It may also be worth noting that, contrary to what we observe in the area of *Gaul*, on the basis of our figures, the merger of Latin /ē/ and /ĭ/ in unstressed syllable preceded this merger in stressed syllable in this area.[44]

A few examples of deviations follow:

> *misoro* (=*mensorum* for *mensium*) (D4578 a. 291)
> *difunctus* and *difuncta* (D2146 a/b a. 395)
> *riciessit* (=*recessit*) (D2824N. a. 370)
> *dipositus* (D2927 a. 397) and *passim*
> *diposita* (2971AN a. 394/96) and *passim*
> *ficerunt* (D3502 a. 392); *distructum* (77a a. 565)
> *disiderio* (D2134N); *dinarios* (D3841)
> *dimisit* (D4567); *lictoris* (D3814), etc.

3.2 Intertonic

Latin /ē/ in this position occurs very infrequently (e.g. a single occurrence in *Gaul*). The handful of instances of *i* spelling occur in the *Southern Italian* area and *Rome*, as follows:

---

[43] Cf. Pei, *Italian Language*, p. 36.

[44] Vidos (p. 196) states that the merger of Latin /ē/ and /ĭ/, being attested in such forms as *senapis, eneco* for *sinapis, enico* in Plautus, began in the unstressed syllable at a very early date, in any event before the middle of the second century B.C., when the first inscriptional examples of this merger in stressed syllable occur. (In this respect this scholar disagrees with Bourciez, *Éléments* (pp. 42/43), who places this merger not before the third century A.D.). Leaving aside the question of chronology (cf. our conclusions regarding stressed Latin /ē/ and /ĭ/ *supra*, The Accented Vowels, p. 68), there is little doubt that the merger of these vowels may have taken place in some areas in unstressed syllable before the merger in stressed syllable, but the possibility that the reverse might have taken place in other areas should not be left out of account.

Area		Century	/ē/>e	/ē/>i
(a)	So. Italy	III-IV	0	0
		V	2	0
		VI-VII	0	1
(b)	Rome	III-IV	14	1
		V	4	0
		VI-VII	2	0

Examples:

(a) *in cimiterium* (=*coemeterium*) (D2000, VII cent.)
Sebirinus (=*Severinus*) (D2951B)

(b) *Viricunda* (D3444 a. 397); *in cimiterio* (D2119)
Sibirinus (D3823); *quisscenti* (=*quiescenti*) (D3098)
et passim

The fact that deviations were found in these two areas only would seem to be in accord with our study of this vowel in initial syllable, where it was observed that, in the *Italian* area, examples of *i* spelling for Latin /ē/ came from the same regions.

3.3 Final

Area	Century	/ē/>e	/ē/>i	%
Baetica	IV-VI	0	0	
	VII	1	0	
Lusitania	IV-VI	0	0	
	VII	0	0	
Tarraconensis	IV-VI	2	0	
	VII	1	0	
Narbonensis	IV-V	2	0	
	VI-VII	8	4	33.3
Lugdunensis	IV-V	0	0	
	VI-VII	3	1	(25.0)
No. Italy	IV-V	2	0	
	VI	4	0	

Area	Century	/ē/>e	/ē/>i	%
Ce. Italy	III-IV	2	0	
	V	1	0	
	VI-VII	2	0	
So. Italy	III-IV	1	0	
	V	1	0	
	VI-VII	8	0	
Rome	III-IV	8	0	
	V	6	0	
	VI-VII	4	0	

Our table of Latin /ē/ in *final* syllable (non-morphological endings) would indicate that the area of *Gaul* is once again ahead of other areas in the matter of the apparent vowel confusion in this position, not unlike the situation observed in connection with final Latin /ĕ/, cf. *supra*, p. 118, although a sporadic *i* spelling was also found in some non-dated inscriptions from the *Italian* area.

Examples of deviations follow:

B. *Gaul*

  (a) *Narbonensis*

    pridi (=*pridie*) (D270 a. 562); *pridii* (D2222A VI cent.)
    decis (=*decies*) (D1215 a. 559)
    oxciis (=*octies*) (3554 a. 546)

  (b) *Lugdunensis*

    cleminx (= *clemens*) (D1075 a. 630)

C. *Italy*

  (b) *Central*

    pridii (D2994AN)

D. *Rome*

    priii (= *pridie*) (D2950N); *lati longi* (D3824)

Changes in morphological endings are illustrated in the following table.

3.4 Noun Endings

A. Third decl. nom. pl.
B. Third decl. acc. pl.
C. Fifth decl. nom. sg. and pl.
D. Fifth decl. abl. sg.

Area	Century	A es	A is	A %	B es	B is	B %	C es	C is	C %	D e	D i	D %
Baetica	IV-VI	0	0		8	0		1	0		5	0	
	VII	0	0		7	0		0	0		13	0	
Lusitania	IV-VI	0	0		2	0		0	0		9	0	
	VII	0	0		0	0		0	0		5	0	
Tarraconensis	IV-VI	0	0		2	2	?	0	0		7	0	
	VII	0	0		0	0		0	0		3	0	
Narbonensis	IV-V	0	0		2	1	(33.3)	1	0		6	0	
	VI-VII	0	0		7	5	41.6	5	0		10	0	
Lugdunensis	IV-V	0	0		4	3	42.8	2	1	(33.3)	4	0	
	VI-VII	0	0		1	3	75.0	4	2	33.3	3	0	

3.4 Noun Endings (Continued)

Area	Century	A			B			C			D		
		es	is	%	es	is	%	es	is	%	e	i	%
No. Italy	IV-V	1	0		6	3	33.3	3	0		10	0	
	VI	1	0		4	2	33.3	4	0		7	0	
Ce. Italy	III-IV	9	0		16	1	5.8	8	1		2	0	
	V	0	0		4	0		0	0		6	0	
	VI-VII	0	0		3	2	40.0	3	0		8	0	
So. Italy	III-IV	5	0		2	2	50.0	3	0		4	0	
	V	0	0		3	1	25.0	2	0		9	0	
	VI-VII	3	0		7	3	30.0	5	0		12	1	
Rome	III-IV	12	3	20.0	37	19	33.9	37	1	2.6	39	1	
	V	1	1	(50.0)	20	3	13.0	3	1	25.0	33	0	
	VI-VII	1	1	(50.0)	2	2	50.0	7	0		2	0	

3.4 Noun Endings

It will be readily seen from this table that most of the deviations occur in the accusative plural of third declension nouns, which may not be surprising in view of the free variation between the endings *es* and *is* of this case in classical times.[45] However, there are a number of instances of *is* spelling in the nominative plural of this declension and a few in fifth declension nouns as well.

Seeing that the *is* ending in the *accusative* plural is found in all areas except *Baetica* and *Lusitania*,[46] a few examples of this phenomenon will suffice:

A. *Iberian Peninsula*

In the *Tarraconensis* area two instances of the form *mensis* (V253, ca. late IV/early V cent.) were found, both on the same inscription, so that, as with all cases of single deviations, it is difficult to say just how widespread this phenomenon may have been.

B. *Gaul*

(a) *Narbonensis*.—Deviations are confined to the form *mensis* in both dated and non-dated inscriptions.

(b) *Lugdunensis*.—Apart from several examples of *mensis* in both dated and non-dated inscriptions, the *is* spelling is also found in the following forms:

> *litis* (D1075 a. 630); *opis* (D1076 a. 633)
> *parentis suus* (D2340 ca. VII cent.)
> *inter.... senioris* (D552)

---

[45] Cf. Sommer, pp. 385/386.

[46] In connection with the *is* accusative plural ending, Carnoy states that «l'accusatif en -*is* n'apparaît en Espagne que dans les inscriptions officielles d'un latin rigoureusement classique. Ce fait est en conformité avec la nature de cette terminaison *is* qui n'est pas primitive en latin et n'a jamais eu de racines bien profondes dans la langue populaire» (p. 219). (For a contrary opinion cf. Sommer, p. 382). We have no example of an official inscription in our material but, judging from the form *mensis* found in the *Tarraconensis* area, it would seem that the plural accusative in *is* was not totally unknown in popular speech.

C. *Italy*

In all three areas there are several instances of *mensis* (also appearing as *mesis*), but in connection with other nouns the *is* spelling in the accusative plural appears in the *Northern* area only, as follows:

>   *nominis sui* (for *nomina sua*) (D849, IV/V cent.)
>   *sedis* (D39 a. 528)

D. *Rome*

In dated material only *mensis* is found. In non-dated material, in addition to this form (also spelled *mesis, minsis, misis*), the *i* spelling appears in the following:

>   *de tres fratris cursoris* (D381B)
>   *sororis suas* (D808AN); *innocentis* (D2500B)
>   *presentis omnis* (D3761)

Instances of *is* ending for *es* in the *nominative* plural attested as far back as Republican times,[47] are found in the following areas:

B. *Gaul*

(b) *Lugdunensis.*—There are no examples in dated inscriptions but in non-dated material there are several instances of *patris* (D1371; D1682; D2455N, *et passim*), in the meaning of *parentes,* and one occurrence of *inocentis* (D3102).

C. *Italy*

(a) *Northern.*—The following forms represent nominative plurals:

>   *parentis dolientis* (D847; D1366);
>   *parentis* and *patris* (*passim*)

in non-dated inscriptions.

---

[47] Cf. Sommer, p. 385.

(b) *Central.*—No example.
(c) *Southern.*—A single example in *parentis* (D4616).

D. Rome

In dated material there are several occurrences of *parentis* (D2626 a. 366; D2627 a. 346; D353 a. 367), as well as a form *fratris* (D4146FN a. 400) and *consulis* (D2139 a. 531/33).

In non-dated material we also read *parentis* (*passim*) and *superstitis* (D2372).

An occasional *is* spelling is also found in the fifth declension accusative plural form *dies* in those areas in which this ending is used with some frequency in the accusative plural of third declension nouns, e.g.

ubi ficet.... diis (D2910N a. 466)
ubi ficit.... dis (D2352, VII cent.) } *Lugdunensis*

dis (D4266D) — Northern Italy

diis (D265a a. 355; D2576A a. 450)
zis (D4006); *dis* (D4034) } Rome

The question has been raised whether in these instances of *is* for *es* spelling we are faced with an orthographic confusion and the indiscriminate use of *e* and *i*, reflecting a change in pronunciation, as suggested by Grandgent (pp. 103 ff), or a survival and extension of the free variation of two morphological endings attested in connection with certain nouns in classical Latin already, or indeed, the change of Latin /ē/ to /i/ through the influence of a following (in this case final) /s/.[48]

---

[48] This problem has been recently discussed by B. Löfstedt (p. 40 ff.) with a critical review of various theories advanced to account for the development of the final /i/ in the plural of third declension Italian nouns of the *cane - cani* type. In his conclusions, this scholar seems to lend his support to the phonetic explanation of this plural formation, i.e. the very close [e] or even [i] pronunciation of the vowel of the ending and considers the frequent *-is* spelling found in Late Latin texts as a link («Zwischenglied») between Latin *canes* and standard Italian *cani*. He does not reject, however, other explanations of this Italian plural formation, particularly the theory advanced by Pei, namely that «*cani* may be the phonetic continuator of *canes*, with the fall of final *s* and *i* outcome for final *e*» in view of the frequent /i/ outcome of Latin /ĕ/ and /ĭ/ in final syllable, cf. Pei, *Italian Language*, pp. 73/74. The reader will also find (*loc. cit.*) a short summary of the various theories advanced in this connection.

Whatever the phonetic explanation in back of the seemingly constant interchange of *es* and *is* may be, it must be noted that it occurs almost exclusively in morphological endings, pointing to a primarily morphological phenomenon, i.e. a free variation on the level of form. As a matter of fact, it is possible that in some areas (the whole *Italian* area covered by our material) [49] where the *is* spelling for *es* occurs in noun endings exclusively, this apparent change is of a purely morphological nature, [50] while in some other area (the *Lugdunensis* area in our case), where *is* appears for *es* in final syllable also, i.e. other than morphological ending, there may have been a combination of both the phonetic and morphological factors. [51]

The ablative singular of the fifth declension noun *dies* sporadically appears spelled with *i* for /-e/, but this phenomenon is limited, in our material, to a single example in the *Southern Italian* area (*sub dii* (D3185D a. 517)) and a couple of examples in the area of *Rome* (*dii* (D4378 a. 378; D604A)), where this deviation also occurs in adverbs. (In accordance with what has been said in connection with the ablative singular of third declension nouns spelled with *i* (e.g. *in paci*), we shall revert to this phenomenon after examination of the ablative singular of third declension adjectives. cf. *infra*, p. 181 ff.

3.5 The orthographic change of *es* to *is* in *verb forms* (involving second conjugation 2nd person singular present active indicative and first conjugation 2nd person singular present active subjunctive forms) is attested in a few instances in the Italian area but the occurrence

---

[49] We have excluded from this discussion the only Spanish area where this phenomenon is found, namely the *Tarraconensis* area, in view of the small sampling at our disposal and the fact that the *is* spelling occurs twice in a single inscription only.

[50] Marie Elizabeth Goff concludes in her study entitled «The Language of the Eighth Century Documents of Central Italy» (unpublished PH.D. Dissertation, Columbia University, 1958) that the vowel change before -*s* is of a morphological nature and the closing influence of -*s* on the preceding vowel is irrelevant» (p. 89), thus rejecting any phonetic explanation of this phenomenon, cf. our note # 48.

[51] From the point of view of the eventual outcome of final syllables in French, the apparent change reflected in the *is* spelling for *es* is not particularly significant, seeing that the vowel of the Latin *es* disappeared anyway, cf. Pei, *Texts*, p. 45.

of verb forms ending in Latin /ē/ is quite infrequent (no occurrence in dated material) and does not warrant a tabular representation.

Here are the few deviations found in both dated and non-dated material:

> ne.... *sepulcrum meum violis* (D3864 a. 568) — No. Italy
> *abis* (=*habes*) (D1356 a. 359) — So. Italy
> *semper refrigeris in pace* (D2304); [52] *abis* (D2142) — Rome

Regarding the /i/ outcome of the second person singular present indicative of the second conjugation Latin verb in standard Italian, as well as the various theories advanced in this connection, cf. Pei, *Italian Language*, p. 94.

A few deviations in the present participle -*ens* ending of Latin second and third conjugation verbs were found in the *Lugdunensis* and *Northern Italian* areas, as follows:

> *dolis ficet* (=*doliens fecit*) (D3401) — No. Italy
> *cluins... potins... passiins* (=*patiens*) (D1075 a. 630) [53] — Lugdunensis

This participle ending occasionally occurs in other areas as well, particularly the *Narbonensis* and *Rome*, where it appears correctly spelled. [54]

We may now attempt to establish a possible chronology of the merger of Latin /ĕ/ and /ē/ in unstressed syllable, as proposed in our introductory remarks on the treatment of these vowels, cf. p. 106 ff.

First of all, we believe that for the purpose of comparing the treatment of Latin /ĕ/ and /ē/ (and /ŏ/ and /ō/) in unstressed syllable, each position must be examined individually. It is possible, for instance, that these vowels may have merged in the medial (i.e.

---

[52] The use of the subjunctive side by side with the imperative form *refrigera* is probably due to the formula *deus refrigeret spiritum tuum*, cf. Diehl, ILCV, Vol. I, pp. 450 ff.

[53] That this deviation is not necessarily limited to one scribe's orthography can be seen from the fact that the form *passiins* is also found in another inscription (D4826).

[54] For a phonetic explanation of the change of Latin /ē/ to /i/ before a nasal plus consonant, cf. accented Latin /ē/ in checked position, p. 55, and our reference to Väänänen, p. 36.

intertonic and penult) and final positions at a time when there was still a qualitative distinction between them in the initial syllable.[55]

Not included in our comparative analysis will be Latin /ĕ/ and /ē/ in morphological endings, because of the presence of morphological, rather than phonological factors, nor in penult and intertonic positions. There are too few occurrences of Latin /ē/ in the latter to make comparison meaningful and there are no occurrences of /ē/ in penult at all. The two tables that follow show a comparison of these two vowels in initial and final positions only.

Before proceeding with our analysis, however, it must be pointed out that the abundance of occurrence of /ĕ/ in some instances, as against the scanty sampling of /ē/, makes our task rather difficult, if not impossible, and that our conclusions, if any can be reached at all, must necessarily be tentative, unless, in a given area, there is sufficient material for a clear pattern to emerge. Let us also recall that our criterion for establishing a qualitative difference between originally long and short /e/ in classical Latin will be the percentage of *i* spelling for either vowel and the significant difference that may exist in the deviations. Should we find, for instance, that, at a given period of time, the percentage of *i* spelling for Latin /ē/ is significantly higher than for /ĕ/, we might be safe in assuming that there was still enough of a qualitative difference between the two.

If, on the other hand, we should find that the difference in deviations is either negligible or non-existent (e.g. where there are no deviations for either vowel), we would either have to assume that there was no longer any qualitative difference between /ĕ/ and /ē/,[56] at the time covered by our inscriptional material, or reluctantly admit that the problem is impossible of solution, at least as far as our corpus is concerned.

---

[55] For the classification of unstressed vowels according to position, viz. initial being the most resistant, final and medial vowels the weakest, cf. Grandgent, pp. 91/92; Vossler-Schmeck, p. 91 ff.

[56] Our premise, of course, is the generally admitted theory that the classical Latin *quantitative* system had given way to a *qualitative* system in postclassical Latin, cf. Lausberg, I, p. 95.

Comparative Table Concerning the Treatment of Latin /ĕ/ and /ē/ in the *Initial* Syllable

Area	Century	/ĕ/>e	/ĕ/>i	%	/ē/>e	/ē/>i	%
Baetica	IV-VI	45	0		4	0	
	VII	36	1		17	0	
Lusitania	IV-VI	86	2	2.3	9	0	
	VII	10	0		5	0	
Tarraconensis	IV-VI	48	0		8	0	
	VII	9	1		1	0	
Narbonensis	IV-V	45	0		3	0	
	VI-VII	97	2	2.0	8	1	(11.2)
Lugdunensis	IV-V	43	0		7	0	
	VI-VII	83	0		2	1	(33.3)
No. Italy	IV-V	129	0		29	1	
	VI	69	0		14	0	
	III-IV	33	0		17	0	
Ce. Italy	V	32	0		8	0	
	VI-VII	54	0		22	0	
	III-IV	28	1	(3.6)	23	0	
So. Italy	V	35	1	(2.8)	16	1	
	VI-VII	99	2	2.0	53	0	
	III-IV	207	1	(0.4)	162	10	5.8
Rome	V	131	1	(0.7)	95	10	9.4
	VI-VII	88	4	3.2	38	6	13.6

Comparative Table Concerning the Treatment of Latin /ĕ/ and /ē/ in the *Final* Syllable

Area	Century	/ĕ/>e	/ĕ/>i	%	/ē/>e	/ē/>i	%
Baetica	IV-VI	4	0		0	0	
	VII	3	0		1	0	
Lusitania	IV-VI	4	0		0	0	
	VII	0	0		0	0	
Tarraconensis	IV-VI	10	0		2	0	
	VII	2	0		1	0	
Narbonensis	IV-V	1	0		2	0	
	VI-VII	7	0		8	4	50
Lugdunensis	IV-V	1	0		0	0	
	VI-VII	7	0		3	1	(33.3)
No. Italy	IV-V	26	0		2	0	
	VI	3	0		4	0	
Ce. Italy	III-IV	7	0		2	0	
	V	2	0		1	0	
	VI-VII	12	0		2	0	
So. Italy	III-IV	4	0		1	0	
	V	4	0		1	0	
	VI-VII	13	0		8	0	
Rome	III-IV	49	0		8	0	
	V	20	0		6	0	
	VI-VII	7	0		4	0	

(a) Initial Syllable

As will be seen from the table, the clearest pattern of chronology of the merger of /ĕ/ and /ē/ in this syllable appears in the area of *Rome*, where our figures would indicate that the merger of /ē/ and /i/ must have preceded that of /ĕ/ and /i/ by a couple of centuries; hence, the qualitative difference between the two [e] vowel sounds seems to have been correspondingly kept by the speakers for a longer time than in some other areas, at any rate until the sixth century, when the percentage of *i* spelling for /ĕ/ shows a 3 % jump.

In the area of *Gaul,* despite our scanty sampling, a similar pattern seems to emerge in both *Narbonensis* and *Lugdunensis* where, in sixth/seventh century material, the lack of deviation for /ĕ/, despite the relative abundance of occurrences of this vowel with respect to /ē/, would seem to point to a qualitative difference between the originally short and long vowels.[57]

The situation in the *Italian* area seems to be the following:

There would seem to be an indication of a qualitative difference in fourth/fifth century material from the *Northern* area, judging from the fact that, despite the high frequency of occurrence of /ĕ/, deviations were found for /ē/ only, in non-dated material as well. This qualitative difference seems to have been obliterated, however, by the sixth century.

Our evidence does not enable us to reach any conclusions in connection with the seemingly conservative *Central* area.

The *Southern* area seems to present a picture that is of some interest. Even though in fifth century material there seems to be a spread in percentage figures, it must be noted that in the previous centuries (keeping in mind that the bulk of the material is from the fourth century) the number of occurrences of /ĕ/ and /ē/ is approximately the same, with a deviation found for /ĕ/ only (paralleling the situation in sixth/seventh century material). Since, furthermore, it is in this area that approximately the same number of deviations were found in both dated and non-dated inscriptions (cf. *supra*, pp. 110 and 131), it would seem that the conclusion as to a merger of /ĕ/ and /ē/ by the fourth century may not be unjustified.

---

[57] Pei, *Texts*, finds that «unaccented long *e* appears in the documents more frequently as *i* than does short *e*» (p. 45), which may, indeed, point to a relatively late merger of Latin /ĕ/ and /ē/.

146   AN INQUIRY INTO LOCAL VARIATIONS IN VULGAR LATIN

Our evidence from the *Iberian* area makes it almost impossible to try to establish any kind of chronology of the merger of /ĕ/ and /ē/, especially in the areas of *Baetica* and *Lusitania,* while in the *Tarraconensis* our seventh century material would seem to point in this direction, although it is difficult to say whether a merger may not have taken place at an earlier time.

(b) Final Syllable

Several *i* spellings for Latin /ē/ as against a seeming stability of /ĕ/, pointing to the possibility of a qualitative difference between the originally long and short vowels as late as the sixth century, are found only in the *Narbonensis*. As to the *Lugdunensis* area, it must be kept in mind that final /ĕ/ sometimes also appears spelled with *i* (in non-dated material), so that it is difficult to detect a similar qualitative difference.

The other areas do not yield sufficient evidence that would justify separate treatment of those vowels in this position.

To the extent that our material authorizes us to draw any conclusions, it would seem that there is some justification for treating Latin /ĕ/ and /ē/ separately, at least in the *initial* syllable, seeing that in some areas there may have been a qualitative difference between them until later than is generally assumed. [58]

4. *Latin /ĭ/, represented by the letter i.*

4.1 Initial

Area	Century	/ĭ/>i	/ĭ/>e	%
Baetica	IV-VI	7	0	
	VII	10	1	
Lusitania	IV-VI	14	0	
	VII	1	1	

---

[58] Cf. Bourciez, *Éléments* (p. 43), who claims that, in the spoken language unstressed /ĕ/ and /ē/ merged to a close [e] by the third/fourth centuries in *all* positions.

Area	Century	/ĭ/>i	/ĭ/>e	%
Tarraconensis	IV-VI	11	0	
	VII	3	0	
Narbonensis	IV-V	4	1	(20.0)
	VI-VII	18	4	18.1
Lugdunensis	IV-V	3	1	(25.0)
	VI-VII	13	1	(7.1)
No. Italy	IV-V	25	3	10.7
	VI	15	1	(6.2)
Ce. Italy	III-IV	10	0	
	V	10	0	
	VI-VII	17	0	
So. Italy	III-IV	15	0	
	V	13	2?	?
	VI-VII	15	0	
Rome	III-IV	88	2	2.3
	V	38	6	13.6
	VI-VII	12	0	

Examples of *e* spellings for Latin /ĭ/ are as follows:

A. *Iberian Peninsula*

(a) *Baetica*.—The only deviation occurs in the proper name *Eliberri* (V455 ca. VI cent.) for *Iliberri*, the name of present-day *Elvira* near *Granada*.[59]

---

[59] Lewis & Short, p. 885, give *Illiberi* and the alternate forms *Ili-* and *-erri*, while Rafael Lapesa, *Historia de la Lengua Española* (4th ed.; Madrid, 1959) cites *Iliberris* or *Illiberis* as the Latinized form of *Iriberri* «new city» which, in turn, he calls «un vestigio toponímico de hablas primitivas ligadas al vascuence» (p. 25). The third declension noun ending must probably be taken as an analogical extension of such place names as *Hispalis* and the form *Eliberri* in our inscription would then appear to be in the locative case. It is also of interest to note that in the *Catálogo* of Mateu y Llopis the name of this place consistently appears as *Eliberri* (p. 323 ff.). It is, of course, only by way of reconstruction that we can determine the quantity of the initial /i/ and the assumption that it must have been short is solely based on its eventual outcome in Spanish, viz. *Elvira*. (Cf. Menéndez-Pidal, *Gramática*, (p. 69), for initial /ĭ/ developing to /e/ in mod. Spanish).

(b) *Lusitania.*—An *e* spelling for /ĭ/ appears in the form *enperio* (V366 a. 641) for *imperio*. [60]

(c) *Tarraconensis.*—No example in dated inscriptions.

In a non-dated item we read *Fredenandus* (V369) for *Fridenandus*. [61]

Just as in the case of Latin /ĕ/ in the initial syllable (there were no deviations at all for Latin /ē/ in this position), our sampling is much too insufficient to allow for any conclusions as to a merger of /ĭ/ and /ĕ/, although, of course, it must always be kept in mind that orthographic tradition on the part of the stonecutters may have been particularly strong in the Iberian area, thus concealing the true state of affairs as far as the spoken language is concerned.

B. *Gaul*

Regarding the treatment of Latin /ĭ/ in pretonic and posttonic syllables in Christian inscriptions, Pirson states the following:

> A l'ĭ *protonique ou posttonique* du latin littéraire correspondait souvent un *e* dans les textes archaïques ou d'origine vulgaire. Cet *e* se rencontre aussi dans les documents épigraphiques de la Gaule. Les inscriptions chrétiennes en font un si fréquent usage qu'il y est devenu pour ainsi dire la voyelle normale de la syllabe atone et qu'il constitue un des traits caractéristiques de la langue latine des ve et vi^e siècles (p. 32).

Deviations in the initial syllable in both dated and non-dated inscriptions are not as frequent as Pirson would lead us to believe.

Examples are as follows:

(a) *Narbonensis.*—In both dated and non-dated inscriptions we find the following spellings:

> *fedelis* (D2454 a. 472); *megravit* (D1687 a. 527)
> *ab heneunte etate* (D1670 a. 557/572)
> *meserecordiae* (D3467 a. 547); *meserecordia* (D1677)

---

[60] This form would also suggest an etymological reconstruction and the possibility that the Latin preposition *in* may have already assumed its Hispano-Romance form *en* in this area. Cf. the form *en* for *in* in the *Lusitanian* inscription V340. Cf. supra, p. 65.

[61] For the treatment of /i/ in Latinized forms of Germanic names as a short vowel (*Fridenandus* > *Fernando, Hernando*), cf. Jennings, pp. 34/35.

(b) *Lugdunensis*.—In dated inscriptions we find deviations in two proper names only:

> dep. *Selentioses* (=*Silentiosae*) (D3-39 a. 334)
> *Felocalus* (=*Philocalus*) (D3562 a. 518)

In non-dated inscriptions we find the following:

> *trebunus* (D437); *fedilis* (D1372); *Vectoris* (D202)

The lack of consistency in our figures from this latter area may be merely coincidental, in that in our dated material we did not find more than one deviation out of 13 occurrences. This does not necessarily mean, we believe, that in this particular region the merger of Latin /ĭ/ and /e/ (possibly both long and short) may not have been well along its way also, as evidenced by *e* spelling in non-dated inscriptions. The consistency of pattern reflected in our figures from the *Narbonensis* area would seem to, point to such a merger, supporting, at the same time, the figures obtained for Latin /ē/ in initial syllable for the comparable period, cf. p. 130.

C. *Italy*

(a) *Northern*.—The following forms show *e* spellings for Latin /ĭ/:

> *prencepalis* (D370, IV/V cent.); *Prencepia* (D1500a a. 409)
> *decata* (D3454 a. 488)
> *Cellican(is)* (=gen.sg. of *Cillica*) (D1158 a. 519)

A number of *e* spellings occur in non-dated inscriptions also:

> *vertutem* (D811b); *fedelis* (D847) and *passim;*
> *cressiani* (=*christiani*) (D1337)

(b) *Central*.—A single deviation in a non-dated inscription in the form *fedelis* (D4722).

(c) *Southern*.—The *e* spelling was found in two proper names: *Felippo* (D2801 a. 408) and *Recemedes* (=*Ricimeris*) (D31185A a. 460), as well as *crestiani* (D1331) in a non-dated item. Because of the number of alternate spellings of the name of *Ricimer*, the consul *ordinarius*,[62] we placed a question mark in our table next to the figure showing deviations, since there would be some doubt attached as to its validity. We, nevertheless, decided to include this form in our material because it does represent an interesting spelling, also on account of the change of /r/ to /d/.

There would seem to be little doubt that of the three *Italian* regions it is the *Northern* one which most clearly shows a trend towards the merger of Latin /ĭ/ and /ĕ/ and would, thus, seem to be drawn into the «sphere of influence» of the area of *Gaul* (cf. Latin /ĭ/ and /ē/ in stressed syllable, p. 67).

D. *Rome*

In both dated and non-dated inscriptions there is a fair amount of forms in which Latin /ĭ/ appears as *e*. A few examples follows:

> *Vencentia* (D4428 a. 307) (but note both *Vincentia* and *Vincentianus* in the same item); *fedelis* (D1351 a. 404, *et passim*, also in non-dated inscriptions);
> *Stelicone* (D3003BN a. 405); *Epolytum* (=*Hippolytum*) (D3754F a. 430); *trebunus* (D440); *vescandente* (=*biscandente*) (D2129); *descessit* (D2851); *Espanis* (D4447), etc.

It would seem that, despite the lack of deviation in our sixth/seventh century material, the progression shown in the fifth century as against previous centuries, coupled with all instances of *e* spelling for Latin /ĭ/ in non-dated material, would confirm the situation found in connection with Latin /ē/ in initial position (cf. supra, p. 132) and the merger of these vowels.

---

[62] Cf. Schönfeld, p. 189 ff., where some of the following spellings of this Suebian name are given: *Ricimer, Ricemer, Recimer, Ricomer, Ricomedes, Ricomedus*.

4.2 Intertonic

Area	Century	/ĭ/>i	/ĭ/>e	%
Baetica	IV-VI	5	0	
	VII	13	2	
Lusitania	IV-VI	7	1	
	VII	2	0	
Tarraconensis	IV-VI	10	1	(9.0)
	VII	3	0	
Narbonensis	IV-V	10	1	
	VI-VII	18	7	28.0
Lugdunensis	IV-VI	7	1	(12.5)
	VI-VII	10	8	44.4
No. Italy	IV-V	36	5	12.2
	VI	10	0	
Ce. Italy	III-IV	11	0	
	V	10	0	
	VI-VII	23	2	8.6
So. Italy	III-IV	13	0	
	V	11	1	
	VI-VII	14	1	
Rome	III-IV	83	1	
	V	54	0	
	VI-VII	12	1	

Deviations in this position occur as follows:

A. *Iberian Peninsula*

(a) *Baetica*.—Two instances of *e* spelling in the Germanic proper name *Belisarius*, appearing as *Belesari* (V157), and the adjective *Emeretensis* (V113), both from our seventh century material.

(b) *Lusitania*.—A single deviation in *relegiosa famula* (V494 a. 587).

(c) *Tarraconensis*.—A single *e* spelling in *era DV*[...] *indectione* (V68).

Although a few cases of *i* spelling for Latin /ĕ/ were also found in these regions, our sampling would seem to be much too scanty and inconsistent to draw any conclusions on the treatment of these vowels in this position. (It will be remembered that in this area there were very few occurrences of Latin /ē/ in intertonic syllable and no deviations).

B. *Gaul*

Pei finds in his texts from Northern France that the overwhelming majority of *e* spellings for Latin /ĭ/ appear in the intertonic syllable and the posttonic in proparoxytons, «the two positions in which unaccented *i* was definitely doomed in French» (p 46), and attributes the *e* spelling in these positions to the «weakening of the vowel sound into the *schwa* that was the forerunner of total disappearance» (*ibid.*).

A glance at our table for Latin /ĭ/ in intertonic position (and, by way of anticipation, at the table showing the treatment of this vowel in penult position, cf. *infra*, p. 154) will show us that Pei's findings are foreshadowed in our inscriptional material from this area and that *Gaul* (the *Lugdunensis* apparently more so than the *Narbonensis*) is quite innovating in the treatment of this vowel, in relation to other areas under study.

A few examples of deviations are as follows:

(a) *Narbonensis*: *virgenalis* (D1734 a. 491); *semplecetate* and *noveletate* (=*nobilitate*) (270 a. 563); *penetentiae* (D1687 a. 527); *indexioni* (D3279 a. 564); *dignetatem* (D88); *meserecordia* (D1677); *relegiosa* (D1673), etc.

(b) *Lugdunensis*: *humanetate* (D1749 a. 487); *pakefecare* (D1075 a. 630); *arceprb.* (=*archipresbyter*) (D1125 ca. VI cent.); *sanctemunialis* (D1679 a. 564); *Lopecenos* (=*lupicinus*) (D3563 a. 523) *edefic(avit)* (D1812); *karetate* (D3858), etc.

C. *Italy*

Sporadic occurrences are found here and there but, except for the *Northern* area, they are generally limited to proper names.

Examples are as follows:

(a) *Northern*: *camped(octor)* (D457a); *prencepalis* (D370); *lapedario* (D654) (ca. IV/V cent. all three); *Baselisci* (D2737a a. 466); *sempeternis* (D3454 a. 488) (analogy with *aeternus?*)
(b) *Central*: *Apolenaris* (D622 a. 575; D695 a. 549) *arcediaconus* (D1197)
(c) *Southern*: *Recemedes* (D3185A a. 460) (cf. *supra*, Latin /ĭ/ in initial syllable and our note # 62); *Caretosa* (=*Charitosa*) (D1205 a. 565)

Just as in the case of Latin /ĭ/ in the initial syllable, there would seem to be little doubt that the *Northern* area is the most innovating, conforming to the pattern of *Gaul*, rather than the other Italian areas.

D. *Rome*

Relatively few instances were found where Latin /ĭ/ appears as *e*. In some instances, such as *retenetur* (D1603 a. 369) and *possedatur* (D840 a. 522), the deviation may be more apparent than real, since these forms are probably influenced by the active forms *tenet* (*retenet* being an obvious etymological reconstruction) and *possedet* (for *possidet*).[63]

Deviations also occur in the following forms:

Filicetate (766A); *inemitabili* (D3343)

both in non-dated inscriptions.

It would seem from our evidence that Latin /ĭ/ in this position is relatively stable.

In view of our anticipation of Latin /ĭ/ in penult position in connection with our discussion of *Gaul*, we are reversing our sequence and shall now present the treatment of this vowel in this syllable.

---

[63] The form *posedet* is attested by Lewis & Short, p. 1403. This, incidentally, is the form that we must postulate for standard Italian *possiede*.

4.3 Penult

Area	Century	/ĭ/>i	/ĭ/>e	%
Baetica	IV-VI	20	2	9.0
	VII	24	0	
Lusitania	IV-VI	13	2	13.3
	VII	6	0	
Tarraconensis	IV-VI	16	5(?)	23.8(?)
	VII	7	0	
Narbonensis	IV-V	16	1	(6.2)
	VI-VII	17	15	46.8
Lugdunensis	IV-V	15	2	11.7
	VI-VII	16	20	55.5
No. Italy	IV-V	66	7	9.6
	VI	21	3	12.5
Ce. Italy	III-IV	20	0	
	V	16	0	
	VI-VII	31	0	
So. Italy	III-IV	46	0	
	V	20	0	
	VI-VII	51	0	
Rome	III-IV	249	0	
	V	132	2	1.5
	VI-VII	63	1	(1.4)

Latin /ĭ/ in this position is represented by *e* in the following forms:

A. *Iberian Peninsula*

    (a) *Baetica*: clarissima *femena* (V131 a. 545);
                   genetor (V364 a. 573)

    (b) *Lusitania*: *soledos* (V69 a. 579)
                  in *nomene* (V185 a. 510)

    (c) *Tarraconensis*: *spiretus*, in *nomene* Dei, *fecit*... *benemereto* come from the same inscription (V211) and might represent one stone-cutter's orthography.

The *e* spelling also appears in the forms *tegetur* and *credetur* (V276 a. 550); however, the spelling *-etur* for *-itur* may also represent a morphological phenomenon, in that these passive forms may be built on the active forms *teget* and *credet*, since the *-it* ending of the third person present indicative of third conjugation verbs is not infrequently spelled *-et* (cf. *infra*, Latin /ĭ/ in verb endings, p. 167 ff.)

The penult, Grandgent (p. 99) tells us, being the weakest of the posttonic syllables of proparoxytons, was more exposed to syncope and the orthographic confusion of *i* and *e* in late Latin texts and inscriptions reflects the weakening of the vowel in this position. Since the penult generally disappears in Spanish,[64] it is most likely that the deviations found in this area do reflect what Menéndez-Pidal calls «la vocal relajada», i.e. the weakening of the vowel as the first step towards syncope.

B. *Gaul*

There seems to be very little doubt that the vowel in this position was particularly weak, cf. *supra*, Latin /ĭ/ in intertonic syllable, p. 152.

A few examples in both dated and non-dated inscriptions follow:

(a) *Narbonensis*: *decema* (D1213 a. 536); *nomene* (D2454 a. 472) *penetens* (D1554N a. 578); *venerabelis* (D1672 a. 540); *pauperebus* (D4728 a. 563); *omnebus* (D1554N a. 578) *femena* (D1341); *provedus* (D1167); *nobelis* (D1648); *domeni* (D2420), etc.

(b) *Lugdunensis*: *septe[mo]* *[de]cemo* (D4404 a. 448); *artefex* (D662 ca. VI cent.); *nuvelis* (=*nobilis*) (D1075 a. 630); *umenetas* (D1169 a. 557) *condetum* (D1237 ca. VI cent.); *omnevos* (=*omnibus* (D4824); *altarebus, dulcissemus* (D1076 a. 632); *amabeles* (D3301); *egetur* (D1075 a. 630); *tegetur* (D1218 a. 548),[65] etc.

---

[64] Cf. Menéndez-Pidal, *Gramática*, p. 75. The forms *femena, soledos* and *nomene* appear in Mod. Spanish as *hembra, sueldos* and *nombre*, respectively.

[65] The forms *egetur* and *tegetur* may, of course, also be built on the present indicative forms *eget* and *teget* (cf. *supra* in re *tegetur* and *credetur* found in the *Tarraconensis* area, p. 155). The ending *et* for *it* in the third person singular present active indicative of third conjugation verbs is not

C. Italy

Except for the *Northern* area, the vowel of the penult appears to be quite stable.

A few examples from the *Northern* area follow:

> *ex comete* (D254 ca. V cent.); *capete* (D1500b a. 409)
> *milete* (D545 a. 396/402); *penetens* (D1733c a. 463)
> *penalebus* (D3454 a. 488); *deposeta* (D1431 a. 535);
> *septema* (D2356 a. 544); *femena* (D3124), etc.

It would seem quite clear that the treatment of Latin /ĭ/ in this position also parallels the situation observed in *Gaul* and, thus, detaches itself from the rest of the *Italian* area (including *Rome*, cf. *infra*).

D. Rome

The low percentage figures for dated material and the occasional appearance of an *e* spelling for Latin /ĭ/ would suggest that in this area the penult was quite stable.

An infrequent *e* spelling occurs in the following forms:

> *Leonedes* (D2974B a. 456); *Vitalessema* (D4394B a. 425)
> *deposeta* (D3115D a. 550); *nomeni* (D854);
> *Aselleca* (D1561A); *karisseme* (D4637); *superstetes* (D1537)

This would appear to be a small sampling of deviations to be significant.

Speaking of the vowel in the penult syllable and the orthographic confusion of *i* and *e* (as well as *o* and *u*), Grandgent finds that

> The treatment of this vowel.... was apparently very inconsistent in Vulgar Latin and the conditions differed widely in different regions. There was probably a conflict between cultivated and popular pronunciation, both types being preserved in the Romance languages: thus while the literary and official world said *(h)omines* (>It. *uomini*), the uneducated pronounced *'om'nes* (>Pr. *omne*)... (p. 99).

---

infrequent in *Gaul;* however, even if we left these forms out of our count, the deviations would still outnumber the correct forms.

There is little doubt that our material is quite in agreement with this scholar's statement about the conditions differing widely in different regions, foreshadowing, it would seem, an important phonological rift, viz. the essentially proparoxytonic syllable structure of standard Italian and Sardinian (our material from *Ce. Italy* includes this area), as against the generally paroxytonic nature of Spanish, Portugese, Catalan, Provençal, French (which, however, since the Middle Ages has become oxytonic) and the Northern Italian dialects.[66]

4.4 Hiatus

Area	Century	/ĭ/>i	/ĭ/>e	%
Baetica	IV-VI	46	0	
	VII	40	0	
Lusitania	IV-VI	94	2	2.1
	VII	20	1	(4.7)
Tarraconensis	IV-VI	56	0	
	VII	9	0	
Narbonensis	IV-V	50	0	
	VI-VII	179	0	
Lugdunensis	IV-V	52	0	
	VI-VII	92	1	
No. Italy	IV-V	172	2	1.2
	VI	74	0	
	III-IV	48	1	
Ce. Italy	V	46	0	
	VI-VII	56	0	

---

[66] Cf. Lausberg, I, p. 153 ff.; Elcock, pp. 41-42, on the «paroxytonic tendency of Vulgar Latin;» Menéndez-Pidal, *Gramática*, p. 77, on instances of the preservation of the penult in Spanish; Pei, *Italian Language*, pp. 30-31, on the resistance to the paroxytonizing trend in Italian as being due to conservative forces. This scholar points out, however, that these forces were not uniformly distributed, but rather restricted to certain sections and social classes, as indicated by the abundance and variety of Italian dialects, cf. section on Italian dialects, *ibid*, p. 154 ff.

So. Italy	III-IV	55	0
	V	49	0
	VI-VII	108	0
Rome	III-IV	313	0
	V	180	0
	VI-VII	110	0

For references regarding the development of vowels in hiatus, cf. Latin /ĕ/ in hiatus, p. 115 and our note #32.

In the light of the generally admitted frequent orthographic confusion of *e* and *i* as an indication of the reduction of the vowel in hiatus to a semi-vocalic quality, it may be surprising to find an abundant sampling of Latin /ĭ/ appearing as *i* in spelling. This, however, may be due to the fact that the majority of instances in which this vowel appears in hiatus are represented by such traditional and stereotyped formulae as *bonae memoriae* and *hic requiescit*[67] which would be least likely to be misspelled.

Nevertheless, sporadic *e* spellings for Latin /ĭ/ do appear, as follows:

A. *Iberian Peninsula*

No deviations were found in *Baetica* and *Tarraconensis*.

The following forms taken from *Lusitanian* inscriptions show an *e* spelling for Latin /ĭ/:

terteo (V93 a. 525); *noxea* (V291 a. 593); *Adulteus* (V79 a. 679); *atrea* (V359)[68]

---

[67] The form *requiescit*, however, often appears spelled *requescit* (for the spelling *requiiscit* and *requiscit* cf. stressed Latin /ē/ in closed syllable, p. 55), showing an apparent loss of the hiatus vowel. It may be of interest to note that *requescit*, as well as such forms as *requevit, quescas, cesquent,* etc., appear in virtually all areas (*Baetica* and *Tarraconensis* being the exceptions), the earliest examples coming from the area of *Rome*. (For the form *queti* for *quieti* already attested in Pompeian inscriptions and the Romance forms *cheto* (It.), *coi* (Fr.) *quedo* (Sp. and Pg.), cf. Väänänen, p. 47).

[68] Although it is generally conceded that the orthographic confusion of *e* and *i* in hiatus stands for reverse spellings, indicating yodization of Latin /ĕ/ and /ĭ/, Carnoy (pp. 35-43) offers an entirely different interpretation of what he chooses to call «ce phénomène lusitanien». Not satisfied with the

Whether these instances of apparent reverse spelling that show up in one area only are coincidental, or whether there is indeed a regional difference to be noted in connection with this phenomenon, is a matter that is difficult to decide. For one thing, there is a complete absence of the reverse phenomenon, viz. Latin /ĕ/ in hiatus appearing as *i* (which would seem to be the more usual way of indicating yodization); for another, even if we assume that the reduction of /ĕ/ and /ĭ/ to a semi-vowel may not be as old in the Iberian area as in *Italy*, the date of these examples (sixth and seventh centuries) would seem to make it unlikely that so widespread a phenomenon in Vulgar Latin[69] should not have been operative in *Baetica* and *Tarraconensis* at this time as well.

B. *Gaul*

Only two deviations were found in the *Lugdunensis* area:

memoreae (D1169 a. 557/626); *Veator* (D2554)

C. *Italy*

Reverse spelling is shown in the following forms:

bearcus (= *biarchus*) (D516/D522b),

both found on inscriptions from the military cemetery at *Concordia, No. Italy*, and

cristaeanus (D1334 a. 343/376)[70]

found in the *Ce. Italian* area.

---

reverse spelling explanation, he argues that the quality of hiatus /ĭ/ tended towards /e/ in this region, as a result of possible Celtic influence. To support his claim he offers a rather lengthy list of non-Latin names found in pagan inscriptions from this area, in which final *ius* and *ia* almost always appear as *eus* and *ea*, and advances the hypothesis that the open pronunciation of hiatus /ĭ/ was later extended to Latin words also.

[69] Cf. Väänänen, p. 47.
[70] For the spelling *ae* for Latin /ĕ/ as an orthographic hypercorrection, cf. *infra*, the diphthong /aj/ in unstressed syllable, p. 250/251.

D. Rome

A few cases of *e* spelling for hiatus /ĭ/, both pre- and posttonic, were found in non-dated inscriptions, as follows:

Licineus (D414); *Laurenteus* (D2192); *Sebasteano* (D3742)

Since reverse spelling would merely seem to confirm the semi-vocalization of both /ĭ/ and /ĕ/ in hiatus, rather than being an indication of a regional difference, we do not believe that any particular significance can be attached to the fact that deviations are most infrequent in the very area which seems to be the focal point of this phenomenon. [71]

4.5 Final

Latin /ĭ/ in the final syllable of non-morphological endings occurs rather infrequently and, except for the area of *Gaul*, no deviations were found in either dated or non-dated inscriptions.

The situation in *Gaul* parallels closely the one found in connection with Latin /ē/, as follows:

		Century	/ĭ/>i	/ĭ/>e	%
(a)	*Narbonensis*	IV-V	0	0	
		VI-VII	0	2	
(b)	*Lugdunensis*	IV-V	1	0	
		VI-VII	1	1	

Deviations occur mainly in numerals compounded with *decem*. Examples in dated and non-dated inscriptions:

(a) *Narbonensis*: *sates* (D270 a. 563); *duodece* (D2892N a. 541) *tredece* (D1280)

(b) *Lugdunensis*: *sates* (D1169 a. 557/626); *sedece* (D1690); *tredecem* (D3242A); *duodecem* (D3566), etc.

---

[71] Cf. *supra*, Latin /ĕ/ in hiatus, p. 115.

Although one might see in these numerals an analogy with *decem,* it must be remembered that the forms *decim* (D438N) and *septim* (D1574) also occur, so that it would seem to be reasonable to assume that by the sixth century, in this area, Latin /ĭ/ and /ē/ —and possibly even /ĕ/— had completely merged in the final syllable. The merger of these vowels in this position is of considerable importance when it comes to determining whether the *e* spelling in morphological endings is to be interpreted as a phonological phenomenon, i.e. merely a graphic representation of a sound that had become a *schwa*[72] or a close [e],[73] or else as a reflection of a morphological substitution, as when *tegit* and *requiescit* become *teget* and *requiescet*, taking a second conjugation present indicative active ending for the expected *it*, which is characteristic of the verb class to which these forms belong, namely the third and fourth Latin conjugations. For a further discussion of this problem, cf. *infra,* Latin /ĭ/ in noun-adjective and verb endings.

The purpose of the following tables showing the treatment of Latin /ĭ/ in noun-adjective and verb endings is twofold:

(a) to show deviations with respect to classical Latin spelling, and

(b) to present a comparison with the treatment of Latin /ĕ/ in morphological, particularly verbal endings.

---

[72] Cf. Grandgent, p. 103.

[73] Cf. Pirson: «cet *e* vulgaire correspondant à l'*i* de la langue littéraire avait évidemment un son fermé» (p. 36).

162 AN INQUIRY INTO LOCAL VARIATIONS IN VULGAR LATIN

4.6 Noun-adjective Endings

A. Third decl. nom. sg.
B. Third decl. nom. sg.
C. Third decl. gen. sg.
D. Total of nom. and gen. deviations (A and C)

Area	Century	A			B			C			D		
		is	es	%	ix	ex	%	is	es	%	is	es	%
Baetica	IV-VI	4	1		0	1		1	0		5	1	
	VII	6	0		1	0		9	0		15	0	
Lusitania	IV-VI	1	0		1	1		1	0		2	0	
	VII	0	0		1	0		2	0		2	0	
Tarraconensis	IV-VI	6	2	25.0	2	1		5	1		11	3	21.4
	VII	0	0		0	0		2	0		2	0	
Narbonensis	IV-V	4	0		0	0		3	0		7	0	
	VI-VII	3	2	40.0	0	0		12	5	29.4	15	7	31.8
Lugdunensis	IV-V	2	0		0	0		5	0		7	0	
	VI-VII	6	1	14.3	1	0		8	2	20.0	14	3	17.6

4.6 Noun-adjective Endings (Cont.)

A. Third decl. nom. sg.
B. Third decl. nom. sg.
C. Third decl. gen. sg.
D. Total of nom. and gen. deviations (A and C)

Area	Century	A			B			C			D		
		is	es	%	ix	ex	%	is	es	%	is	es	%
No. Italy	IV-V	13	1		3	0		12	0		25	1	(3.8)
	VI	1	0		0	0		10	3	23.0	11	3	21.4
Ce. Italy	III-IV	2	0		0	0		4	0		6	0	
	V	4	0		0	0		5	1		9	1	
	VI-VII	1	0		0	0		16	0		17	0	
So. Italy	III-IV	3	1	(25.0)	5	0		3	0		6	1	(14.3)
	V	2	1	(33.3)	1	0		11	3	21.4	13	4	23.5
	VI-VII	3	1	(25.0)	2	0		31	2	6.0	34	3	8.1
Rome	III-IV	16	4	20.0	5	0		35	1		51	5	8.9
	V	15	2	11.7	3	0		26	0		41	2	4.6
	VI-VII	9	0		3	0		12	1	(7.6)	21	1	(4.5)

THE UNACCENTED VOWELS 163

Examples of deviations in the various areas occur as follows:

A. *Iberian Peninsula*

The spelling *es* for *is* occurs mainly in the third declension nominative singular:

(a) *Baetica*: *dulces ani*[*ma*] (V115 a. 485)
Filex (=*Felix*) (V105)
(b) *Lusitania*: *Bracarius felex* (V18 a. 381)
(c) *Tarraconensis*: *utere felex* (V520a) ⎫
...[*fi*]*deles* (V197) ⎬ (IV-VI cent.)
tristes... coniunx (V295) ⎭

The only instance of an *es* spelling in the genitive singular occurs in this region: *tetulum Victoes* (= *Victoris*) (V239).

B. *Gaul*

Deviations occur in both the nominative and genitive singular forms in dated and non-dated inscriptions; however, it may be of interest to note that, at least as far as dated inscriptions are concerned, none of them are earlier than the first half of the sixth century, contrary to what we observe in some of the other areas under investigation. (Unfortunately, none of the examples from *Tarraconensis* are accurately dated.)

A few examples of *es* spelling for *is* follow:

(a) *Narbonensis*: *fedeles famula* (D1432N a. 514)
Apriles (proper name) (D2891AN a. 530)
iuniores (D1808 a. 530)
riges (=*regis*) (D2910 a. 518/33)
consoles (D3279 a. 564); *cruces* (D1512)
resurrecxiones (D1677), etc.
(b) *Lugdunensis*: *Eugenia neptes* (D1676 a. 552)
ic pausat Amabeles (D3301)
principales (D373); *civitates* (D1919)
recordaciones (D1463), etc.

C. *Italy*

Examples of *es* spelling in nominative and genitive singular forms are found in all Italian areas, either in dated or non-dated inscriptions, although the *Central* region offers the least.

THE UNACCENTED VOWELS 165

(a) *Northern*: *cives* (D4440 a. 424)
fedeles (D1360)
omnes (D1741)
comites (D116 a. 512)
Iohannes (D848 a. 539)
in somno paces (D305)
marteres Xpi (D2015N) [74]

(b) *Central*: *cives Gallus* (D1474C)
fideles... fuisti (D2312)
in somnum paces (D3181 a. 442)
die Veneres (D4402A)

(c) *Southern*: *cives Romana* (D4430 a. 551)
Dianeses innocens (=*Dianensis*) (D2932A a. 397)
mites (D3114 a. 469)
infates (=*infantis*) (D3029 a. 401)
Iuniores (D248 a. 508)
die Martes (D2777A) [75]
etc.

D. *Rome*

Here are a few examples of deviations in nominative and genitive singular forms, in both dated and non-dated inscriptions:

incomparaviles (=*incomparabilis*) (D2732 a. 368)
cibes (D4461 a. 345); *dulces* (D4623 a. 388)
inimitabiles (D1722 a. 409); *natales* (D2114A)
staviles (=*stabilis*) (D2500B); *fideles* (D1353C)
recordationes (D301 a. 396); *Bictores* (D3408)
die Veneres (D2372); *dies Soles* (D4389), etc.

Comparing our evidente regarding Latin /ĕ/ (cf. *supra*, p. 120 ff.) and /ĭ/ in noun-adjective endings, we find that the *is* spelling for *es* is quite infrequent and that the general trend would seem to be in the direction of *es* for *is* in all areas under study, pointing to a morpho-

---

[74] This example would seem to illustrate the fact that Greek *upsilon* had become an [i] sound in the spoken language and, in turn, was subject to merger with Latin /ĕ/ in unstressed position. Cf. Väänänen, p. 38; Pirson, p. 40.

[75] Cf. Spanish *martes*, standard Italian *martedì* (<*martes dies*).

logical extension of a single ending in the singular of third declension nouns and adjectives. [76]

---

[76] For the reduction of the classical Latin system of noun and adjective declensions to a two-case declensional system in Vulgar Latin, cf. Muller-Taylor, pp. 54 ff.; also Vossler-Schmeck, p. 103. Specifically for the singular of third declension nouns and adjectives, cf. Sittl, «Zur Beurteilung des sogenannten Mittellateins,» *Archiv für lateinische Lexikographie und Grammatik,* zweiter Jahrgang, Leipzing, 1885), pp. 566/557. For the interpretation of this phenomenon as merely due to «l'incertezza -*es*/-*is* nella finale,» cf. Pisani, *Testi,* p. 121.

4.7 Verb Endings

A. Third conj. pres. ind. 2nd pers. sg.
B. Third/fourth conj. pres. ind. 3rd pers. sg.
C. First/second/third/fourth conj. perf. ind. 3rd pers. sg.

Area	Century	A		B			C		
		is	es	it	et	%	it	et	%
Baetica	IV-VI	0	0	7	1		63	0	
	VII	0	0	2	1		29	0	
Lusitania	IV-VI	2	0	0	1		108	2	1.8
	VII	0	0	1	0		16	0	
Tarraconensis	IV-VI	1	1	11	11	50.0	41	2	4.8
	VII	0	0	0	0		6	0	
Narbonensis	IV-V	0	0	8	2	20.0	23	6	20.6
	VI-VII	0	0	42	10	19.2	93	21	18.4
Lugdunensis	IV-V	0	0	10	1	(9.0)	42	1	(2.4)
	VI-VII	2	0	23	9	28.1	64	14	16.6

4.7 Verb Endings (Continued)

Area	Century	A			B			C		
		is	es	%	it	et	%	it	et	%
No. Italy	IV-V	0	0		21	10	32.2	111	8	6.6
	VI	0	0		33	6	15.4	48	4	7.7
Ce. Italy	III-IV	0	0		3	2	40.0	29	1	(3.3)
	V	0	0		8	2	10.0	23	0	
	VI-VII	0	0		20	4	16.6	38	4	9.5
So. Italy	III-IV	0	0		2	1	(33.3)	39	1	(2.5)
	V	0	0		13	2	13.3	27	0	
	VI-VII	0	0		52	1	(1.8)	57	1	(1.8)
Rome	III-IV	1	1		11	15	57.6	257	8	3.0
	V	0	0		29	13	30.9	138	6	4.1
	VI-VII	0	0		49	4	7.5	64	3	4.3

The verb endings that occur most frequently are those of the third person singular forms of the present and perfect active indicative of third conjugation verbs.[77] The spelling *et* for *it* appears in connection with both present and past tense forms, although it would seem that deviations are more likely to occur in the present tense (except for the area of *Gaul*, cf. *infra*), which is especially represented by the verb form *requiescit*, alternating constantly with the spelling *requiescet*.

Some examples of deviations in our material are as follows:

A. *Iberian Peninsula*

   (a) *Baetica*:   *vivet* (V151, IV/VI cent.)
                             quiescet (V156, VII cent.)
   (b) *Lusitania*:   *requiescet* (V87 a. 487)
                               requiesset (V184)
   (c) *Tarraconensis*:

The only verb form in which the expected *it* ending appears as *et* is *requiescet*, alternating with the correct spelling in a 50:50 ratio.

A few examples of *et* spelling for *it* in the perfect are found in the areas of *Lusitania* and *Tarraconensis*, as follows:

    fecet (V14 ca. V cent.); *recesset* (V185 a. 510)
    fuet (V186) — *Lusitania*
    posuet (V2 a. 362); *recesset* (V198 ca. V cent.) — *Tarraconensis*

The *is* ending of the second singular present active indicative appears in one instance spelled with *es*, *quiesces* (V208 ca. V cent.) on an inscription from the latter area, possibly by influence of *requiescet*.

The trend to replace the ending *it* of third and fourth conjugation present active indicative third singular forms by *et*, which is a second conjugation ending, seems to be best illustrated in the *Tarraconensis*, more particularly in the *Tarragona* (Northeastern Spain) region, where *requiescit* and *requiescet* constantly alternate; however, it may be worth noting that in the *Lusitania* where the formula *hic requiescit* is extremely rare (the consecrated expression being *hic requievit in pace*, see-

---

[77] This, of course, is due to the strongly formulaic nature of tomb inscriptions, of which the bulk of our material is made up.

mingly in the meaning of 'was put to rest'), the only occurrence of this verb form in fourth/sixth century material appears spelled with *et* (cf. *supra*). Even though our sampling from both this region and *Baetica* is not abundant, it might not be unreasonable to assume that, given a larger corpus, we would find an extension of the *et* ending in the present indicative, similar to the one observed in *Tarraconensis*.[78]

In the perfect, which is almost exclusively represented by verbs belonging to the classical third and fourth conjugations, the spelling *et* for *it* is much less frequent than in the present tense, but the fact that we find such forms as *recesset* and *vixsit* side by side in the same inscription (V198 ca. V. cent., *Tarraconensis*) would seem to suggest the same kind of formal variation of these two endings that we observe in the present tense.[79]

There seems to be little doubt that of the three Spanish areas, the *Tarraconensis*, in particular the Northeastern part, i.e. what is today the area of *Catalonia*, is the most innovating as regards the treatment of these verbal endings.

B. *Gaul*

With the exception of the form *teget* (D1217 ca. VII cent.) on an inscription from *Narbonensis*, the third person present is represented

---

[78] The extension of this ending would seem to point to a morphological merger of the second, third and fourth conjugation *et* and *it* endings, with a concomitant loss of opposition, leaving two formal devices used in free variation to designate the third person indicative active form of a verb belonging to any of these classes. Cf. the concurrent use of the spelling *it* for *et* and *et* for *it* in one and the same inscription, e.g. *iacit - requiescet* (V192 a. 459, *Tarraconensis*); *continet - lugit* (V287 a. 624, *Baetica*).

The reshuffling of the classical conjugational system seems to be further evidenced by the regularization of irregular forms, so-called athematic verbs, like *offero* which, in the third person singular present indicative active appears almost exclusively as *offeret* on various votive objects, although a few instances of the correct form *offert* are also found. Would the reconstructed form not also show the speakers' preference for the third person singular *et* ending?

[79] The fact that we find the *it* ending in the perfect in the overwhelming majority of cases is not surprising, seeing that it occurs mainly in the forms *vixit* and *requievit* which, due to their stereotyped nature, the stonecutter was not too likely to misspell. Also, in the perfect tense, there was no possibility of a morphological merger of the second, third and fourth conjugations (the third person singular ending being *it* in all three of them) and this fact may have contributed to the relative stability of this ending.

by the forms *requiescet* and *quiescet*, in both dated and non-dated inscriptions.

A few examples of *et* spelling in perfect forms:

(a) *Narbonensis*: *recesset* (D446AN a. 489) (but *vixit*)
viset (=*vixit*) (D1665 a. 508/9)
transiet (D1734 a. 491); *obiet* (D1215 a. 559)
fuet (D270 a. 562) (but *fulsit, reliquid*)
rapuet (D1512), etc.

(b) *Lugdunensis*: *sublecetavet* (=*sollicitavit*) (D1075 a. 630)
transiet (D1169 a. 557/626) (but *vixit, fuit*)
vixe (D1674 a. 520; *ficet* (D2456 ca. VII cent.)
obiet (D2903 a. 501) (but *vixit*)
posuet (D426N), etc.

In addition to these deviations, in an inscription from the *Narbonensis* we found the form *leges* (D2354) for *legis*.

It is of interest to note that in this area the spelling *et* for *it* occurs in both the present and perfect endings in approximately the same ratio. On the other hand, the *e* spelling for Latin /ĭ/ in the final syllable is not limited to morphological endings (cf. *supra*, p. 160) and this fact must be kept in mind when passing judgment on the conclusions of those scholars who see in the confusion of *it* and *et* spelling in verb endings a phonological, rather than a morphological phenomenon, at least for what concerns the area of *Gaul* (cf. *supra*, Latin /ĕ/ in verb endings, p. 125 ff). Indeed, the evidence offered by our material and the comparison of the treatment of both Latin /ĕ/ and /ĭ/ in verb endings would seem to favor Grandgent's theory to the effect that the *e* spelling for final /ĭ/ and, conversely, the *i* spelling for final /ĕ/, merely reflect the *schwa* quality of the final vowel.[80]

C. *Italy*

The verb form in which the spelling *et* appears for *it* most frequently in the present indicative is *requiescet, quiescet* (also spelled *quiesquet, quesquet, cesquet*) and examples in both dated and non-dated inscriptions are quite abundant, so that only deviations in other than this verb form will be given for this tense.

---

[80] P. 103. The fact that the merger of these vowels into a single sound also brings about a morphological merger of the third singular present of the second and third/fourth conjugations seems rather evident, cf. Pirson, p. 36.

(a) *Northern*

1. present: *leget* (D2356 a. 544); *teget* (D2168) *dormet* (D3197), etc.
2. perfect: *precepet* (D39 a. 528/29) *vixet* (D2829A a. 486; D1698 a. 471) (where we also read *requiescet* and *recesset*); D4198 (where *vixet* and *vixit* occur side by side), *et passim*; *recesset* (D2828 a. 435) *et passim*; *posuet* (D3143); *fecet* (811e); etc.

(b) *Central*

1. present: The only verb form found spelled with *et*, outside of *requiescet, quiescet*, etc., is *teget* (D114N ca. VI cent.).
2. perfect: There are comparatively few deviations in relation to those found in the present tense. In non-dated inscriptions, for instance, only two deviations were found, *vixet* and *requiebit* (both in D1153).
   The spelling *et* in dated material occurs in *recesset* (2827 a. 350; D253 a. 570) (also *vixet* and *requiescet*) and *vixet* (*passim*).

(c) *Southern*

The situation in this area rather closely parallels the one observed in the *Central* area, namely a relative abundance of deviations (i.e. *et* spelling) in the present tense, just about limited to *requiescet, quiescet*, etc., and few deviations in the perfect. [81]

1. present: *me vincet amor* (D1356 a. 359) (but *vincis*) [82]
2. perfect: *recesset* (D2837 a. 391); *bixet* (D4677 a. 529) *fecet* (D4156); *vicxet* (D1737)

It would seem, on the basis of our evidence culled from both dated and non-dated inscriptions, that the *et* spelling for *it* in the present

---

[81] The forms *requiescet*, etc. are particularly frequent in non-dated material.
[82] The morphological implications of the *et* ending in the third singular seem to be established by the mod. Italian *vince* (<*vincet*), as against the second person *vinci* (<*vincis*). (For the final /i/ from Latin /ĭ/, cf. Pei «Latin and Italian Final Front Vowels» in *Studies*, p. 79-84).

tense verb forms occurs in all areas with considerable frequency, while the same deviation in the perfect tense, although attested as early as the one in the present tense, is much less frequent, except for the *Northern* area. In fact, the situation in this latter region would seem to parallel that in the area of *Gaul,* setting it apart from the rest of *Italy.*

D. *Rome*

Apart from the frequent occurrences of *requiescet, quiescet,* etc. in both dated and non-dated inscriptions, the *et* spelling for *it* in the present and perfect tenses occurs as follows:

1. present: *badet* (D4379 a. 386); *bendet* (D685b)
   iscribet (D4177 a. 404); *sitet* (D2477)
   bibet (=*vivit*) (D3373C), etc.
2. perfect: *decesset* (D1296 a. 367; D2807AN a. 359)
   bixet (D693 a. 406) and *passim* in both dated and non-dated inscriptions,
   viset (D2607 a. 405; D591 a. 530); *vixet* (*passim*)
   visse (D2576AN a. 564);[83] *bise* (D2951A) (=*vixit*)
   fecet (D2633 a. 393) (but *vixit*), and *passim* in both dated and non-dated inscriptions,
   fece (D3523I; D4231)[84]
   militabet (D562); *pausabet* (D1468 a. 401)
   emet (D3739) and *passim,* etc.

Latin /ĭ/ appears spelled as *e* in some other verb forms also:

bibates (=*vivatis*) (D861A)
vives (D1736) and *passim*
cesques (=*quiescis*) (D3100)

all these forms occurring in non-dated inscriptions. The same verb forms also appear correctly spelled.

Our material shows that the *et* spelling in the perfect is not as infrequent as our figures seem to indicate, even though the percentage of deviations is quite low. This, however, may not be surprising if one keeps in mind that the most frequent perfect form is *vixit,* a stereotyped

---

[83] Cf. The mod. Italian perfect form *visse* 'he lived.'
[84] Cf. The mod. Italian perfect form *fece* 'he did, he made.'

form least subject to misspelling. Nevertheless, there would seem to be some justification to state that the *et* ending in the present tense exceeds by far the same ending in the perfect and that chronologically the use of *et* and *it* as a formal device in free variation in the present tense antedates the same phenomenon in the perfect.

It may be well to summarize our findings in connection with Latin /ĭ/ in these verbal endings, especially in the light of what has been said with regard to the *it* spelling of the third singular present indicative active of second conjugation verbs (cf. *supra*, p. 129). First of all, it must be noted that the orthographic confusion in the present tense moves in two directions, i.e. *it* > *et* and *et* > *it*, rather than in one direction only, even though the trend seems to be towards the replacement of *it* by *et*. While it is undeniable that the alternation of these two formal devices has morphological implications viz. the morphological merger of the third person singular of second and third/fourth conjugation verbs, the fact that there is a confusion in spelling, reflecting a similar confusion on the phonological level, rather than a clear-cut movement in one direction, say *it* to *et* to the exclusion of *et* to *it*, would seem to justify the theory that «phonetic change preceded and was the cause of morphological change.» [85]

The transitional nature of these two formal devices seems to be quite well illustrated by two studies of Latin documents in Spain. In his examination of the language of the eighth century *Forum Judicum*, Cooper [86] reports the orthographic confusion of *i* and *e* in verb endings, while in his study of the *Cartulario de San Vicente de Oviedo*, a set of documents dating from the ninth to the eleventh centuries, Jennings [87] finds that there is a definite one-way shift from *it* to *et* and never the reverse phenomenon.

It is well known that in the area of *Gaul* the endings in both the present and the perfect tenses disappeared before one or the other had had a chance to win out, [88] while in the Spanish and Italian areas the ending *et* was generally extended. [89]

---

[85] Cf. Pei, *Texts*, p. 42 and our note #33 in re scholars favoring this theory. Also cf. Bloomfield's statement: «Homonymy and *syncretism*, the merging of inflectional categories, are normal results of sound-change» (p. 388).
[86] Cf. p. 63.
[87] Cf. p. 120.
[88] Cf. Pei, *Texts*, pp. 45 and 49.
[89] This is universally true as far as the third person present tense form is concerned. As for the perfect, except for the regular Latin first and fourth

5. *Latin /ī/, represented by the letter i.*

As was stated in connection with Latin /ī/ in stressed syllable (cf. *supra*, p. 69), it is the consensus of Latin and Romance scholars that, of all Latin vowels, this one was the least liable to change. [90]

5.1 Latin /ī/ in unstressed position

As far as our inscriptional material is concerned, Latin /ī/ occurs only in the initial, intertonic and final syllables but the occurrence of this vowel is far from frequent and, except for morphological endings, there are no deviations to report in either dated or non-dated inscriptions. Hence the absence of any tabular representation in these positions.

5.2 Latin /ī/ in morphological endings.

Since the only verbal ending in which this vowel occurs is represented by the first person perfect active indicative form, which is quite infrequent and, when it appears, is never misspelled, our discussion will be limited to noun-adjective endings, as illustrated in the following table. It will be noticed that some case endings occur very infrequently and that, consequently, even a single deviation may show a high percentage of change. It goes without saying that, on the basis of a small sampling, it is not possible to reach any definite conclusions and that,

---

conjugation verbs, the third person singular ends in /e/ in Italian, e.g. *vixit>visse; fecit>fece; perdidit>perdette* Cf. Pei, *Italian language*, pp. 98-100. For the development of the perfect tense in Spanish, cf. Menéndez-Pidal, *Gramática*, p. 310 ff., and in Portuguese, cf. Vazquez-Cuesta and Mendes da Luz, p. 350 ff.

On the coexistence of alternative methods, on the plane of expression, of indicating a single category on the plane of content, cf. William Diver, «On the Diachronic Role of the Morphological System,» *Miscelánea Homenaje a André Martinet* «*Estructuralismo e Historia*», T. 11. (1958), where this scholar makes the following statement: «When a morphological system decreases in size, in that certain oppositions that had existed on the plane of content are no longer made use of, the forms that had served to mark these oppositions may either remain in the language or fall into disuse» (p. 47).

[90] To illustrate this point, Lindsay offers the following examples: «Ital. beve, from Latin *bĭbĭt*, misi from Latin *mīsī*» (p. 23).

5.2 Noun and Adjective Endings

A. Second decl. gen. sg.
B. Third decl. dat. sg.
C. Third decl. abl. sg.
D. Third decl. acc. pl.

Area	Century	A						B			C			D		
		i	e	%	i	o	%	i	e	%	i	e	%	is	es	%
Baetica	IV-VI	38	0					2	0		2	0		0	0	0
	VII	42	0					0	0		1	3	75.0	0	0	0
Lusitania	IV-VI	71	0					1	0		0	0		0	0	0
	VII	6	0					2	0		1	0		0	0	0
Tarraconensis	IV-VI	18	0					7	0		0	0		0	0	0
	VII	12	0					0	0		0	0		0	0	0
Narbonensis	IV-V	28	0					0	0		1	0		5	0	0
	VI-VII	53	1					0	0		1	0		9	6	40.0
Lugdunensis	IV-V	12	0					3	0		0	0		2	1	(33.3)
	VI-VII	38	2*		38	14	26.9	1	0		0	0		10	1	(9.0)

* Found in the same inscription.

5.2 Noun and Adjective Endings (Continued)

A. Second decl. gen. sg.
B. Third decl. dat. sg.
C. Third decl. abl. sg.
D. Third decl. acc. pl.

Area	Century	A i	e	%	A i	o	%	B i	e	%	C i	e	%	D is	es	%
No. Italy	IV-V	78	0		78	5	6.0	9	1		2	1		8	4	33.3
	VI	33	0		33	1	(3.0)	0	0		0	0		5	1	(16.6)
Ce. Italy	III-IV	9	0					19	0		2	0		1	10	90.0
	V	15	0					2	0		0	0		2	2	50.0
	VI-VII	41	0		41	1		1	1		1	0		4	0	
So. Italy	III-IV	17	0					16	0		1	0		2	0	
	V	25	0					7	0		0	0		2	4	66.6
	VI-VII	57	0					1	0		1	0		15	3	16.6
Rome	III-IV	52	0		52	8	13.0	131	2	1.5	4	0		20	18	47.3
	V	98	0		98	4	3.8	23	0		2	0		11	8	42.1
	VI-VII	67	0		67	2	1.8	2	0		2	1		9	0	0

at best, only certain trends can be established with respect to a given linguistic phenomenon, as reflected in orthography.

(a) Second Declension Genitive Singular.

A. *Iberian Peninsula*

This case always appears spelled with *i*.

B. *Gaul*

The spelling *e* for *i* is very rare. The only examples are the following:

> *adolescens integre carnis* (D1747 a. 547)
> *ingenie, consile* (=*consilii*) (D1075 a. 630)

from the *Narbonensis* and the *Lugdunensis,* respectively.

These examples, being of a rather late date, may well indicate the general weakening of final vowels in this area.[91]

Of greater interest for the morphology of the noun and adjective are instances in which the genitive singular appears spelled with *o*, pointing to what would seem to be the development of a single oblique case.[92]

Examples of this phenomenon are the following:

> *membra ad duus fratres Gallo et Fidencio qui foerunt fili Magno* (D150)[93]

---

[91] Cf. Grandgent, p. 103.

[92] In classical Latin all cases, except the nominative and vocative, are sometimes called *oblique cases,* cf. Allen-Greenough, p. 16.
In Romance development, *oblique* is defined as «the single case form which combined the function of all non-nominative Latin cases» (Hall, *Linguistics,* p. 329), or «the single form resulting from the phonetic merger of classical Latin oblique cases, where such merger took place» (Pei, *Italian Language,* p. 76 (Note #5). For the merging of inflectional categories as the «normal result of sound change,» cf. Bloomfield, p. 338, and our footnote #85.

[93] This particular inscription illustrates more than one interesting point. Apart from the use of *Gallo, Fidencio, Magno,* referred to as «genitivos del caso oblicuo merovingio» (cf. Díaz y Díaz, p. 122), for *Galli, Fidentii, Magni,* respectively, it also shows the replacement of the genitive by a prepositional construction: *ad duus fratres* for *duorum fratrum,* with *ad* indicating possession, used with the classical accusative plural, cf. *terra ad ipsus imptoris* quoted by

post consulato Inportuno (D4823 a. 510)
anno IX regno.... (D1220 a. 500/527) [94]
an XXXXVI rig. Clotario (D1169 a. 557/626)
in mensi Iulio.... diae Sabato (D3129 ca VI cent.)
etc.

It is worth noting that all examples of apparent oblique extension come from the *Lugdunensis* area. [95]

C. *Italy*

There are no examples of any *e* spelling for *i* in the genitive singular.

In the *Northern* area, a few instances of the apparent extension of the oblique case can be observed, as follows:

consulato Aeti et Valerio (D343 a. 432)
davit fisco viribus.... (D436 ca IV/V cent.)
(cf. *virib. fisci dabit....*) (D457 same period)
arca Ursicini lapedario (D654 ca. IV/V cent.) [96]
p.c. (=*post consulatum*) *Arcadio et Honorio* (D1501 a. 402)
etc.

Muller-Taylor, p. 63, from a Merovingian document. This construction is generally considered to be the forerunner of mod. French «ce livre à moi» (cf. Díaz y Díaz, *loc. cit.*).

[94] The correct form should, of course, be *regni* (cf. *anno.... rigni domi. Chlotharii regis* (D1218 a. 548/621)). An occasional replacement of the genitive by a prepositional construction is evidenced by the phrase *ano V e rigno Dagoberti* (D1076 a. 632/3).

One of the *Formulae Andecavenṣes* (probably composed during the reign of King Childebert in the sixth century in Angers, although the manuscript dates from the eighth century) begins as follows: *Annum quarto regnum domni nostri Childeberto reges....* and is commented upon by Muller-Taylor in the following terms: «In spite of the apparent confusion of forms, this first line obeys very clearly the linguistic laws. *Annum quarto* marks the merging of the accusative and the general oblique case; *regnum* for the genitive is due to the same law; however the genitive of possession remains alive longer, and we find *domni nostri reges* (*regis*) *Childeberto*, which shows the tendency to discard all forms except the general oblique for proper names» (p. 186, footnote #1). Cf. *supra, an. XXXXVI rig. Clotario* (D1169 a. 557/626).

[95] Pei, *Texts*, finds that «the use of the oblique case for the genitive is one of the most striking and frequent phenomena in the syntax of our texts» (p. 218), a state of affairs that our inscriptions from this area would seem to foreshadow.

[96] It would be possible to interpret *lapedario* also as a dative of possession (cf. Allen-Greenough, p. 232), in which case the proper name should read *Ursicino*. Be it as it may, there seems to be a fair indication of a confusion of cases in the stonecutter's mind.

In the *Central* area, we found only one instance of -*o* spelling for the genitive singular:

reposita est super pectum abunculo suo (D846 ca. VI cent.)

D. *Rome*

The genitive singular, when used in its classical Latin function, is always spelled with *i*.

Instances of *o* spelling for the genitive are shown in the following examples:

magnalia Xpo (D1139 a. 535)

as well as in several formulae indicating consular years:

post cons. d.n. Gratiano II et Probo (D2795 a. 372)
sub consulatu Modesto.... (D2976 a. 372)
consulatum F. Honorio... et Evodio (D2978C a. 386)
conss. dn. Arcadi... et Rufinio (D4219B a. 392)[97]
etc.

In connection with these expressions, there is also the possibility of a confusion in the stonecutter's mind of several stereotyped formulae, rather than the use of a single oblique case, namely the so-called ablative absolute construction *consulibus* followed by the names of the consuls in the ablative,[98] and *post consulatum* or *consulatu* followed by the genitive, as shown in such expressions as *post consulatu(m) Gratiani et Dagalaifi* (D2943 a. 367) or *consulatu Nicomaci Flabiani* (D3822 a. 394). Evidence of such confusion would seem to be furnished by such hybrid constructions as

consulatu Symmaci et viris consulibus (D694 a. 522)
consulatu Maximo et Paterio vv.cc. consulibus (D4387 a. 433),
et passim

Whichever way we may interpret the causes that lead to the *o* spelling of the genitive singular in these constructions there would seem

---

[97] A hesitation between the endings *i* and *o* in *Rufinus?*
[98] Cf. Allen-Greenough, p. 267.

to be justification in stating that these deviations reflect a general confusion of the classical Latin system of cases.[99]

(b) Third Declension Dative Singular.

A sporadic *e* spelling for the expected *i* is found in the following examples:

Olebrio.... et Nepote (D1191) — *Lugdunensis*
arca Manioni milite (D545 a. 394/402) }
innocenti.... petente (D1507) } —*No. Italy*
domno (=*domino*)... *Victore* (D1840A a. 539/546) }
benemerente Cassanete (D2851C)[100] } —*Ce. Italy*
Mirurianete (=*Mercurianeti*) *filiae* (D2948A) — *So. Italy*
benemerente filio (D2942 a. 366), and *passim* in both dated and non-dated inscriptions;
clarissime... coniuge (D158 ca. III cent.), and *passim*;
fratre (D4104); *patre* (D4651);
quiescente (D2452A); *Innocente* (D2876), etc.

this latter group from the area of *Rome*.

Since we believe that the spelling *e* in dative forms for the expected *i* is closely related to the same orthographic change in the ablative of *i*-stem nouns and adjectives, an attempt to interpret this phenomenon will be made after examining the situation with respect to this latter case.

(c) Third Declension Ablative Singular of I-stem Nouns and Adjectives.

There are very few occurrences of this case (none at all in some areas) and, accordingly, deviations are also few in number, except for the area of *Baetica* where, out of four occurrences in seventh century material, three are spelled with *e*, as follows:

in medio... altare (V313 a. 637)
cum virginibus... nobile cetu (V286 a. 649)
in fundum... suburbio Obolconen(s)e (V323, VII cent.)

---

[99] That this confusion is not limited to the second declension is shown by the following example: *p.c. Lampadi et Oreste* for *Orestis* (D318 a. 531).

[100] For the new declensional type in *etis, eti*, cf. our note #24.

Carnoy states in his study of Spanish inscriptions, p. 218, that there is a progressive disappearance of this /ī/ ending in these ablatives since the second century and that by the time of the bulk of Christian inscriptions, we find that it has been replaced by the /e/ ending of non i-stem nouns and adjectives. Our material would seem to confirm this view.

Sporadic *e* spelling in other areas are shown in the following examples:

> *de civitate Mursese* (D370 ca. IV/V cent.) — *No. Italy*
> *de loco Kasense* (=*Casensi*) (D4451B) — *Ce. Italy*
> *Fl. Iohanne orientale* (D318 a. 538) — *Rome*

Scanty as our sampling may be, these instances of *e* spelling would, nevertheless, seem to point to a trend to extend the ablative singular ending in /e/ to i-stem nouns and adjectives. This seeming hesitation between two endings,[101] as reflected in orthography, would also seem to be the case in the dative, as evidenced especially in the area of *Rome*, pointing to a morphological merger of the two cases.[102]

Would it not, therefore, seem justified to see, with Pei (cf. *supra*, p. 119), in the *e* spelling for Latin /ī/ and, conversely, the *i* spelling for Latin /ĕ/ in these particular endings the reflection of a morphological, rather than phonological factor at work, as well as an indication of the creation of a single oblique case?

(d) Accusative Plural of Third Declension Adjectives

According to the tenets of traditional Latin grammar, the accusative plural ending in *is* was permissible only when the genitive plural ended in *ium*, and this was applicable to both adjectives and nouns.[103] Furthermore, these so-called i-stem nouns and adjectives also end in *i* in the ablative singular.[104] According to this rule, the substantival adjec-

---

[101] Cf. Latin /ĕ/ in Noun-Adjective endings, *supra*, pp. 120 ff. for instances of *i* spelling in the ablative singular.

[102] Cf. Battisti in re the orthographic replacement of the third declension dative /ī/ ending by *e*: «bisognerà ammettere che le incertezze dell'ablativo siano state trasportate al dativo, che cosi viene conguagliato» (p. 207).

[103] Cf. Sommer, p. 386.

[104] Although adjectives of one termination are originally consonant stems, they have shifted to the i-stem class also by virtue of the abl. sg. and gen. pl. *i* and *ium* endings, respectively. Cf. Kieckers, *II*, p. 51.

tives [105] *Aprilis, Septembris, Novembris* and *Decembris* should have the ending *is* in the accusative plural, seeing that they end in *i* and *ium* in the ablative singular and genitive plural, respectively. [106]

Nevertheless, there seems to be hesitation in the use of the endings *es* and *is* in classical Latin authors; [107] on the other hand, some scholars seem to consider forms like *Novembris* [108] and *Decembris* [109] in late Latin inscriptions and texts as deviations from the classical norm.

Following the rule outlined above, we decided to include these adjectives, just about the only ones appearing in the accusative plural in our material, as conforming to the pattern of i-stem adjectives.

Except for the area of the *Iberian Peninsula* where the *is* ending does not occur, there would seem to be the same kind of orthographic interchange between two accusative plural endings that we observed in connection with third declension non i-stem nouns, namely a free variation of two formal devices which, in the case of our material from *Gaul*, may also reflect the merger of final vowels into a *schwa* quality (cf. *supra*, pp. 139/140 ff.).

It may be of interest to note that in three of our Italian areas (*Central, Southern* and *Rome*) our table shows a sharp decrease and even absence of an orthographic change of *is* to *es*, in sixth/seventh century material which may be more than just coincidental and without significance; in fact, we believe that it is a rather good indication of the extension of the *is* ending to those plurals which, in accordance with Latin grammar, show an *es* ending. Furthermore, our table showing the reverse phenomenon, i.e. the spelling *is* for *es* in the accusative of non i-stem nouns (cf. *supra*, p. 136) would seem to indicate that, during the comparable period, orthographic deviations generally increase with respect to earlier centuries.

---

[105] «Substantivische Adjektiva» called by Kieckers, *II*, p. 57.

[106] Cf. *Nonarum Aprilium* and *mense Septembri* attested in Cicero, quoted in Lewis & Short, pp. 145 and 1674.

[107] There seems to be a preference for the accusative plural in *es*, cf. Lewis & Short under *Aprilis* (p. 145); *Septembris* (p. 1674); *Novembris* (p. 1219); *Decembris* (p. 517). Cf. also Allen-Greenough's interpretation of Caesar's *Is dies erat a.d.v. Kal. Apr. L. Pisone A. Gabinio consulibus* as *quintum Kalendas Aprilis* (p. 267).

[108] Cf. Pei, *Texts*, p. 45.

[109] Cf. Sommer, p. 385. This, of course, seems to be in contradiction with the traditional rule that this scholar gives for the *is* ending in the accusative plural but would seem to indicate that usage does not always conform to the rules of the grammarians.

184 AN INQUIRY INTO LOCAL VARIATIONS IN VULGAR LATIN

To the extent that our interpretation of the written evidence is correct, Pei's theory concerning the plural of third declension noun forms in mod. Italian, viz. that a form like *cani* is «the continuator of classical Latin *canīs*» (*Italian Language,* p. 73) finds strong support from our inscriptional material.

6. Latin /ŏ/, represented by the letter *o*.

6.1 Initial

Area	Century	/ŏ/>o	/ŏ/>u
Baetica	IV-VI	7	0
	VII	10	0
Lusitania	IV-VI	17	0
	VII	6	0
Tarraconensis	IV-VI	10	0
	VII	11	0
Narbonensis	IV-V	14	0
	VI-VII	24	0
Lugdunensis	IV-V	15	0
	VI-VII	10	1
No. Italy	IV-V	108	0
	VI	16	0
	III-IV	25	0
Ce. Italy	V	9	0
	VI-VII	20	0
	III-IV	14	0
So. Italy	V	7	0
	VI-VII	29	1
	III-IV	113	0
Rome	V	86	0
	VI-VII	42	0

THE UNACCENTED VOWELS

Already in the Appendix Probi we read *formica non furmica*, evidencing, it would seem, the occasional change of Latin /ŏ/ to /u/ in initial position, as rellected in orthography.[110]

Our material, as can be seen from the preceding table, shows very sporadic *u* spelling for Latin /ŏ/ in this position. The few deviations are the following:

dulure (D1076 a. 633/D4827)[111]
ustiarius (D1288)[112] — *Lugdunensis*
Iuhannis (D1260 a. 511) (D4564)
cunparab [*it*...] (D3759A)[113] — *So. Italy*
Uctobris (D2825)
Nurbanus (D3521B),[114] occurring twice, but
cf. *Norvanus* (=*Norbanus*) (D3521A) — *Rome*

6.2 Intertonic

Area	Century	/ŏ/>o	/ŏ/>u
Baetica	IV-VI	2	0
	VII	4	0
Lusitania	IV-VI	3	0
	VII	1	0
Tarraconensis	IV-VI	1	0
	VII	3	0
Narbonensis	IV-V	2	0
	VI-VII	5	0

---

[110] Cf. Väänänen, p. 36, in re «action fermante » of /r/ plus consonant on the preceding /ŏ/, parallelling, it would seem, the similar change of /ĕ/ to /i/ in the same phonetic context, and considered to be a southern Italian dialectalism. Cf. our note #24 and Sommer, p. 65.

[111] Latin /ŏ/ in unstressed initial position regularly becomes /u/ in modern French, when in free syllable, cf. *douleur*.

[112] There seems to have been in use a popular form *ustium* for the classical Latin *ostium*, attested in Late Latin and not limited to Gaul, cf. Pirson, p. 42. The form *ustiarius* could also be an analogical formation, cf. Fr. *huissier*, It. *usciere*. Also cf. Lindsay, p. 34.

[113] This form could also represent an etymological reconstruction with *cum*.

[114] In connection with this name, Diehl remarks «Norbanus nom. gentile haud rarum» (ILCV, II, p. 229). For the change of /ŏ/ to /u/ before /r/ plus consonant, as a possible dialectal feature, cf. our note #110.

Area	Century	/ŏ/>o	/ŏ/>u
Lugdunensis	IV-V	4	1*
	VI-VII	5	4*
No. Italy	IV-V	16	0
	VI	8	0
Ce. Italy	III-IV	6	0
	V	6	2*
	VI-VII	10	0
So. Italy	III-IV	9	0
	V	13	2
	VI-VII	17	0
Rome	III-IV	45	4*
	V	29	2*
	VI-VII	9	0

The preceding table, showing Latin /ŏ/ in intertonic position, would seem to give evidence of frequent *u* spelling for this vowel in some areas, but it must be noted that the frequency of these deviations is more apparent than real. In fact, this *u* spelling occurs in proper names only, particularly in the name *Theodosius*, the name of several *consules ordinarii*, which appears frequently spelled *T(h)eudosius*, e.g.

        consu. *Theudosi* (D1703 a. 431) — *Lugdunensis*
        Teudosio et Romudoro (=*Rumorido*) (D3036BN a. 403)
                                                      — *Ce. Italy*
        .... *et Theudosio* (D2936A a. 418) — *So. Italy*
        Teudosio III et Eucenio (D2633 a. 393) — *Rome*

In the area of *Lugdunensis* this spelling is also found in the name of the Merovingian kings *Theodoricus* and *Theodobertus*, e.g.

        regno dom. *Theudorici* (D2912 a. 526/27)
        rig. dom. nos. *Teudoberti* (D2914 a. 538/600)

---

* Occurring in proper names beginning with Theo.

The only other name in which Latin /ŏ/ is spelled *u* is *Leuntino* (D2614), appearing on a *Roman* inscription.

Seeing that the apparent change of Latin /ŏ/ occurs in the same phonetic context in every instance, one might interpret these deviations as a reflection of *synaeresis*, i.e. the semi-vocalization of the /ŏ/ in hiatus and its merger with the preceding vowel into a diphthong, a phenomenon not uncommon in the spoken language,[115] so that the *u* spelling would reflect the semi-vocalic /ŏ/, rather than a change of /ŏ/ to /u/ in this position.

6.3 Penult

Area	Century	/ŏ/>o	/ŏ/>u
Baetica	IV-V	0	0
	VII	3	1
Lusitania	IV-VI	2	0
	VII	0	0
Tarraconensis	IV-VI	1	0
	VII	3	0
Narbonensis	IV-V	0	0
	VI-VII	3	0
Lugdunensis	IV-V	0	0
	VI-VII	3	1
No. Italy	IV-V	4	0
	VI	3	0
Ce. Italy	III-IV	1	0
	V	5	0
	VI-VII	9	0
So. Italy	III-IV	2	0
	V	3	0
	VI-VII	4	0
Rome	III-IV	10	0
	V	9	0
	VI-VII	4	0

---

[115] Cf. Navarro-Tomás, p. 154.

Deviations shown in the table concerning Latin /ŏ/ in *penult* position appear, almost exclusively, in Greek loan words only, as follows:

diacunus (V174 a. 649, *Baetica*), (D1220N ca. a. 540, *Lugdunensis*), (D1208, *Ce. Italy*)
episcupo (V354., *Tarraconensis*)

It has been suggested that the *u* spelling in these loan-words is an attempt to represent the close quality of Greek *omicron*,[116] so that the validity of these examples for the treatment of Latin /ŏ/ in this position would seem to be weakened.

The only instances of *u* spelling in Latin words appear in the forms *pecture* and *curpure* (D4827 from the *Lugdunensis* area.[117]

6.4 There are very few occurrences of Latin /ŏ/ in the *final syllable* (non-morphological endings), none at all in some areas. As a matter of fact, the *u* spelling was found in three identical forms only in the area of *Rome*, viz. *quatur* (also spelled *quattur*) (D4400B a. 399/ D2612N/D2952A), which would seem to be a contracted form of **quattuur*,[118] alternating with the form *quator* (D2921 a. 431/D2810E).

In view of the scanty sampling at our disposal, this would seem to be hardly enough evidence to draw any conclusions regarding the treatment of Latin /ŏ/ in the final syllable in this particular area; however, seeing that this Latin numeral eventually turns into mod. Italian *quattro* by a process of metathesis,[119] it may not be unreasonable to interpret the alternation of the *or* and *ur* spelling as a reflection

---

[116] Cf. Carnoy, p. 60; Meyer-Lübke, *Einführung*, p. 148.

[117] An analogical explanation for these forms is offered by Prinz as follows: «...nominativi singularis vocalis etiam in alios casus translata esse videtur» (p. 78). Also cf. Pei, *Texts*, p. 53, for a similar interpretation.

[118] Prinz comments: «Haec forma ex '*quattuur' orta esse videtur... 'Quattordici' Italianorum referendum est ad '*quatturdecim' (p. 81). For the loss of hiatus /ŭ/ before /u/ and /o/, cf. Lindsay, p. 414; Battisti, p. 103; Sommer, pp. 137 and 221; Väänänen, p. 48.

[119] Cf. Pei, *Italian language*, p. 80. The same process is also reflected in Fr., Prov., Cat. *quatre*, Sp. *cuatro*, Pg. *quatro*. (Meyer-Lübke, REW, 6945, p. 520). The survival of the form *quattor*, however, seems to be attested in Sicilian *battor* and Logudorese *battoro* (Lindsay, p. 414 and Meyer-Lübke, *ibid.*).

of the weakening of the final vowel into a *shwa* sound, much like the Engadine form *kuattər*,[120] as the first step in this process.

Latin /ŏ/ in morphological endings is illustrated in the following table. It will be seen that these endings are quite infrequent and occur, with one exception (not shown in the table), in the nominative singular of third declension nouns.

---

[120] Cf. Kieckers, II, p. 118.

190 AN INQUIRY INTO LOCAL VARIATIONS IN VULGAR LATIN

6.5 Noun and Adjective Endings

A.)
B.) Third decl. nom. sg.
C.)
D.)

Area	Century	A			B			C			D		
		or	ur	%	ox	ux	%	os	us	%	o	u	%
Baetica	IV-VI	2	0		0	0		0	0		1	0	
	VII	1	0		0	0		0	0		3	0	
Lusitania	IV-VI	2	0		0	0		0	0		0	0	
	VII	0	0		1	0		0	0		2	0	
Tarraconensis	IV-VI	0	0		2	0		0	0		0	0	
	VII	2	0		0	0		1	0		2	0	
Narbonensis	IV-V	1	0		0	0		0	0		0	0	
	VI-VII	2	0		2	0		0	0		1	0	
Lugdunensis	IV-V	3	0		1	0		0	0		2	0	
	VI-VII	3	4	57.1	0	1		0	0		1	0	

6.5 Noun and Adjective Endings (Continued)

A.
B. } Third decl. nom. sg.
C.
D.

Area	Century	A or	ur	%	B ox	ux	%	C os	us	%	D o	u	%
No. Italy	IV-V	8	0		0	0		0	0		0	0	
	VI	1	0		0	0		0	0		0	0	
Ce. Italy	III-IV	4	0		0	0		0	0		6	0	
	V	2	0		0	0		0	0		0	0	
	VI-VII	3	0		0	0		0	1		1	0	
So. Italy	III-IV	2	0		0	0		0	0		1	0	
	V	1	0		0	0		0	0		7	0	
	VI-VII	5	0		0	0		0	0		15	0	
Rome	III-IV	12	0		2	0		0	1		16	0	
	V	13	0		1	0		0	1		12	0	
	VI-VII	4	0		0	0		0	1		2	0	

Examples of deviations are the following:

B. *Gaul*

(a) *Narbonensis*: The spelling *ur* for *or* appears in non-dated inscriptions only:

> *lectur* (D1280); *Bellatur* (D2900); *oxsur* (D3580)

(b) *Lugdunensis*:

> *Senatur* (D662 ca. VI cent.); *Vigur* (D1374)
> *amatur, doctur* (D4733A ca. VII cent.)
> *inux* (=*innox*) (D2340 ca. VII cent.) [121]

To these nouns must be added the comparative adjective form *nuviliur* (=*nobilior*) (D1075 a. 630), appearing in an inscription of similar content (verse inscription to honor a church personality) also as *novilior* (D1076 a. 632).

Although our examples from the *Narbonensis* area are not dated, it may be of some interest to note that those from dated material in the *Lugdunensis* area do not occur before the sixth century. Cf. Grandgent's statement: «It is likely that final vowels were especially obscure in Gaul in the sixth and seventh centuries» (p. 103).

Prinz has attempted to explain these forms in *ur* by analogy of the present passive infinitive ending,[122] although his explanation does not seem to us altogether convincing. Granted this scholar's interpretation as regards nouns spelled *tur* for *tor*,[123] the analogical extension of the passive infinitive ending to forms like *oxsur*, *Vigur* and *nuviliur* is not immediately evident.

More obvious may be the interpretation of *inux* as an analogical formation after the pattern of *coniux* or even the nominative singular

---

[121] The word *innox*, in the meaning of 'innocent, pure' is not infrequent in Christian inscriptions as a descriptive adjective used with a proper noun, e.g. *inux Aigulfus*, in this particular epitaph.

[122] «Quae confusio ab iis vocabulis orta videtur esse, in quibus substantivum et verbum paene congruebant, velut 'amator : amatur'» (p. 77).

[123] Pei, *Texts*, p. 257, does find the survival of the classical passive form ending in *r* in Merovingian documents. But was the use of the passive in the spoken language extensive enough to exert an analogical pull?

of second declension masculine nouns, assuming that the final consonant transcribed by *x* had already become a sibilant. [124]

The *u* spelling for Latin /ŏ/ in noun endings appears sporadically in the *Italian* area (including *Rome*) but it is limited to two forms where there is little doubt of analogy at work.

In the *Central Italian* area and in *Rome* there are several instances of the word *nepus* (D1131 a. 405; D846 ca. VI cent., *et passim*) which, incidentally, seems to be the only spelling in our inscriptional material. In this latter area, we also found a single occurrence of *innus* (=*innox*) (D4664 a. 393). [125]

The analogical support from second declension masculine nouns seems rather evident in connection with these two forms.

It is worth noting that the only examples in which the spelling *ur* occurs for the expected *or* in noun and adjective endings come from the area of *Gaul*, i.e. the very area in which the opposite phenomenon was also found, namely the *or* spelling for *ur* in the present passive indicative cf. *infra*, p. 233.

7. Latin /ō/, represented by the letter o.

7.1 Initial

Area	Century	/ō/>o	/ō/>u
Baetica	IV-VI	0	0
	VII	7	0
Lusitania	IV-VI	10	0
	VII	1	0

---

[124] Instances of *s* spelling for /ks/, represented by *x*, appear in Gaul around the fifth century, e.g. *viset* (D1665 a. 485/509), *Narbonensis* and *vicxit* (D44 ca. early V cent., *Lugdunensis*) and become quite frequent thereafter. The apparent shift from /ks/ to /s/ would seem to be further attested by inverse spelling, viz. *titolux* (D3592A) and *cleminx* (D1075 a. 630). Our example being of a rather late date, it is likely that the word was pronounced /inus/. Cf. the identical example from *Rome* (*supra*).

[125] The *s* spelling for *x* would seem to indicate that the velar element in /ks/ had been lost by this time. Inverse spellings are not lacking and it may be of interest to note that the earliest example, *vicxit* (D3888) dates back to the year 298 A.D.

Area	Century	/ō/>o	/ō/>u
Tarraconensis	IV-VI	4	0
	VII	3	0
Narbonensis	IV-V	4	0
	VI-VII	11	1 (?)
Lugdunensis	IV-V	5	0
	VI-VII	7	1
No. Italy	IV-V	11	0
	VI	4	0
Ce. Italy	III-IV	8	0
	V	3	0
	VI-VII	12	0
So. Italy	III-IV	12	0
	V	2	0
	VI-VII	7	0
Rome	III-IV	67	0
	V	27	1
	VI-VII	15	0

As can be seen in the table, there are few instances where Latin /ō/ is spelled with *u* in the *initial* position. The few deviations appear in the following forms:

(a) *Narbonensis*: Upilione... console (D2747 a. 524)[126]
(b) *Lugdunensis*: nuviliur (=nobilior) (D1075 a. 630)
(c) *Rome*:   cunsulatu (D1306b a. 498)
             Custantia, Custantius (D2952N)
             Furtunia (D3999N)

It may be more than just a coincidence that the *u* spelling for /ō/ in the area of *Rome* occurs before /r/ plus consonant and the consonant group /ns/.[127] The «closing influence» exerted by the former group

---

[126] For the alternate spelling *ūpilio* for *ōpilio* 'shepherd', cf. Lewis & Short, p. 1269.
[127] For the fall of /n/ before /s/ (e.g. *Custantia* for *Constantia*) attested already in early Latin inscriptions, viz. COSOL in the Scipio epitaph, cf. Väänänen, pp. 66-67 and the Appendix Probi, e.g. *mensa non mesa*.

on a preceding /ĕ/ and /ŏ/, said to be dialectal feature (cf. our note #24), has already been pointed out. As to the /ns/ consonant group, we already observed that stressed Latin /ē/ in closed syllable (cf. *supra*, p. 54 ff.) often appears spelled with *i* when followed by this group (e.g. *minsis*), both in the areas of *Gaul* and *Italy*, whereas the *u* spelling for stressed /ō/ in the same phonetic context was found only in the *Italian* area, including *Rome*, e.g. *cunsule, tussor* (=*tonsor*) (cf. *supra*, p. 85).

Our examples of *u* spelling for initial /ō/ followed by the consonant group /ns/ would seem to parallel the situation found in connection with /ō/ in stressed position and point to a dialectal feature, similar to the one observed for /ŏ/ before /r/ plus consonant.

It is generally assumed that the *u* spelling for Latin /ŏ/ reflects a very close [o].[128]

7.2 Intertonic

Area	Century	/ō/>o	/ō/>u
Baetica	IV-VI	0	0
	VII	1	0
Lusitania	IV-VI	1	0
	VII	1	0
Tarraconensis	IV-VI	2	0
	VII	0	0
Narbonensis	IV-V	1	0
	VI-VII	3	0
Lugdunensis	IV-V	0	0
	VI-VII	0	2
No. *Italy*	IV-V	5	2
	VI	5	0
	III-IV	3	0
Ce. *Italy*	V	0	0
	VI-VII	2	1

---

[128] Cf. Pirson, p. 41.

Area	Century	/ō/>o	/ō/>u
So. Italy	III-IV	2	0
	V	3	1
	VI-VII	3	0
Rome	III-IV	12	3 (?)
	V	6	0
	VI-VII	3	0

Sporadic *u* spelling for Latin /ō/ in this position is found in the areas of *Gaul* and *Italy* (including *Rome*). Deviations occur in the following forms:

B. *Gaul*

(a) *Narbonensis*: *Matrona scēmuniales* (=*sanctimonialis*) (D1677)
(b) *Lugdunensis*: *Droc[berta?] sanctemunialis* (D1679 a. 564)
    neguciatoris (D2483 a. 601)
    octugenta (D3565)

C. *Italy*

(a) *Northern*: *Victurinus* (D481, IV/V cent.)
    negutiator (D675, IV/V cent.)

both forms found in the restricted area of the *Concordia* military cemetery.

(b) *Central*: *octuginta* (D1005 a. 570)
(c) *Southern*: *Victurina* (D3028A a. 462)

D. *Rome*

Deviations in dated material appear in the proper name *Neoterius*,[129] the *consul ordinarius*, spelled *Neuterio* (D2977/D4643 a. 390), *Neuteri* (D3501 a. 390). However, the validity of this example is doubtful since, just as in the case of *Teudosius* for *Teodosius* (cf. *supra*, Latin /ŏ/ in intertonic position, pp. 186/187), the *u* may merely

---

[129] We have assumed that the /o/ in this name is long, on the theory that the proper name may be connected with the adjective *nĕōtericus*, cf. Lewis & Short, p. 1200.

reflect the semi-vocalic nature of Latin /ō/ as a result of the resolution of the hiatus into a diphthong through *synaeresis*.

The only instance where /ō/ appears spelled with *u* in a common noun occurs in *laburantibus* (D4325B).

Admittedly, our sampling is much too scanty to draw any specific conclusions, but it may, nevertheless, be of interest to note that in the *Lugdunensis* the only occurrences of Latin /ō/ in this position are spelled with *u*.

An interesting instance of an *a* spelling for /ō/ was found in the *Baetica*, viz. *octagensima* (V287 a. 642), appearing on a verse inscription couched in good Latin. There would seem to be little doubt that this new form of the ordinal *octogensima* is derived from an analogically remodelled form *octaginta* (or *octuaginta*) [130] which is generally considered to be the etymon of Spanish *ochenta*. [131]

Occurrences of Latin /ō/ in the *final* syllable (non-morphological endings) are very infrequent (a total of two occurrences each in the *Iberian* area and *Gaul* and about a score in the whole *Italian* area) and there are no deviations to be reported.

Before turning to a brief discussion of Latin /ō/ in morphological endings, a word concerning the separate treatment of Latin /ŏ/ and /ō/ may be in order. (cf. *Supra*, Preliminary Note on the Treatment of Latin /ĕ/ and /ē/ and Latin /ŏ/ and /ō/ in Unstressed Syllable, p. 106 ff.)

As was observed in connection with /ĕ/ and /ē/, in some areas there appeared to be justification in a separate treatment of these vowels, but only in specific positions, and the qualitative difference between the open and closed vowel sound may have lasted, in these positions, longer than is generally assumed. [132]

A comparative table of the treatment of /ŏ/ and /ō/ in both *initial* and *intertonic* positions, for instance, would hardly show any appreciable difference and it would appear that unstressed /ŏ/ and

---

[130] The form *octuaginta* is, in fact, attested in an eighth century manuscript containing a verse inscription in honor of a certain bishop Victorianus (V284, *Tarraconensis*).

[131] Cf. Menéndez-Pidal, *Gramática*, p. 243. In a verse inscription from *Tarraconensis* we found the form *septagesima* for *septuagesima* (V315 a. 737), which, in turn, would suggest the cardinal form *septaginta*, the etymon of Spanish *setenta*. The form *octaginta* is obviously remade on the analogy of *septaginta* and *nonaginta*.

[132] Cf. Bourciez, *Éléments*, p. 43.

/ō/ are subject to *u* spelling, where this spelling occurs at all, in about the same ratio.[133] In accordance, therefore, with our criterion set forth in the introductory remarks (cf. *supra*, pp. 107/108), it would seem that we would have to assume that speakers no longer made any qualitative difference between originally long and short /o/ in unstressed syllable and that in those areas in which there seems to have been a qualitative difference between /ĕ/ and /ē/, particularly the area of *Rome*,[134] through at least the fifth century, the merger of /ŏ/ and /ō/ occurred at an earlier date.

On the basis of our evidence, therefore, there would seem to be no valid reason not to treat Latin /ŏ/ and /ō/ in unstressed syllable under the same heading, as suggested by Pirson and B. Löfstedt (cf. *supra*, p. 106).

To summarize our conclusions on the treatment of /ĕ/, /ē/, /ŏ/ and /ō/ in unstressed syllable, it would seem that there was some justification in dealing with these vowels separately, if only to show on the basis of negative evidence that in many instances it is difficult to establish a chronology of merger; we believe, on the other hand, to have also shown by the separate treatment of these vowels that statements like «dans le latin parlé, l'ẹ et l'ọ lorsqu'ils ne portaient pas l'accent, étaient remplacés par ẹ et ọ»[135] without specifying areas and syllabic positions, i.e. without leaving room for exceptions, are not altogether accurate.

---

[133] In the *Lugdunensis* area, for instance, we find, in sixth/seventh century material, one *u* spelling for Latin /ŏ/ and one for /ō/ in *initial* position, in approximately the same amount of material.

[134] The area of *Rome* offers unquestionably the clearest pattern of qualitative difference between /ĕ/ and /ē/ in initial syllable, cf. *supra*, table on p. 143.

[135] Bourciez, *Éléments*, p. 43.

7.4 Noun and Adjective Endings

A. Second decl. dat. sg.
B. Second decl. abl. sg.
C. Second decl. acc. pl.

Area	Century	A			B			C		
		o	u	%	o	u	%	os	us	%
Baetica	IV-VI	0	0		17	0		23	0	
	VII	0	0		26	0		13	0	
Lusitania	IV-VI	2	0		16	0		36	1	
	VII	1	0		8	0		4	0	
Tarraconensis	IV-VI	8	0		15	3	16.6	8	0	
	VII	0	0		19	0		3	0	
Narbonensis	IV-V	1	0		33	0		4	3	42.8
	VI-VII	1	0		71	3	4.0	13	28	68.3
Lugdunensis	IV-V	3	0		33	1	(2.9)	6	7	53.8
	VI-VII	2	0		59	2	3.2	13	26	66.6

7.4 Noun and Adjectives Endings (Continued)

A. Second decl. dat. sg.
B. Second decl. abl. sg.
C. Second decl. acc. pl.

Area	Century	A			B			C		
		o	u	%	o	u	%	os	us	%
No. Italy	IV-V	46	0		162	2	1.2	30	8	21.0
	VI	1	0		48	0	0	14	6	30.0
Ce. Italy	III-IV	26	0		43	0	0	9	0	37.5
	V	12	0		27	2	6.8	5	3	37.5
	VI-VII	1	0		52	0	0	1	12	92.3
So. Italy	III-IV	29	0		46	1	(2.4)	3	2	40.0
	V	5	0		38	2	5.0	8	5	38.4
	VI-VII	62	0		62	4	6.0	17	16	48.4
Rome	III-IV	90	0		432	11	2.5	59	33	35.8
	V	21	0		163	10	5.7	23	28	54.9
	VI-VII	2	0		86	4	4.4	8	19	70.3

7.5 Latin /ō/ in morphological endings.

Virtually the only endings in which Latin /ō/ appears are the classical Latin dative and ablative singular and the accusative plural of second declension nouns and adjectives, as shown in the preceding table. The occurrence of this vowel in the first person singular verbal ending is most infrequent and is always spelled with *o* whenever it appears.

(a) Dative Singular.

There are only two instances of an *u* spelling for Latin /ō/ in our whole inscriptional material, both found in the area of *Rome*:

Asellu benemberenti (sic) (D1970b)
dno Ze[su Xpo Nazar]enu (D3858A)

In the *Northern* and *Southern Italian* areas, furthermore, a few instances of *i* spelling were found in words which we would expect to function as classical dative cases, as follows:

i. *North*: *dabit poenam fisci auri p. duum* (D504) [136]
Ateri Florenti.... fecimus (D1942)

both from fourth/fifth century material from the *Concordia* military cemetery. In a non-dated inscription we read:

ii. *South*: *...T]heodoto diaconi iuncta pudica* (D1719)
spirito requiescenti karissimi (D3400) [137]

Although the occurrence of Latin /ō/ in the classical dative function is quite infrequent in some areas (apart from those where it is absent), it may be of interest to note that in those regions in which it is found with some frequency, this vowel is just about always spelled

---

[136] This form was not discussed under Latin /ō/ in the final syllable (non-morphological ending) since it does not involve a phonological phenomenon. In fact, it would rather seem that the *um* spelling shows the kind of hypercorrection found in connection with the ablative singular (cf. *infra*) and that this numeral has been drawn into the orbit of the noun-adjective declensional system.

[137] Influence of the preceding word?

with *o*. The two exceptions would seem to be influenced by the occasional *u* spelling in the ablative, cf. *infra*.

As to the few instances of *i* spelling for Latin /ō/, it may be worth noting that it occurs mainly in the *Northern* area where we also found a few *o* spellings for Latin /ī/ in the classical genitive singular ending, cf. *supra*, p. 179. [138]

(b) Ablative Singular.

The *u* spelling for Latin /ō/ in the classical ablative ending occurs with some frequency, in almost all areas. A few examples follow:

A. *Iberian Peninsula*

No example from *Baetica* and *Lusitania*.

(c) *Tarraconensis*: *depositus...d. quintu kl. Ianuari* (V192 a. 459)
...*Vol]asianu[...con]sule* (V194 a. 503)
consulatum Eugeni Augusti primu (V189 a. 393) [139]

from the *Tarragona* region, i.e. Northeastern part of *Tarraconensis*. In non-dated material, from the Southern part of this area, the form *tertiu idus Feb.* (V261) was found.

---

[138] It may be of interest to note this genitive-dative confusion is attested in Rumanian by the morphological merger of these two cases, both in the singular and plural of masculine and feminine nouns and pronoun-adjectives (except personal pronouns), e.g. *domnului - domnilor* and *casei - caselor*. Cf. Elcock, p. 89, also Alain Guillermou, *Manuel de langue roumaine* (Paris, 1953), p. 25.

A similar merger has taken place, but only in the plural, in French, Catalan and Italian where the Latin dative plural *illis* gave place to the genitive plural *illorum*, becoming *leur(s)*, *llur(s)* and *loro*, respectively, which forms now function as both indirect object pronouns and possessives, both pronominal and adjectival. Cf. Ewert, pp. 156 and 162; Pei, *Italian Language*, p. 88; Entwistle, p. 90 and A. Griera, *Gramàtica històrica del català antic* (Barcelona, 1931), pp. 106/107.

[139] We are, of course, left wondering whether this construction was meant to be a classical ablative absolute, *consulatu.... primo*, or a so-called accusative absolute, *consulatum.... primum*, not uncommon in late Latin literature, cf. Charles H. Beeson, *A Primer of Medieval Latin* (Chicago, 1953), p. 17.

B. *Gaul*

    (a) *Narbonensis*:   LXVII *aetatis anu* (D1687 a. 527)
                              in hoc titolu (D3580N ca. VI/VII cent.)
                              die septimu idus (D2831)

    (b) *Lugdunensis*:   *vero* (=*viro*) *clarissimu consule* (D1749 a. 487)
                              ordeneque rictu (D1075 a. 630)
                              idus... annu XVI (D2916 a. 612)
                              (but *regno*)

C. *Italy*

    (a) *Northern*:   n]*onu k. Agust.* (D3527CN a. 434)
                             die tertiu kal. (D560)
                             se vibu (=*vivo*) (D1337)
                             qintu kal. Gen. (D2841B)

In what we would expect to be a classical ablative absolute construction we read *Symmacum v. c. cs.* (D2738A a. 485).[140]

    (b) *Central*:   *dep...sextu decimu kal.* (D256 a. 469)
                           in seculu (D2277); *in coniugiu* (D4294N)
                           excepto Ursu et muliere (D3852)

In this area we also find two instances of *um* spelling for /ō/, namely *die quintum kal. Iuliarum* (D4813 a. 420) and *die... septimum kal. Octobres* (D1549).

    (c) *Southern*:   *die septimu kal.* (D2883N a. 380)
                             Ellu...cons. (D1029A a. 478) (i.e. the consul *Illus*)
                             c. (=*cum*) *maritu fecit* (D260 a. 538)
                             in oratoriu (D3860 a. 612); *in psalmu* (D3861)
                             se bibu (=*vivo*) (D3759A)
                             a dzaconu (D3763), etc.

---

[140] Instances of *um* spelling for Latin /ō/ are not included in our table. There are relatively few of them and will be noted separately. This spelling seems to point clearly to a morphological confusion of the classical accusative and ablative cases and needs no particular comment. In some cases it may, indeed, reflect a legitimate classical accusative case, cf. *supra*, our note #139.

D. *Rome*

Examples in both dated and non-dated inscriptions are quite abundant. A small sampling follows:

> *quartu id. Maias* (D966 a. 352/366)
> *a Martianu fossore* (D3754 a. 378)
> *vixit annis...mense unu* (D2945AN a. 380)
> *lectoris de Belabru* (D1271 a. 482)
> *se bibu conpara[vit]* (D3727CN a. 481) [141]
> *pro votu* (D1905a ca. V cent.)
> *cum maritu* (D634 a. 537/553)
> *in hoc locu* (D467); *in Cristu* (D2222)
> *ispiritus in bonu quescat* (D2285A)
> *in deu* (D3366A); *in heaeternu (sic)* (D3491A)
> *depositus....octabu decimu kal* (D3515C)
> *a fossore...amicu* (D3757), etc.

The question as to whether the *u* spelling for Latin /ō/ in these and many other instances reflect a phonological merger of the back vowels /ō/ and /ŭ/ or an inverse spelling of *u(m)* for *o*, i.e. a morphological confusion of the classical Latin accusative and ablative cases, has occupied many scholars working on both inscriptional and documentary material. [142]

In his special study devoted to the problem of the treatment of Latin /ŏ/ and /ŭ/ in inscriptional material, Prinz (p. 120 ff.) discusses the problem of the *u* spelling for /ō/ in declensional endings and attempts to ascertain whether this spelling in the ablative singular is due to a *permutatio vocalium* or, indeed, reflects a morphological confusion, i.e. the use of the classical accusative case for the ablative, even though the final *m* has been omitted. [143]

---

[141] The construction *se vivum* is not infrequent and we are left in doubt whether to interpret the spelling *vivu* as an ablative or an accusative case, in the light of Latin grammar. We also find *se vivu* and *se vivo* side by side in the same inscription (D3830). Cf. *infra*, our analysis of Prinz' discussion.

[142] For a summary of opinions, cf. Prinz, p. 4 ff.

[143] For the frequent orthographic omission of final *m* in inscriptions cf. Diehl, *De m finali*, p. 190 ff, in which an attempt is made to explain many of the omissions of this consonant on the basis of various factors, such as abbreviations, lack of space (*margine urgente*), attraction to a following word in a different case, etc. Nevertheless, Diehl himself has to admit that in at

On the basis of the frequency of occurrence of such forms as *tertiu idus, se vivu, vixit annu*, etc. this scholar sets out to show that in inscriptions from *Gaul, Northern Italy, Rome* and the rest of the *Italian* area the *u* spelling reflects a classical accusative case, the final *m* having been omitted by the stonecutter for reasons suggested by his eminent teacher, Ernst Diehl (cf. our note #143), while in the *Iberian* area and in *Africa* the *u* spelling would seem to stand for the classical ablative.[144] In order to account for this spelling in the latter instance, Prinz brings analogical considerations into his discussion,[145] but he is forced to admit, even before completing his analysis, as an apparent admission of defeat,

> difficillimum est discernere, utrum in U
> terminatione accusativus M finali omissa
> an ablativus O vocali mutata subsit (p. 120)[146]

---

least 1,200 instances the omission of final *m* defies explanation. Cf. also Carnoy's skepticism regarding this scholar's attempt to account for the orthographic omission of final *m* in each individual instance and his observation «Il est obligé de reconnaître qu'en douze cents cas au moins on ne peut trouver aucune raison à l'omission de l'*m*» (p. 206).

For a more recent *mise au point* regarding the problem of Latin /m/, cf. Robert K. Higgins, «Research Into the Phenomena Involving Latin Final M» (unpublished Master's Essay, Department of French and Romance Philology, Columbia University, 1951).

[144] The criterion used by Prinz seems to be the frequency of occurrences of the classical ablative case in /ō/, spelled *o, u* and *um* (what would appear to be an inverse orthography). Whenever he finds that the *o* spelling appears almost to the exclusion of the other spellings, he interprets this evidence as pointing to the orthographic *u* representing the ablative case, whereas in those instances in which he finds frequent *u* and *um* spellings besides *o* spellings, he feels that the *u* rather reflects classical accusative forms where the final *m* has been omitted for one of several reasons (p. 121 ff.). Just how cautious Prinz is in advancing these hypotheses appears from his general conclusion «Difficillimum est iudicare, utrum in U terminatione accusativus an ablativus subsit» (p. 130).

[145] «Cum 'domus' et quartae et secundae declinationis terminationes exhibeat, ablativum ad analogiam terminationum declinationis quartae interdum in U exire mirum non est» (p. 120).

In a somewhat similar vein, Carnoy (p. 220) ascribes the *u* spelling for Latin /ō/ in the ablative ending to hypercorrections of semi-literate stonecutters who are vaguely conscious of the difference between the ablative endings of the second and fourth declesions, but no longer remember which noun or adjective belongs to which class.

[146] More recently, B. Löfstedt, discussing the *u* spelling for Latin /ō/ in the classical ablative case in connection with his documentary study, also comes to the conclusion that «bei den Belegen.... unmöglich zu sagen, ob wir

In view of the above, there seems to be no point in further belaboring the issue of whether the *u* spelling stands for final Latin /ō/ in the classical ablative ending or an *m*- less accusative form, apart from the fact that this is not the purpose of our study. Be it as it may, due to the fact that this spelling is most unusual whenever final Latin /ō/ appears in a dative ending and does not occur at all in non-morphological final syllable, the phonological explanation of a *permutatio vocalium* does not seem altogether satisfactory. Limited as this phenomenon seems to be to a specific declensional ending it would rather seem that it is of a morphological nature, whether it be a case confusion reflected in the interchange between the classical accusative singular spelling *u(m)* and the ablative singular *o*, suggesting an opposition on the plane of expression only, or, indeed, a neutralization of the opposition of the second and fourth declension ablative singular endings (cf. reference to Carnoy in our note #145), or even an analogical ablative form in /u/ patterned along the lines of first, third and fourth declension nouns, in accordance with the equation, e.g. *diem:die :: annum:annu*. [147]

---

es eigentlich mit einer Akkusativ oder einer Ablativform, d.h. mit einer Schreibung *u* für *um* oder *u* für *o* zu tun haben» (p. 115). As to the various explanations that have been adduced to account for the orthographic omission of final *m* (and here this scholar seems to level indirect criticism against Diehl in the first place) and the attempt by Prinz to decide, albeit tentatively, on the basis of individual instances, whether an *u* spelling represents the classical accusative or the ablative forms, Löfstedt is most critical. Speaking of the omission of final *m* on inscriptions and the various factors believed to be responsible for it (cf. our note #143), this scholar states: «All dies kann indessen die Auslassung eines *m* nur erklären und als möglich erscheinen lassen, nicht aber b e w e i s e n» (p. 116). As to the study undertaken by Prinz, he concludes: «M.E. ist es, wenn es sich um spätere Inschriften handelt, gundsätzlich verfehlt, in jedem Falle mit Bestimmtheit entscheiden zu wollen, welches *u* ein Akk. und welches ein Abl. ist: die Steinmetzen hätten es oft selbst nicht sagen können. Der Akkusativ und der Ablativ hatten sich frühzeitig einander syntaktisch angenähert; .... Diese Vermischung der beiden Kasus wurde auch durch morphologische Faktoren... und durch die phonetische Ähnlichkeit der Endungen u. a. im Sing. der 2. und der 4. Dekl. gefördert» (*ibid.*).

[147] In connection with the plural accusative in *us* the following analogy has been suggested by Diehl: «vocalis *u* orta est ex numero singulari ad analogiam '*horam horas, diem dies, mensem menses, manum manus*' potius quam ex vocali *o* mutata in *u*» (ILCV, Vol. III, p. 485). Since in the great majority of instances the only difference between the classical accusative and ablative singular was the presence or absence of /m/ is it not possible that, with the general breakdown of grammatical oppositions, a stonecutter or scribe,

THE UNACCENTED VOWELS

Except for the seemingly conservative areas of *Baetica* and *Lusitania*, it would appear that the *u* spelling for Latin /ō/ in the classical ablative ending is represented in all areas, suggesting that this morphological phenomenon must have been rather widespread.

(c) Accusative Plural.

A striking feature of Christian inscriptions from *Gaul* and the whole *Italian* area is the *us* spelling of the classical accusative plural in /ōs/.[148] Since this spelling occurs most frequently in the form *annus*, in both dated and non-dated inscriptions, only those examples will be given in which it occurs in other words.

A. *Iberian Peninsula*

We found no example besides *annus*, also occurring in two non-dated inscriptions, V64a, *Lusitania* and V200, *Tarraconensis*.

B. *Gaul*

(a) *Narbonensis*: annus duus (3552 a. 597)
(b) *Lugdunensis*: ad duus fratres (D150)
livertus (=libertos) (D1749 a. 487)
vervis (=verbis) ...pacefekare ferus (D1075 a. 630)
ter denus gesserat annus (D1218 a. 548/621)
pro parentis suus (D2340 ca VII cent.).

C. *Italy*

(a) *Northern*: at superus (D4725)
(b) *Central*: No example except *annus*.
(c) *Southern*: inter iustus (D3350)

---

vaguely recalling his classical Latin case endings, may have set up this kind of analogical equation? This kind of transfer of a linguistic feature from one part of a system to another part of the same system seems to go on all the time, cf. Hall, *Linguistics*, p. 323 ff.

[148] It is, therefore, not accurate to state, as Grandgent does, that «the accusative plural in *us* was particularly common in *Gaul*» (p. 103).

D. *Rome*

Except for *se vibus* (=*vivos*) (D1137 a a. 521), all examples are taken from non-dated inscriptions:

> *retro sanctus* (D2153); *santus* (D3358)
> *filius suus* (D4568) and *filius* (*passim*)
> *se vivus* (D3757A), etc.

An analogical explanation for this phenomenon was first advanced by Carnoy, as follows:

> Le succès de cette forme dépend sans doute de la phonétique, en ce que *o* et *u* finals se confondirent et de la morphologie, en ce qu'elle est le résultat d'une analogie. On aurait fait la proportion:
>
> $$\frac{rosa(m)}{rosas} = \frac{annu(m)}{annus} \quad \text{(p. 49)}$$

Diehl entertains a similar idea (cf. our note #147) except that he leaves any phonological consideration out of account. Prinz follows suit, stating further that this *us* ending in the accusative originally spread from the *Italian* area under Greek influence.[149]

Grandgent, on the other hand, believes that the accusative plural spelling *us* for *os* is a result of the intermediate confusion due to the transfer from the fourth to the second declensions which «began in Classic Latin and continued in vulgar and late speech» (p. 148).[150]

B. Löfstedt objects to any analogical explanation that proceeds from the accusative singular case on the ground that the classical accusative *um* ending was probably pronounced as [o], as reflected in

---

[149] «US terminationem vi analogiae ortam esse puto: U ex accusativo singulari in pluralem translata est, ut in declinatione altera eodem modo quo in ceteris declinationibus accusativi singularis et pluralis vocalis par redderetur. Praeterea US terminationem lingua Graeca iutam esse arbitror, quod in titulis vetustissimis, qui US exhibent, vestigia linguae Gracae occurrunt et haec terminatio in Italia, ubi vis linguae Graecae maxima erat, orta est» (pp. 135-136).

[150] Cf. Pei's critical comment: «What evidence there is for this stand it is difficult to state, since in all other cases, both in the singular and in the plural, the movement appears to be from the fourth to the second declension rather than the opposite.» (*Texts*, p. 56). For a similar criticism cf. B. Löfstedt, p. 87.

the frequent *o* spellings, so that the analogy postulated by Carnoy and Prinz would have rather resulted in the preservation of the classical accusative *os* ending.[151] If there is any analogy involved in the *us* spelling at all, this scholar would rather see an orthographic influence of the nominative singular *us* ending, the more so since the *us* spelling for *os* in the accusative plural seldom occurs in words whose nominative singular does not end in *us*.[152]

Apparently not convinced by his analogical explanation either, this scholar seems to lean towards a phonological one, arguing that the *us* spelling indeed reflects a very close back vowel due to the closing influence of final /s/ on the preceding /ō/, parallelling the spelling *is* for Latin /ēs/ in the third declension accusative plural, for which he also postulates the influence of final /s/ (cf. our note #48). The weakness of this theory, however, would seem to be shown by the frequent *es* spelling for *is* in the third declension accusative plural of adjectives and the third declension nominative and genitive singular forms and the general trend in the direction of the extension of the *es* ending in this latter instance, cf. *supra* p. 165.

It would seem to us that because the *u* spelling for Latin /ō/ occurs in morphological endings only, we must interpret the *us* ending in the accusative plural as a morphological phenomenon, possibly as a free variation of two classical Latin endings as a result of the neutralization of opposition on the plane of expression. Our interpretation would also lend support to Grandgent's hypothesis that the *us* for *os* spelling reflects an intermediate confusion on the formal level, due to the shift of nouns and adjectives of the fourth declensional class to the second class, a confusion aided by the kind of analogical influence suggested by Carnoy, Diehl and Prinz (cf. *supra*).

---

[151] «Hiergegen ist aber einzuwenden, dass die alte Akk.—Endung *um* in später Zeit wahrscheinlich *o* ausgesprochen und auch sehr häufig *o* geschrieben wurde; im Spätlatein wurde also die von Carnoy und Prinz vermutete Analogie eher Beibehaltung der alten Akk.—Endung *os* zur Folge gehabt haben» (p. 87).

[152] «Natürlicher ist es m.E. an einen Einfluss vom Schriftbild der Nominativendung *us* her zu denken, die selten *o* geschrieben wird und in der sich die Aussprache *u* vielleicht länger als im Akk. erhalten hat.... Dass in der Tat die Nominativendung *us* for *os* im Akk. Plur. selten bei denjenigen Wörtern eintritt, die im Nom. Sing. nicht auf *us* enden» (*ibid.*).

8. *Latin /ŭ/, represented by the letter u.*

8.1 Initial

Area	Century	/ŭ/>u	/ŭ/>o
Baetica	IV-VI	5	0
	VII	9	0
Lusitania	IV-VI	1	1
	VII	1	0
Tarraconensis	IV-VI	2	0
	VII	2	1*
Narbonensis	IV-V	4	0
	VI-VII	6	1
Lugdunensis	IV-V	4	0
	VI-VII	4	2*
No. Italy	IV-V	17	0
	VI	2	0
Ce. Italy	III-IV	5	0
	V	3	0
	VI-VII	13	0
So. Italy	III-IV	13	0
	V	3	0
	VI-VII	7	0
Rome	III-IV	62	0
	V	16	0
	VI-VII	11	1

The occurrence of Latin /ŭ/ in this position is quite infrequent in some areas, as can be seen from the preceding table, and where it does occur with some frequency it is rarely spelled with *o*. In many instances, furthermore, this spelling is limited to proper names, some of

---

* Germanic proper names.

them Germanic, whose validity might be questioned on the ground of lack of orthographic tradition, thus increasing the likelihood of misspelling, just as we are likely to misspell a proper name with whose spelling we are not familiar.

Examples of *o* spelling for Latin /ŭ/ are the following:

A. *Iberian Peninsula*

(a) *Baetica*: No example.

(b) *Lusitania*: Deviation in the proper name *Orbanus* (V28 a. 518).

(c) *Tarraconensis*: In seventh century material the name of the Visigothic king *Gundemarus* appears as *Condemarus* (V456). This spelling also appears on a Visigothic coin inscription from this area (V456a), but F. Mateu Llopis informs us that the spelling with *o* is characteristic of all coins issued under this king in the *Tarraconensis*, whereas in coins from other areas the name appears as *Gundemarus*.[153]

B. *Gaul*

(a) *Narbonensis*: *fondabet* (D1808 a. 530)
orbisque magister (D1062b)[154]

(b) *Lugdunensis*: *Gondobadus* (D3303 a. 636)[155]
Lopecenos (D3563 a. 523)[156]
colπacion[e] (D1281)

C. *Italy*

(a) *Northern*: *a fondamen. do. iobante* (=*iuvante*) (D1854).

(b) *Central*: No example.

(c) *Southern*: *docisime memorie* (D4358).[157]

---

[153] Cf. «Los nombres hispanos de lugar en el numerario visigodo,» *Analecta Sacra Tarraconensis*. XIII (1940), 66-74. For the hesitation between the *o* and *u* spelling in Germanic proper names whose first element is *Gund-*, cf. Jennings, p. 238.

[154] Prinz believes in a confusion of *orbis* and *urbs* «quod significationes harum vocum non multum diversae erant» (p. 31). Cf. *decus orbis* (D1307) from a verse inscription from Rome.

[155] For the Burgundian name *Gundobadus*, cf. Schönfeld, p. 116.

[156] Cf. *Lopa* (D3472) and *Lopolus* (D3584).

[157] This form was found on an inscription from *Sardinia* where both stressed and unstressed /ŭ/ do not merge with /ō/, cf. Log. *dulke* (Meyer-Lübke, *Wörterbuch*, #2792, p. 215).

D. Rome

Several instances of the *o* spelling occur in the word *uxor*, appearing as *oxure* (D840 a. 522), *oxore* (D4240) and *ocxore* (D4240A), both in non-dated inscriptions. Cf. the nominative form *oxor* (D293, D4135H) from this area. The fact that initial /ŭ/ is spelled with *o* only in a single word would seem to weaken the evidence of a merger of /ŭ/ and /ō/ in this syllable. Indeed, it would appear that in this area, and the *Italian* area in general, Latin /ŭ/ in the initial syllable is quite stable, whereas in the other areas our material is too scanty and the validity of some deviations too doubtful to draw any conclusions.

8.2 Intertonic

Deviations, i.e. *o* spelling for Latin /ŭ/ in this position are somewhat more numerous than in the initial, as shown in the following table, and in some areas even seem to outnumber the correct forms. Of special interest may be the fact than in the area of *Rome* we find quite a number of *o* spellings for /ŭ/, whereas the *Central* and *Southern* Italian areas appear to be rather conservative.

Area	Century	/ŭ/>u	/ŭ/>o	%
Baetica	IV-VI	2	0	
	VII	1	1	
Lusitania	IV-VI	11	0	
	VII	0	1	
Tarraconensis	IV-VI	5	1	
	VII	1	0	
Narbonensis	IV-V	1	0	
	VI-VII	2	7	77.7
Lugdunensis	IV-V	4	0	
	VI-VII	1	1	(50.0)
No. Italy	IV-V	14	2	12.5
	VI	0	0	
Ce. Italy	III-IV	7	0	
	V	3	0	
	VI-VII	9	0	

Area	Century	/ŭ/>u	/ŭ/>o	%
	III-IV	5	0	
So. Italy	V	0	0	
	VI-VII	5	1	
	III-IV	31	3	8.8
Rome	V	20	1	(4.7)
	VI-VII	7	2	22.2

Examples of deviations are as follows:

A. *Iberian Peninsula*

In all three areas deviations occur in either proper or place names.

(a) *Baetica*: *Obolconen(s)e* (V323, VII cent.) (=adjective derived from *Obulco*, today the town of *Procuna* (*Jaen*).
(b) *Lusitania*: *Portocale* (V451, VII cent.), for an attested form *Portucale* which, in turn, is a contraction of *Portus Cale*, the modern *Oporto*.[158]
(c) *Tarraconensis*: ....*Vol*]*osianu* [...*con*]*sule* (V194 a. 503)[159]

B. *Gaul*

(a) *Narbonensis*: *adoliscens* (D2747 a. 524) (analogy with *adolesco*(?)).
Volosiano (D2889 a. 503)
volontate (D1432 a. 551/566)
secolares (D1670 a. 557/602) (but *in seculo*)
consolis ....*post consolato* (D1672 a. 540) (*passim*)
monomen[*to*... (D3631)
(b) *Lugdunensis*: *post consolato* (D4823 a. 510)
Exsoperantia (D3590B)

There is little doubt that in the *Narbonensis* the merger of /ŭ/ and /ŏ/ in this position is an accomplished fact by the sixth century.

---

[158] Cf. Silva Neto, p. 162.
[159] The name of this *consul ordinarius* also appears as *Volosianus* in inscriptions from *Narbonensis* and *Rome*. The name *Volusius*, with a short intertonic /u/ is attested by Lewis & Short, p. 2013.

214   AN INQUIRY INTO LOCAL VARIATIONS IN VULGAR LATIN

The scanty sampling in the *Lugdunensis* does not permit us to make the same definite statement, but seeing that these two areas generally go hand in hand in matters of innovation (e.g. Latin /ĭ/ in intertonic and penult syllables, *supra,* pp. 151 and 154, and Latin /ŭ/ in the penult, *infra,* p. 215 it would seem quite reasonable to state that, given a larger corpus, we would have found a similar situation.

C. *Italy*

    (a) *Northern*: *Erolorum* (=*Herulorum*) (D464, IV/V cent.)
                      depotata (D3454 a. 488)
                      Secondinus (D1335)

    (b) *Central*:   No example

    (c) *Southern*: *sepoltura* (D3869 a. 558)
                      adolescen[*t*....] (D4109)

D. *Rome*

Examples from this area are as follows:

> *consolatu* (*Gratiani*) (D2968N a. 371) and *passim*
> *ortolanu*[*s*... (=*hortulanus*) (D592 a. 486)
> *cons. Volos*[*iano*... (D2176 a. 503)

In order to compare the treatment of Latin /ŭ/ in what is considered to be the weakest unstressed positions, namely the intertonic and the penult (cf. Grandgent, p. 99), we shall now turn to the latter with a tabular analysis.

8.3 Penult

Area	Century	/ŭ/>u	/ŭ/>o	%
Baetica	IV-V	25	3	10.8
	VII	15	1	(6.2)
Lusitania	IV-VI	46	0	
	VII	20	0	
Tarraconensis	IV-VI	6	1	
	VII	0	0	

THE UNACCENTED VOWELS 215

Area	Century	/ŭ/>u	/ŭ/>o	%
Narbonensis	IV-V	4	0	
	VI-VII	9	22	70.9
Lugdunensis	IV-V	11	3	21.4
	VI-VII	14	17	54.4
No. Italy	IV-V	35	4	10.2
	VI	34	5	12.8
	III-IV	3	0	
Ce. Italy	V	8	0	
	VI-VII	5	2*	
	III-IV	7	0	
So. Italy	V	3	0	
	VI-VII	9	1	
	III-IV	38	0	
Rome	V	22	0	
	VI-VII	8	0	

Deviations in this position occur as follows:

A. *Iberian Peninsula*

   (a) *Baetica*: *operarios vernolos* (V303 a. 594)
              famola Dei (V106 IV/VI cent.)
              Cordoba (V437) and *passim* [160]

   (b) *Lusitania*: No example

   (c) *Tarraconensis*: A single example in *tomolo* (V276 a. 550)

B. *Gaul*

Except for the forms *coiogi* (D433) and *abstolit* (D1218 a. 548/621) from the *Lugdunensis* area, in both this one and the *Narbonensis* the *o* spelling occurs exclusively in words of the *ulus, ula* type, as follows:

---

* occurring in the same inscription.
[160] The name of the city also appears on several Visigothic coins included in the Vives collection and it may be of interest to note that in Mateu y Llopis, *Catálogo*, p. 326 ff., the name of this city consistently appears as *Cordoba* on all Visigothic coins.

> *tomolo* (D2910 a. 515/6) and *passim*
> *tumolo* (D3556 ca. V cent.) and *passim*
> *secolo* (D2747 a. 524) and *passim*
> *famolus* (D1421 a. 571) and *passim*
> *famola* (D1432 a. 551/566) and *passim*
> *console* (D1676 a. 552) and *passim*
> *titolu(m)* (D3580 ca. VI/VII cent.) and *passim*
> *regolas* (D1652), etc.

The abundance of these forms does not mean that the correct spelling *tumulus, famulus, titulum,* etc. never occurs but, as shown in the table, deviations outnumber the correct forms.

C. *Italy*

(a) *Northern*: Just as in the case of *Gaul*, all *o* spellings occur in words of the *ulus* type, especially in the form *secolo* (D1693 a. 481) and *passim*. Other examples are the following:

> *cel[l]ola* (D1805 a. 542/565)
> *famola* (D1431 a. 535)
> *parvolus* (D2829 a. 447) [161]

(b) *Central*: In one and the same inscription we read *parvola* (D377 a. 574?), both times used as an adjective. In view of the alternate spelling of this adjective in classical Latin (cf. our note #161) the validity of this example is doubtful, although given and commented upon by Prinz (p. 25) as a deviation from the classical norm.

(c) *Southern*: A single example of *o* spelling found in *console* (D4417 a. 568).

D. *Rome*

Contrary to what we found in the intertonic syllable, there are no examples of *o* spelling for Latin /ŭ/ in this position.

There would seem to be little doubt that, on the basis of deviations, the *Central* and *Southern Italian* areas and *Rome* are quite conservative in the treatment of Latin /ŭ/ in the penult.

---

[161] According to Lewis & Short, p. 1310, *parvolus* used as an adjective is an accepted alternate spelling, but in the sense of «child,» as used in our inscription, the correct spelling is *parvulus*.

In view of the striking parallellism with the treatment of Latin /ĭ/ in penult and the frequent *e* spellings in the very areas in which we also find frequent *o* spellings for Latin /ŭ/, we would like to interpret these deviations in the light of Grandgent's view to the effect that the orthographic confusion between *o* and *u* in the penult reflects the weakening of the vowel in this position (p. 99). The apparent conservatism in the *Italian* area (except the *Northern* area), we believe, merely reflects «the conflict between cultivated and popular pronunciaciation» (Grandgent, *ibid.*) (the conservative areas representing the cultivated pronunciation) and confirms the cleavage between the areas of paroxytonic and proparoxytonic syllable structures that our inscriptional material seems to foreshadow. (Cf. *supra*, Latin /ĭ/ in the penult, p. 154 ff.).

8.4 Hiatus

The Appendix Probi censures the forms *cluaca* and *poella*,[162] i.e. the orthographic confusion of *o* and *u* before another vowel, which is generally interpreted as the reflection of the semivocalic quality of Latin /ŏ/ and /ŭ/ in hiatus, cf. Väänänen, p. 47.

In the main, Latin /ŭ/ in this position is represented by *u*, although an occasional *o* spelling is found, especially in the area of *Gaul*, more particularly in the *Narbonensis* (the only area where deviations in dated material were found), as follows:

(a) *Narbonensis*: *Febroarias* (D1808 a. 530)
    nonas Ienoarii (D2222A V/VI cent.)
    Genoarias (D2891A a. 530)
(b) *Lugdunensis*: *Febroari dies* (D2803)
    foerunt (D150)[163]

In the *Italian* area two instances of *o* spelling were found, as follows:

---

[162] No. 86 *cloaca non cluaca* and No. 131 *puella non poella*, cf. Pisani, *Testi*, pp. 175-176.

[163] Pirson (p. 46) states that the /u/ was long originally and later weakened due to the unstressed position. To account for the Old French *furent* a long /u/ is, indeed, postulated (cf. Bourciez, *Éléments*, p. 341), but in classical Latin it appears to have been short, cf. Allen & Greenough, p. 82.

actoarius (D1311) — *Northern Italy*
Deo annoente (D290) — *Rome*

In some instances hiatus /ŭ/ has fallen. The form in which this phenomenon occurs most frequently is *Febrarius,* the earliest attestation of which in Christian inscriptions is found in a third century epitaph from *Rome,* where we read *nonas Febrarias* (D158). In what appears to be the oldest dated Christian inscription from *Gaul (Lugdunensis* area), we also read *kal. Febraris* (D3039 a. 334).[164] Further occurrences of this form are also found in the *Narbonensis* (D1434 a. 516), the *Northern* (D421) and *Central Italian* (D3227 a. 344) areas. The fall of hiatus /ŭ/ in this particular word must be of an early date, since it is attested in Pompeian inscriptions several times.[165]

Other examples of the fall of /ŭ/ in this position are as follows:

Genarius (D2803Ba) — *Lugdunensis*[166]
Zemnara (=*Ianuaria*) (D2698N) — *Rome*

and two instances of *dodeci(m)* (D1361) and (D2687), from the *Northern Italian* area and *Rome,* respectively,[167] in pretonic position, while in the posttonic syllable we found the forms *posi* (D3706) and *posit* (D462) (*passim*) from these same areas.

Grandgent informs us that « [hiatus] *u* after all consonants fell before unaccented *u* probably by the middle of the first century, before *o* by the second century» (p. 95). In fact, *mortus* is attested in Pompeian inscriptions seven times (cf. Väänänen, p. 48) and the Appendix Probi censures forms like *cocus* and *ecus*.[168]

With the exception of a single occurrence of *innocus* (D2441) in the *Northern Italian* area, examples are limited to the area of *Rome,* as follows:

---

[164] Cf. Diehl's note to this inscription, ILCV, Vol. II, p. 120.

[165] Cf. Väänänen, p. 47. In inscriptions from the *Iberian* area the form was either correctly spelled or abbreviated to *Febr.* However, all Romance forms show the loss of hiatus /ŭ/, cf. Meyer-Lübke, REW, #3231, p. 243.

[166] But cf. Fr. *janvier,* Prov. *genvier* showing consonantization of hiatus /ŭ/, as against It. *gennaio,* Cat. *gener,* Sp. *enero,* Pg. *janeiro* showing the loss of this vowel. Cf. Meyer-Lübke, REW, #4576, p. 330.

[167] Cf. It. *dodici* and all Romance forms evidencing the fall of hiatus /ŭ/ in this form, cf. Meyer-Lübke, REW, #2799, p. 215.

[168] #37 *equs non ecus* #38 *coqus non cocus,* #40 *coqui non coci* (cf. Pisani, *Testi,* p. 172). For *cocus* and *ecus* attested in Cicero, cf. Battisti, p. 103.

quator (D2921 a. 431) and *passim*
innocus (D2921 a. 431)
innoco (D4636)
innoca (D4623 a. 388; D4663)
mortus est (D2787); morta (D2788)
domnae morte (D1482a a. 394)

Grandgent (*ibid.*) treats under the same heading the forms *sus* and *tum*, for *suus* and *tuum*, respectively, despite the fact that the vowel in hiatus is accented, probably because they seem to have arisen as a result of proclitic or enclitic use of the possessives.[169]

Evidence of such short forms of the Latin possessive is not lacking in our inscriptional material, with examples from the *Iberian* and *Italian* areas, as follows:

genetor sus (V364 a. 573) — Baetica

tum... corpus (V285 a. 630) — Tarraconensis [170]

vivo so... fecit (D811e)
filium tum (D2287A) — Northern Italy

cum fratrem sum (D1602)
filio so (D4133G)
[...] cin(i)um (=virginium?) sum (D1735N a. 355)
isspiritus tus (D2316N)
uxor sa (D2619), etc. [171] — Rome

Our material would seem to show that these short forms of the possessives were not limited to a specific area [172] and the reason why none were found in *Gaul* and some *Italian* areas may be due to the rather infrequent occurrence of the possessive and the fact that when it does occur, it happens to be correctly spelled.[173]

---

[169] Cf. Sommer, pp. 413-14; Kieckers, II, p. 127; Väänänen, pp. 48 and 133.

[170] Cf. the Old Spanish possessive forms *to* and *so* (Menéndez-Pidal, *Gramática*, p. 257).

[171] For the enclitic use of short forms in dialectal *fratemo*, *sorata*, etc. cf. Pei, *Italian language*, p. 88.

[172] A short form *sa* was also found on an inscription from *Noricum* (D1879 IV/V cent.).

[173] Pirson mentions no short possessive form in his study but the fact that they «gain universal extension in French» (Pei, *Italian language*, p. 88) would seem to indicate that they were in use in the spoken tongue.

8.5 Final

Occurrences of Latin /ŭ/ in the final syllable, other than morphological endings, are mainly limited to the adverb *minus*,[174] with an occasional *iterum, secundum, tantum* and *mecum* completing the list.
Instances of *o* spelling in this position are as follows:

A. *Iberian Peninsula*

No deviations in the *Baetica* and *Lusitania*.
In the *Tarraconensis*, in fourth/sixth century material, we found two occurrences of *mecum*, once appearing as *meco* (V211). It is also in this area that *com* was found for *cum* (cf. *supra*, Latin /ŭ/ in monosyllables, p. 92).[175]

B. *Gaul*

(a) *Narbonensis.*—The adverb *minus*, occurring a total of 23 times in this area, appears four times spelled *menos* (D2831; D2896; D2898; D4426), each time spelled also with *e* for Latin /ĭ/.
The adverb *iterum*, which occurs a total of eight times, appears once as *eterom* (D2889A a. 524?) (in the same inscription we also read *Eulogios* (=*Eulogius*) and *anos*).

(b) *Lugdunensis.*—We found no occurrence of these adverbs, either correctly or incorrectly spelled. A single occurrence of the adverb *tantum* was found.

C. *Italy*

(a) *Northern.*—Eight occurrences of *minus* to one *menos* (D4179BN) were found and a single instance of *secos* (D2287A) for *secus*.[176] On the latter inscription one can also read *Marcellinos Dio-*

---

[174] Due to the frequent occurrence of the formula *vixit plus minus....annos*.

[175] This form would seem to illustrate the substitution of *com* for *cum* in combination with a pronoun. The form *meco* did not survive in mod. Spanish, the etymon of *(con)migo* being *mīcum* (attested in documents), but it did give rise to Old Portuguese *mego* and Italian *meco*. Cf. Menéndez-Pidal, *Gramática*, p. 251. For the Italian form cf. Elcock, p. 79.

[176] Used as a preposition in *secos filiun* [sic] *tum*, cf. Lewis & Short, p. 1657.

THE UNACCENTED VOWELS   221

nysati uxori.... and this leads Prinz to wonder whether the *os* spelling in this instance may be due to Greek influence, since this spelling often appears in the nominative singular of Greek proper names which follow the second Latin declensional pattern (p. 113).

No deviations were found in the *Central* and *Southern* areas and in *Rome*.

The traditional explanation of the *o* spelling in *menos* and *eterom* is that it reflects the merger of Latin /ŭ/ and /ŏ/ in the final syllable (cf. Pirson, p. 47), but in connection with these deviations it may be worth noting that the forms *minos and *iterom are never found (but *menus* and *eterum* are, cf. *supra*, stressed Latin /ĭ/ in open syllable, p. 59 ff.) which would seem to point to the fact that in those areas in which final /ŭ/ and /ŏ/ merged as of the period of our inscriptional material, this merger must have been subsequent to that of Latin /ĭ/ and /ē/ in stressed syllable.

The spelling *om* in *eterom* is, furthermore, found in the same area in which a few second declension accusative forms also appear spelled with *om* for *um*, as follows:

> *tomolom* (D4426) (also *Teodemodos* (=*Teudemundus*) and *menos*); ...t]*itulom* (D3631 a. 517?) [177]
> *bonom memoriom Rapso* (D3564)
> *tumulom* (D53) (but also *in seculum*
> and *titolum*) — *Lugdunensis*

Would the fact that in one and the same inscription we find both *om* and *um* spelling used interchangeably, or wherever we find *om* for *um* we also find *os* for *us* not point to the neutralization of Latin /ŭ/ and /ŏ/ in the final syllable in both the areas of *Gaul* and *Northern Italy*? The possibility of a Celtic substratum influence has also been suggested to account for these spellings. [178]

8.6 Latin /ŭ/ in Morphological Endings

The morphological endings in which Latin /ŭ/ occurs are primarily represented by the nominative and accusative singular and the genitive plural of second declension and the dative/ablative plural of third/

---

[177] Actually appearing as....] *iiuiom* and reconstructed by the editor.
[178] Cf. Prinz, p. 112.

fourth/fifth declension nouns and adjectives, as well as the third person present active indicative plural form of third/fourth conjugation verbs.

The following table gives a tabulation of occurrences of these morphological endings in dated inscriptions, showing the kind of deviations found in our material. The table excludes the dative/ablative ending *bus* since, with one exception,[179] it always appears correctly spelled.

(a) Nominative Singular of Second Declension Nouns and Adjectives

1. The spelling *os* for *us*

This spelling occurs mainly in proper names, but an occasional *os* spelling for *us* is found in common nouns and adjectives as well. Examples of deviations are as follows:

A. *Iberian Peninsula*

The nominative singular in both the *Baetica* and *Tarraconensis* is always spelled *us*.

On a Visigothic coin from the *Lusitania* area we read:

Reccaredus.... iustos (V447, ca. VI cent.)

B. *Gaul*

  (a) *Narbonensis*: *Eulogios* (D2889A a. 524?) (*eterom* in same)
  bonememorios (D2892A a. 528) (but *menus*)
  Exoperios (D3984)
  Teodemodos (D4426) (also *tomolom*)
  (b) *Lugdunensis*: *antestetis* (=*antistes*) *est... tuos* (D1075 a. 630)
  Lopecenos (D3563 a. 523)

C. *Italy*

  (a) *Northern*: *Desiderius comitiacos* (D343 a. 432)
  Marcellinos (D2287A) (also *secos* in same)

---

[179] The only deviation occurs in two non-dated inscriptions from the *Lugdunensis* area where twice the form *omnevos* (=*omnibus*) (D4824; D4827) appears.

THE UNACCENTED VOWELS

8.6 Latin /ŭ/ in Morphological Endings

A. Second decl. nom. sg.
B. Second decl. acc. sg.
C. Second decl. gen. pl.
D. Third/fourth pl. pres. ind. 3rd pers.

Area	Century	A us	os	%	A us	o	%	B um	o	%	C orum	oro	%	D unt	ent	%
Baetica	IV-VI	28	0		28	0		1	0		1	0		0	0	
	VII	16	0		16	0		3	0		6	0		1	0	
Lusitania	IV-VI	49	1		49	1		4	0		1	0		0	0	
	VII	9	0		9	0		2	0		2	0		1	0	
Tarraconensis	IV-VI	13	0		13	0		2	0		9	0		0	0	
	VII	14	0		14	1		4	2*		3	0		0	0	
Narbonensis	IV-VI	14	0		14	0		1	2*		1	0		0	0	
	VI-VII	25	2	7.4	25	0		11	1		2	0		0	1	
Lugdunensis	IV-V	15	0		15	0		1	1		2	0		0	0	
	VI-VII	26	2	7.1	26	1		4	1		2	0		2	0	

* Occurring on the same inscription.

8.6 Latin /ŭ/ in Morphological Endings (Continued)

A. Second decl. nom. sg.
B. Second decl. acc. sg.
C. Second decl. gen. pl.
D. Third/fourth pl. pres. ind. 3rd pers.

Area	Century	A os	A us	A o	A %	B um	B o	B %	C orum	C oro	C %	D unt	D ent	D %
No. Italy	IV-V	1	82	0		19	0		32	0		1	0	
	VI	1	36	0		6	0		2	0		0	0	
Ce. Italy	III-IV	0	22	0		9	0		4	0		0	1	
	V	0	11	0		5	0		2	0		0	0	
	VI-VII	0	28	0		4	0		9	0		0	1	
So. Italy	III-IV	0	23	0		7	0		4	0		0	0	
	V	0	19	0		3	0		0	0		0	0	
	VI-VII	0	38	0		11	0		9	0		1	0	
Rome	III-IV	1	111	0		39	1		14	2	12.5	2	0	
	V	1	92	0		31	1		10	2	16.6	1	2	
	VI-VII	0	54	0		14	0		5	0		2	1	

Eioybianos (=Iovianus) Retos (D3170A) (en pace in the same; Greek influence?)
parvos (D2356 a. 544)
(b) *Central*: tibi deos (D2312) (but *omnibus*)
(c) *Southern*: No example.

D. **Rome**

The few examples are mostly limited to proper names, as follows:

dipositos (D2927 a. 397) (but *positus, minus*)
Antiochos candidatus (D490 a. 450)
Asellos (D2999D), Leontios (D3013F)

Lindsay sums up the consensus of Latin scholars when he says that «the [Old Latin] terminations *os, om* became *us, um* towards the end of the third century B.C.» (p. 234) (cf. *filios, Luciom, oino(m)* in the Scipio epitaph), so that it would not seem too likely that the occasional *os* (as well as *om*) spelling is a mere archaism.[180]

Prinz (p. 103 ff.) analyzes these and other examples from Pagan inscriptions and accounts for them in various ways, such as dissimilation (*tuos*), influence of a preceding *v* (*parvos*), Greek influence (especially in names like *Antiochos, Exoperios, Leontios*), etc., and where this scholar does not find a plausible or obvious reason, he simply notes the occurrence.[181]

Whatever the reasons for the *os* spelling for *us* may be, the conclusion reached by Prinz in this connection is of interest to us from the point of view of regional differences. Indeed, this scholar finds that

> OS terminatio nominativi singularis declinationis alterius non raro obviam fit in titulis christianis Galliae Transalpinae (p. 111)

---

[180] Lindsay notes, however, «In Late Latin, when $\breve{u}$ and $\bar{o}$ had come to have nearly, or altogether, the same sound, *o* is often written for $\breve{u}$, so that the older spelling seems to be revived» (p. 237).

[181] Another possible explanation, not evisaged by Prinz, is that in cases like *iustos* or *dipositos*, where we would expect an *us* spelling, the final *s* may be an afterthought, a learned impulse on the part of the stonecutter who realized, after he had written *iusto* and *diposito* (i.e. the use of a single oblique form in the nominative function) that in good Latin the case of the subject ended in an *s*. The form *iusto* is, indeed, found on a Visigothic coin from the *Tarraconensis* area (*Condemarus.... iu(s)to*, V456, VII cent.).

and further observes that in this very area the *om* spelling for *um* in the accusative singular is also found. He interprets these spelling as a reflection of the merger of Latin /ŭ/ and /ŏ/ in the final syllable, rather than a morphological phenomenon, a conclusion to which we would be inclined to subscribe, seeing that the *os* and *om* spelling in this area (as well as *Northern Italy*) also occurs in non-declensional final syllable. [182]

2. The spelling *o* for *us*

An occasional *o* spelling for the expected *us* to show nominative singular function occurs in most areas, as follows:

A. *Iberian Peninsula*

    (a) *Baetica*: No example .
    (b) *Lusitania*: *Cunde Marcianus famulo Dei* (V64b, V cent.) (but *Bebius famulus Dei* in V64a)
    (c) *Tarraconensis*: *Condemarus....iusto* (V456, VII cent.) (Visigothic coin)

B. *Gaul*

    (a) *Narbonensis*: *titulo duor. fratrum* (D3578)
    (b) *Lugdunensis*: *reg. bonememorio Felocalus* (D3562 a. 518) [183]

C. *Italy*

    (a) *Northern*: *bonomemorio Eioybianos* (D3170A)
                    Porcella... cum filis suis duo, uno anoro VII et u(n)o anoro III (D3197C)
    (b) *Central*: *Simon Cananeio* (D1962d) (but *Chananeus* in D1964)

---

[182] Let us recall that in the *Lugdunensis* the *os* spelling was also found in a plural dative / ablative from *omnevos*, cf. footnote #179, while in all other areas the *us* ending in this case is always correctly spelled.

[183] The adjective *bonememorius* (also appearing as *bonomemorius* and *benememorius*) appears to be a new formation based on *bonae memoriae*.

(c) *Southern*: *Ilaro, dulcis anima* (D897)
Petronio deposito in pace (D2973) [184]
Quobuldeo (=*Quodvultdeus*) *requievit* (D3137A) [185]

D. Rome

A single instance of *o* spelling for a nominative in *us*:

Petro et Marcellino....vivi sivi fecerunt (D1545)

In this area we also found an instance of a neuter nominative singular form spelled with an *o*:

erit tibi deus testimonio (D3878)

As can be readily seen from these examples, the occurrence of an *o* spelling for *us* in the nominative singular case ending, an apparent morphological extension of the oblique case in the singular, [186] is very sporadic and the overwhelming majority of instances of correct spelling would indicate that the *us* ending in this grammatical function was quite stable throughout the period covered by our inscriptional material.

(b) Accusative Singular of Second Declension Nouns
and Adjectives [187]

The earliest example of an *o* spelling for *um* seems to be given in an inscription from *Rome* which reads (*h*)*un*(*c*) *titelo moles*[*tet*]

---

[184] The consecrated formula is the following: proper name in the nominative, followed by *depositus in pace*. From the standpoint of Latin grammar this construction could also be interpreted as a dative case, rather than an oblique case form in the nominative function.

[185] In the same inscription we also read *Tecla... requievivit* (sic) which would seem to strenghten the interpretation of *Quobuldeo* as being in a nominative function.

[186] For a definition of the *oblique* case, cf. footnote #92. On the extension of the single oblique case to the nominative case, including the area of *Gaul* where, however, the two-case declensional system survived through the Old French period, as against the single case of Old Spanish and Old Italian, cf. Pei, *Texts*, p. 214 ff.

[187] Our tabulation does not include cases in which we found forms like *anno* for *annum*, i.e. the use of the ablative of time within which for the accusative of time duration, to use the labels given in our traditional grammars,

(D3872) and which Rossi believes to be not later than the early third century. Nevertheless, our table would indicate that wherever the accusative in a direct object function occurs with some frequency, the area of *Italy* in particular, the expected *um* ending rarely appears spelled with *o*. On the other hand, the occurrence of this case in the *Tarraconensis, Narbonensis,* and *Lugdunensis* areas is quite infrequent, so that the occasional *o* spelling for *um* would seem to indicate a high percentage of deviation which, in view of the scanty samplings at our disposal, may or may not accurately reflect the true state of affairs.

Instances of *o* spelling for *um* occur as follows:

A. *Iberian Peninsula*

No examples from either *Baetica* or *Lusitania*.
On an inscription from *Tarraconensis* we read:
 siquis temtaverit isto monumento (V262, VII cent.)

B. *Gaul*

(a) *Narbonensis*: *voto suo fecit* (D1927 a/b a. 470),

appearing twice on the same inscription and once more on a non-dated stone (D1928).

(b) *Lugdunensis*: *deo timens* (D1340 a. 486)
 gesisti sacrum...officio (D1075 a. 630)
 titulo posuit (D3584D)

---

since duration is occasionally expressed by the ablative case already in classical Latin (cf. Allen & Greenough, p. 266); hence, it may not be surprising to find both the accusative and the ablative cases used in expressing this idea, often side by side, e.g. *vixit annos L et uno* (V83 a. 544). Cf. Martin, who sums up the situation found in inscriptional material when he states that «it is not at all rare to find the Accusative and the Ablative side by side in the same expression of time, thus confirming their practical identity to express duration of time» (p. 23).

We also omitted all instances in which an *o* ending follows a preposition which, in accordance with Latin grammar, would require a form in *um*, i.e. where there appears to be a confusion of the classical Latin case government, such as *cum comparem suam* (V205), *cum quem* (D2408), *post consulato* (D323 a. 386), *de saeculum* (D1296 a. 367), found in all areas, not to speak of the frequent use of the preposition *in* with both the accusative in *um* and ablative in *o*, without regard to the idea of *motion* or *state* (cf. Allen & Greenough, p. 133). Our table, therefore, shows occurrences of the classical accusative only in a direct object function.

C. *Italy*

No example.

D. *Rome*

Besides the example quoted above, we further found the following:

Victorina tumulavit Eraclio marito (D362)
voto [posu]it....aepiscopo (D1923 ca. V cent.)
fecimus nobis....arcosolio (D3646)

Purely on the basis of our figures, it would seem that the areas of *Gaul* and *Tarraconensis* are those in which the *o* spelling for *um* occurs with greatest frequency; however, as already pointed out, the scanty sampling of the occurrence of the classical accusative case does not permit us to reach any supportable conclusions as to a clear-cut regional differentiation. Our material would rather seem to indicate that, just as in the case of the nominative case in *us*, the *o* spelling for *um* was not limited to a particular area.

As to the significance of the *o* spelling for *um*, there would seem to be little doubt that, at least in those areas where it appears only in morphological endings, it reflects a morphological phenomenon.[188]

(c) Genitive Plural of Second Declension Nouns and Adjectives

The spelling *oro* for *orum* occurs most frequently in the area of *Rome*, but it can also be found in non-dated inscriptions from the *Northern* and *Central Italian* areas.

Examples of this spelling are as follows:

(a) *Northern*: *annoro* (D3240) et *passim*[189]

---

[188] This, we believe, is also true of the area of *Gaul*, even though in this area a few instances, of *om* spelling for *um* were found (cf. *supra*, pp. 258), which have led to the interpretation of *voto*, etc., as a *permutatio vocalium* and a fall of final *m* (cf. Prinz, p. 112). That the two phenomena, in our opinion, do not seem to be related appears from the concurrent use of a form in *o* and one in *um* in the same inscription, cf. *supra*: *gesisti sacrum... officio* (D1075 a. 630), a purely formal rather than grammatical opposition.

[189] In this and most other instances listed here, the genitive is followed by a numeral to denote the number of years the deceased person has lived

(b) *Central*: *annoro* (D2993; D4118D)

(c) *Rome*: *misoro* (=*mensorum*) (D4578 a. 291) [190]
　　　　vixit annoro (D2976B a. 372) [191]
　　　　annoro V et mensis VII (D1526 a. 407) [192]
　　　　amicus amicoro (D4622 a. 402?)
　　　　mesoro duoro....diero (D4575) [193]
　　　　quoro (D2133); *eoro* (D1948)
　　　　marturoro (D1999A) [194]
　　　　and *annoro passim*.

---

and would appear to be an extension of the classical *genitive of quality* used with numerals to define measures of length, depth, etc. Cf. Allen & Greenough, p. 213. This use of the genitive to express age is not limited to any particular area and is also found in inscriptions from *Spain* and *Gaul*.

[190] An analogical genitive plural formation under the influence of *annorum*, it would seem, due to the frequent use of these forms side by side, e.g. *Maurus annorum quinquae mensorum tres* (D1527), rather than an actual shift of declension. The accusative plural always appears as *menses* or *mensis*, never as **mensos*.

For the fall of /n/ before /s/ attested as early as the third cent. B. C., cf. Väänänen, p. 66.

For Latin /ē/ in the initial position appearing frequently as *i* in the area of Rome, cf. *supra*, p. 132.

[191] Of interest is the use of the genitive to express duration of time. Apparently the frequent use of the genitive to denote age also led people to use it after *vivere*. For the beginnings of the use of the genitive in these constructions, attested in the Latin of the Augustan Age, cf. Martin, p. 15.

[192] The syntactic confusion in the stonecutter's mind is quite apparent. The inscription reads, in part, as follows: *...exsivi(t) pisinnus.... de corpore annoro V et mensis VII*. Could the writer have had *vixit* in mind when he wrote *mensis*, confusing duration of time with the genitive to express age? Or is the stonecutter at all conscious of the syntactic use of the Latin case system and merely uses conventionalized formulae in a haphazard fashion?

[193] The only instance of an *o* spelling for *um* in the genitive plural of a fifth declension noun found in our material. Prinz (p. 116), reports the form *mesero* (CIL VI 2662) from a non-Christian inscription. The form *meserum*, which is attested in our material (D4576), has also been interpreted as «Eine junge Analogiebildung nach dem begriffsverwandten *dierum*» (Sommer, p. 384), rather than a declensional shift. (cf. our note #190 for *mensorum* by analogy of an equally «begriffsverwandten» *annorum*).

[194] For the [u] pronunciation of Greek upsilon in the oldest Greek borrowings and its shift to [i] «among the common people» in the Augustan period under learned influence, cf. Grandgent, p. 80. Väänänen reports that «À Pompéi, les deux succédanés de [y], *u* et *i*, sont en balance» (p. 38). This «balance» is also reflected in our material and we find both *martur* and *martir* side by side with the learned spelling *martyr*, cf. Old Italian *martore*, mod. Italian *martire* (<Lat. *martyr*), but mod. Italian *martoro* (<Lat. *martyrium*) (Meyer-Lübke, REW, #5385/#5386, p. 392.

On the basis of the frequency of its occurrence, this phenomenon would seem to be characteristic of a large region of the *Italian* area [195] where a trace of this genitive plural has survived to this day in the pronoun-adjective form *loro*. [196]

As to the *oro* ending for *orum*, Prinz (p. 115) believes that it is due to an assimilation of the unstressed final vowel to the stressed vowel and supports his argument by the fact that in the first declension the genitive plural *arum* ending never appears as *aro. Although this explanation leaves out of account forms like *diero* and *mesero*, these would seem to be patterned after the more frequent forms in *oro*.

On the other hand, the frequent *oru* spelling of the genitive plural in those very areas in which the *oro* spelling also occurs, e.g.

bracchiatoru (D493); *Mattiacoru* (D553)
(both ca. V cent.) — *No. Italy*

annoru ses (=*sex*) *dieru* (D4128C) — *Ce. Italy*

marturoru (D2119); *anoru* (D3096A)
annoru II mesoru X (D2797), *passim* — *Rome*

would seem to indicate that the *oro* ending is due to the fall of final /m/ [197] and the subsequent merger of the unstressed back vowels,

---

[195] A single occurrence of the genitive plural in *oro* outside this area is found on an inscription from *Thracia*, where we read *Vrsulenthus... de schola secunda scutarioro* (D564). No example of this ending was found in either the *Iberian Peninsula* or *Gaul*.

[196] Cf. Pei, *Italian Language*, p. 83 ff. Regarding the mod. Sardinian form *issǫro*, Lausberg (III, p. 110) points out that Latin *ipsorum* should have given *issǫru (Latin /ŭ/ in the final syllable remains /u/ in Sardinian) and accounts for this irregularity as «eine Ausgleichung an den o- Vokalismus der Plurale» (*ibid.*). In the earliest Sardinian document, however, we do find the form *issoru*, as well as a general confusion of final *o* and *u* spellings, so that the form *issǫro* may also reflect this earlier «phonetic indecision» (cf. Pei, *ibid.*, pp. 194-195).

[197] The fall of final /m/ in post-classical Latin has been generally recognized by both Latin and Romance scholars. It is on the chronology of the eventual disappearance of this phoneme that there seems to be disagreement, although most scholars merely note its orthographic omission in inscriptional and documentary material, without attempting to place this phenomenon in any given century. For bibliographical reference concerning final /m/, cf. Pei, *Texts*, pp. 107-108. For some recent opinions, cf. Väänänen, p. 69 and Battisti, p. 137. Higgins (cf. *supra*, footnote #141) concludes that, on the basis of the evidence furnished by inscriptional studies, it is not possible to draw any conclusions as to the chronology of the loss of final /m/ (p. 21).

i.e. a purely phonological rather than morphological phenomenon. Yet, the concurrent use of forms in *oro* and *orum* in the same inscription as, for instance, *annoro octo mensorum dece* (D2817C) and *annoro VI... annorum...* (D3727HN), both found on a *Roman* epitaph, makes us wonder whether the *o* spelling for *um* in the genitive plural ending might not also be interpreted in a morphological context, much like the same phenomenon observed in the singular of second declension nouns and adjectives, i.e. as a formal variation of two endings on the plane of expression, aided by a conceivable analogical equation, such as *murum:muro* :: *annorum:annoro*.

(d) The Ending *ent* for *unt* in the Third Person Plural Present Indicative Active of Third/Fourth Conjugation Verbs.

The purely morphological phenomenon of the use of the ending *ent* (which is characteristic of the second Latin conjugation) for *unt* is attested in either dated or non-dated inscriptions from all areas, thus offering additional evidence, it would seem, for a phenomenon already observed in other documents of the Vulgar Latin period, as the result of the reshuffling of the classical conjugational system. [198]

A few examples from our material follow:

A. *Iberian Peninsula*

  A single example from *Baetica*: *offerent* (V383)

B. *Gaul*

  (a) *Narbonensis*: *hic requiescent* (D3580 ca. VI/VII cent.)
            (but cf. *requiescunt* (D3176AN))
  (b) *Lugdunensis*: *requiescent* (D3130a)

C. *Italy*

  (a) *Northern*: *votum solvent* (D1885) and *passim* [199]
         caesquent (D3442)
         dum vivent habent...dolorem (D3349)

---

[198] Cf. Pei, *Texts*, p. 185. For the subsequent distribution of *ent* and *unt* verbal endings in the Romance languages, cf. Battisti, p. 251.

[199] From the context it would appear that this form is to be interpreted as a present rather than a future tense, cf. *votum solbunt* (D1890) from the same region (*Aquileia*).

(b) *Central*: hic requiescent (D1494 a. 394/402; D622 a. 548) (but cf. *requiescunt membra* (D1124))
(c) *Southern*: hic dorment (D3205A)

D. Rome

The *ent* ending, with the exception of *dorment* (D3213AN) is limited to the form *requiescent* (D1707 a. 461/482; D3819 a. 544) and *passim* in non-dated inscriptions also.

As to the use of the *ent* ending with verbs of the third/fourth Latin conjugational class, it would seem to be closely related to the use of *et* in the third singular of these verbs (cf. *supra*, Latin /ĭ/ in verb endings, p. 167 ff.), i.e. an analogical extension of the free variation in the singular to the plural.

(e) The Ending *or* for *ur* in the Present Passive Indicative.

In connection with nominative singular forms of third declension nouns and adjectives (cf. *supra*, p. 190 ff.) we found a number of *ur* spellings for *or* (e.g. *lectur*, *amatur*, *doctur*) which, in our material, seem to be limited to the area of *Gaul*. Since it has been suggested that this spelling is due to a confusion of the vowels in the final syllable (cf. Prinz, p. 77) or the fact that «final vowels were especially obscure in Gaul in the sixth and seventh centuries» (Grandgent, p. 103),[200] we would expect to find the opposite phenomenon also, i.e. the spelling *or* for *ur* in the present passive indicative. Indeed, we do find a couple of examples of this spelling in the area of *Gaul* —where, incidentally, there is but a single correct occurrence of the present passive infinitive in dated material in the *Lugdunensis* and none in the *Narbonensis*— as follows:

Χριque vocavetor eres (D1512) — *Narbonensis*
huc conditor (D1340 a. 486) — *Lugdunensis*

A single instance of *or* for *ur* also occurs in the *Southern Italian* area, namely *diponitor* (D1419), although the spelling *ur* for *or* in third declension nouns and adjectives was never found.

---

[200] By «obscure» Grandgent probably means that the final vowels assumed a *shwa* quality. For references to scholars who hold a similar view as regards final vowels in the area of *Gaul*, cf. Pei, *Texts*, p. 51.

In view of the fact that the area of *Gaul* seems to be the only one where we found examples of the spelling *or* for *ur* and vice versa in morphological endings, the conclusion that they reflect a merger of Latin /ŭ/ and /ŏ/ in the final syllable does not seem unjustified.

9. *Latin /ū/, represented by the letter u.*

Except for morphological endings, Latin /ū/ occurs almost exclusively in the initial syllable; however, because of the few occurrences of this vowel, on the one hand, and a single deviation in dated material, in a proper name, on the other hand, we have omitted a tabular representation.

The only example of a deviation in dated material was found in the *Lusitania* where, out of a total of three occurrences in sixth/seventh century material, Latin /ū/ once appears spelled with *o* in the proper name *Orania* (V89 a. 562) for *Urania*.

In two non-dated inscriptions from the *Baetica*, the name of the martyr of Seville, *Rufina*, is spelled *Rofina* (V385) and *Rovina*, respectively, but in another four occurrences this name is correctly spelled. Since this name is not attested in the classical Latin lexicon, there is no way of ascertaining the quantity of the /u/, except that both *Rufina* and *Rufino* are attested Christian names in modern Spanish, so that by way of reconstruction it would seem that the initial vowel was a Latin /ū/.[201]

Two *o* spellings for this vowel were found in the following words:

froniti (cf. *fruniscor*) (D4694)	— Northern Italy [202]
mosivo exornata (D1862)	— Central Italy

Regarding the occasional *o* spelling for Latin /ū/ in the unstressed syllable, Pirson makes the following comment:

---

[201] Cf. Menéndez-Pidal, *Gramática*, p. 73, where it is stated that classical Latin /ū/ is preserved as /u/ in Romance. The name *Rufina* would seem to be related to Rufus, cf. Lewis & Schort, p. 1603.

[202] Cf. *supra*, Latin /ū/ in stressed position, p. 101 for the comment by Prinz regarding the *o* spelling for Latin /ū/ before a nasal, reflecting a regional pronunciation.

THE UNACCENTED VOWELS   235

l'*o* des graphies....auquel correspond dans le latin classique
un *ū*....peut provenir d'un affaiblissement de cette dernière
voyelle en syllabe atone, ou de la réduction de la diphtongue
ou en *o,* qui s'est déjà effectuée à l'époque archaïque et qui
a pu se transmettre d'âge en âge à travers les textes d'origine
ou de caractère populaire (p. 44).

With less than a handful of examples of *o* spelling for Latin /ū/ at
our disposal and excepting the possibility a restricted regional feature
(cf. our footnote #202), it would seem reasonable to conclude that
Latin /ū/ in unstressed position (except for morphological endings)
is quite stable in our material.

9.1 Latin /ū/ in Morphological Endings

The most frequent occurrence of Latin /ū/ is found in the accusative plural of fourth declension nouns and adjectives, particularly in the form *idus*. A few occurrences of the genitive and ablative singular forms are also found.

The following table shows occurrences of these grammatical cases and the deviations found in our inscriptional material.

9.1 Latin /ū/ in Morphological Endings

A. Accusative Plural
B. Ablative Singular } Fourth decl. Nouns and Adjectives
C. Genitive Singular

Area	Century	A			B			C		
		us	os	%	u	o	%	us	i	%
Baetica	IV-V	5	0		0	0		0	0	
	VII	2	0		1	0		1	0	
Lusitania	IV-VI	5	1		0	0		0	0	
	VII	1	0		0	0		0	0	
Tarraconensis	IV-VI	4	1		1	0		0	0	
	VII	3	0		1	1		1	0	
Narbonensis	IV-V	2	0		1	1		3	0	
	VI-VII	6	0		1	2		0	0	
Lugdunensis	IV-V	2	0		0	0		0	0	
	VI-VII	6	0		0	1		0	0	

9.1 Latin /ū/ in Morphological Endings (Continued)

A. Accusative Plural } Fourth decl.
B. Ablative Singular } Nouns and Adjectives
C. Genitive Singular }

Area	Century	A			B			C		
		us	os	%	u	o	%	us	i	%
No. Italy	IV-V	11	0		3	1		0	0	
	VI	9	1		1	0		0	0	
Ce. Italy	III-IV	6	0		0	1		0	0	
	V	1	0		1	0		0	0	
	VI-VII	4	0		1	0		0	0	
So. Italy	III-IV	7	0		0	0		0	0	
	V	5	0		0	0		0	0	
	VI-VII	3	0		0	0		0	0	
Rome	III-IV	40	1		4	0		0	0	
	V	21	0		11	0		1	0	
	VI-VII	7	0		3	0		0	0	

238   AN INQUIRY INTO LOCAL VARIATIONS IN VULGAR LATIN

(a) Accusative Plural.

Instances where the expected *us* spelling appears as *os* are as follows:

A. *Iberian Peninsula*

  (a) *Baetica*: No example.
  (b) *Lusitania*: *construxit arcos* (D363 a. 483).
  (c) *Tarraconensis*: *binos porticos arcos* (D362 a. 589/90).[203]

B. *Gaul*

  (a) *Narbonensis*: *corporis artos* (D1809).
  (b) *Lugdunensis*: No example.

C. *Italy*

A single example from the *Northern* area:

  inclitos.... actos (D326b a. 524).

D. *Rome*

  casos.... iniquos (D4742 a. 345).
  conposuit versos (D3447).
  idos Octobri (D2816N).

There seems to be a little doubt that these forms in *os* are due to analogy with the accusative plural form of second declension nouns and adjectives and that they point to the shift from the fourth to the second declension which, authorities tell us, had already begun in classical Latin and continued throughout the Vulgar Latin period.[204] On the other hand, the fact must not be lost sight of that in a number of instances the spelling *us* for an expected *os* was found in the accusative plural of second declension nouns and adjectives also, suggesting that as a result of the breakdown of the grammatical opposition between the

---

[203] The form *arcos* may offer additional interest in that it would seem to be used here in an adjectival function, possibly as a synonym of *curvus*. If so, the accusative plural in *os* would, of course, be correct.

[204] Cf. Grandgent, p. 148; Battisti, p. 207.

second and fourth declensions, the accusative plural ending *os* and *us* were used in free variation, the latter supported by the kind of analogy advanced by Carnoy, Diehl and Prinz (cf. *supra*, p. 206 ff).

(b) Ablative Singular.

Only two instances were found in our material where an actual ablative singular form in /ū/ appears spelled with *o*, namely

vite curso.... finito (V293 a. 693). —*Tarraconensis*
consulato Aeti.... (D343 a. 432). —*Northern Italy*

The analogical pull of the overwhelming majority of ablative forms in /ō/ would seem to be quite evident, i.e. the shift from the fourth to the second declensional class.

Further evidence of this declensional shift would seem to be offered by the formula *post consulato,* for an expected *consulatum,* the earliest example of which is found in the *Central Italian* area (D323 a. 386), with four more examples from the area of *Gaul*.[205]

The only occurrence of a nominative plural form appears spelled with *i*: *mani eius precidantur* (D545 a. 394/402), found in the *Northern Italian* area. An obvious declensional shift.

---

[205] D1587 a. 491; D1672 a. 540; D3284 a. 563 (*Narbonensis*) D4823 a. 510 (*Lugdunensis*).
In the case of *post consulatu* (D1500b a. 409, *No. Italy*; D1478 a. 370, and *passim* in *Rome*) it is difficult to decide whether we are faced with a legitimate fourth declension ablative form or an *m*-less accusative, as has already been pointed out by Diehl, *De m finali*, pp. 102-103.

Chapter III: Diphthongs

1. *The Diphthong /aj/, represented by the letter ae*

Grandgent states that «the regular change of *ae* to ę took place largely in Republican times in unaccented syllables; in stressed syllables in the first century of our era and later» (p. 88). This scholar's statement reflects the consensus of Latin and Romance scholars, namely that the diphthong /aj/ was reduced to a monophthong, pronounced as an open [e], about the time indicated by Grandgent, although it is pointed out that in certain words a popular or dialect pronunciation of a closed [e] came into general use, e.g. *fenum, preda, seta,* etc., confirmed by such reverse spellings as *faecit, diaebus, diae, requisescit,* etc.[1]

The reduction of this diphthong both in stressed and unstressed positions seems to be attested in Pompeian inscriptions already (cf. Väänänen, p. 39) and both Carnoy (p. 69) and Pirson (p. 18) note the orthographic confusion of *ae* and *e* from the time of the earliest inscriptions found in *Spain* and in *Gaul,* respectively.

This orthographic confusion is also abundantly attested in our material, in both dated and non-dated inscriptions, as will be seen from the following tables illustrating this phenomenon.

A separate table is given for the stressed and unstressed syllables, as well as the conjunction *quae*. The posttonic segment in the table showing the treatment of this diphthong in unstressed syllable exclu-

---

[1] Cf. Niedermann, *Phonétique,* p. 61; Bourciez, *Éléments,* p. 44, Battisti, p. 105; Sommer, p. 72; Pirson interprets these reverse spellings as an indication that in certain words «*ae* a été assimilé à *e fermé*» (p. 21), evidencing «la double valeur de *ae* dans les documents de la décadence» (*ibid.*). This double value would seem to be attested by Sp. *heno,* Fr. *foin* (from Latin *fęnum*) as against It. *fieno* (from Latin *fęnum* (=*faenum*), cf. Meyer-Lübke, REW, #3247, p. 244.

sively represents the genitive and dative singular and nominative plural endings of the classical first declension nouns and adjectives, which are treated under one and the same heading, seeing that the *e* spelling for *ae* would seem to reflect the reduction of the diphthong to a monophthong, i.e. a phonological rather than morphological phenomenon.

In view of the great number of deviations in all areas, a few random examples will suffice.

1.1 The Diphthong /aj/ in Stressed Syllable

Area	*Century*	/aj/>ae	/aj/>e	%
Baetica	IV-VI	4	0	
	VII	2	2	50.0
Lusitania	IV-VI	3	3	50.0
	VII	0	2	100.0
Tarraconensis	IV-VI	1	1	(50.0)
	VII	0	1	(100.0)
Narbonensis	IV-V	0	2	100.0
	VI-VII	0	7	100.0
Lugdunensis	IV-V	0	1	(100.0)
	VI-VII	1	2	66.6
No. Italy	IV-V	7	18	72.0
	VI	11	17	60.7
	III-IV	1	1	50.0
Ce. Italy	V	0	2	100.0
	VI-VII	3	1	25.0
	III-IV	0	0	
So. Italy	V	2	2	50.0
	VI-VII	1	1	(50.0)
	III-IV	8	6	41.4
Rome	V	4	3	42.8
	VI-VII	0	1	(100.0)

A. *Iberian Peninsula*

Our figures from this area do not include the frequent spelling *era* for *aera,* which occurs so frequently in connection with the dating of inscriptions, especially from the *Baetica* and *Lusitania* regions. In the former we find well over 50 instances of *era* against three instances of *aera,* a situation which is duplicated in the latter.

The situation in the *Tarraconensis* is somewhat different, since the specifically dated inscriptions from this area are dated by consular years almost exclusively; but even so, *era* appears four times to one correct spelling *aera.*

Other examples of *e* spelling for *ae* in stressed position are as follows:

(a) *Baetica*: *ab hoc evo* (V163 a. 682); *leta* (V172 a. 649)
  etas (V133); *celos* (V351)
(b) *Lusitania*: *Saturninus penitens* (V42 a. 578)
  hoc seculo (V86 a. 632)
  Bartholomeus, Mattheus (V373)
(c) *Tarraconensis*: *querunt* (V276 a. 550); *seculi* (V315 a. 737)

B. *Gaul*

It will be noted that in this area the *ae* spelling is hardly ever found. Here are a few examples of deviations:

(a) *Narbonensis*: *prebū(it)* (D1806 a. 445); *secolo* (D1670 a. 524)
  sepe (D1687 a. 527); *penetens* (D1554N a. 557)
(b) *Lugdunensis*: *adesit* (=*adhaesit*) (D1076 a. 633)
  secolo (D1340 a. 486); *preses* (=*praesens*) (D202)

C. *Italy*

(a) *Northern*: Except for *presul* (D1060 a. 490) and *penitens* (D1733 a. 463), all deviations are limited to *seculum/seculo.*
(b) *Central*: *pretor* (D67d a. 447); *seculo* (D1667N a. 489) *Ateneus* (D3926); *Bebi* (D4178)
(c) *Southern*: *letus* (D3114 a. 469)
  locus Lete (=*Laetae*) (D3860 a. 612)

D. *Rome*

> *preditus* (D1477 a. 348); *in seculo* (D645 a. 279)
> *premia* (D1590 a. 393); *questor* (D199 a. 472)
> *querunt* (D1139 a. 535), etc.

A few instances of reverse spelling may be of interest:

(1) The spelling *ae* for Latin /ĕ/

(a) *Tarraconensis*: *quaeritur* for *queritur* (from *queror*) (V276 a. 550). In the same inscription we also read *querunt* for *quaerunt*.
(b) *Lugdunensis*: *Braevis* (D3489)
(c) *No. Italy*: *baenae* (D439 a. 434?); *cun quaen* (D4283) *aet* (=*et*) (D4451A)
(d) *Rome*: *aeques* (D278); *aequitum* (D525 III/IV cent.?) *praetium* (D3813); *daeo* (D3366B) *Laee* (D4293), but *ibid.* also *Leo praesbiter* (D1131 a. 405)

(2) The spelling *ae* for Latin /ē/

(a) *Narbonensis*: *requiaescit* (D3126)
(b) *No. Italy*: *faecit* (D3577); *posuaerunt* (D4199) *caesquent* (=*quiescent*) (D3442)
(c) *Ce. Italy*: *faecit* (D2698A); *fecaerunt* (D4170N)
(d) *Rome*: *diaebus* (D404); *maecum* (D2265) *aemet* (=*emit*) (D3739GN) *aeius* (D4125); *quaescit* (D3113)

These reverse spellings would seem to indicate that the diphthong /aj/ was likely to merge with both the originally short and long /e/, illustrating a «hesitation about the way in which the new monophthong was to be assimilated to the system» (Spence, *art. cit.*, p. 3), seeing that the simplification of this diphthong is said to have given rise to a long open [e], cf. Lausberg, I, pp. 136/137 and Weinrich, p. 16.

The Spelling e for ae in Monosyllables

The spelling *que* for *quae*, the feminine form of the relative pronoun, is very widespread, as will be seen from our table.

Of greater interest, however, is the fact that in almost all areas where the forms *quae* and *que* occur, we often find them replaced by *qui,* suggesting the use of the masculine form of the relative pronoun with a feminine antecedent. Since the occurrence of this phenomenon is much too frequent to be either due to misspelling or ignorance of the classical Latin rules of concord, [2] the morphological extension of the masculine *qui* at the expense of the feminine *quae* would seem to be rather obvious and it has been generally interpreted as a morphological phenomenon. [3]

The Relative Pronoun quae

Area	Century	quae	que	qui	%
Baetica	IV-VI	0	2	0	
	VII	0	0	0	
Lusitania	IV-VI	1	0	0	
	VII	0	0	0	
Tarraconensis	IV-VI	2	0	2	50.0
	VII	0	0	1	(100.0)
Narbonensis	IV-V	2	0	1	(33.3)
	VI-VII	6	1	10	58.7
Lugdunensis	IV-V	3	3	3	33.3
	VI-VII	3	0	5	63.5
No. Italy	IV-V	6	9	9	37.5
	VI	6	2	3	27.2
	III-IV	1	5	0	
Ce. Italy	V	3	3	1	(14.3)
	VI-VII	5	2	6	46.1

---

[2] Martin, p. 8, lists the use of *qui* and *quem* with a feminine antecedent under «Lack of Concord».

[3] Cf. Carnoy, p. 269; Pirson, p. 157-58; Menéndez-Pidal, *Gramática*, p. 263; Grandgent, p. 165; Battisti, p. 226; Maurer, *Gramática*, p. 114, Väänänen, p. 133.

DIPHTHONGS 245

Area	Century	quae	que	qui	%
So. Italy	III-IV	4	2	0	
	V	3	3	0	
	VI-VII	10	11	3	12.5
Rome	III-IV	40	55	2	2.0
	V	22	17	5	11.3
	VI-VII	8	6	5	21.0

A few examples, taken at random, will suffice to illustrate this phenomenon:

Amantia qui vixit (V251) — *Tarraconensis*
Constantiola qui (D2830 a. 467) — *Narbonensis*
deo sacrata puella qui (D1703 a. 431) — *Lugdunensis*
dulcissimae Restute qui (D3239 a. 353) — *Rome*
filia comites (=*comitis*) *qui* (D116 a. 512) — *No. Italy*, etc.

Examples are not limited to dated inscriptions and the occurrences of *qui* for *quae* or *que* are very frequent in non-dated epitaphs as well, except for the *Iberian* area, from which our sampling of the relative pronoun is very small.

The earliest attestation of the use of *qui* for *quae* in a dated Christian inscription is found in Rome.[4] Nor is the above example an isolated instance, since in another fourth century epitaph we read *Erculia qui vixit* (D4409 a. 363). Nevertheless, our figures would seem to indicate that the replacement of the feminine by the masculine form is, at this time, rather sporadic and does not occur with greater frequency before the fifth century. Purely on the basis of our percentage figures, it would seem that this phenomenon was very widespread in the areas of *Gaul* (particularly *Lugdunensis*), *No. Italy* and, possibly, *Tarraconensis*[5]

---

[4] Hence, Grandgent is not quite accurate when he states that *qui* for *quae* «occurs in Christian inscriptions from the fifth century on» (p. 36). In other areas, it is true, the occurrence of the masculine relative pronoun for the feminine form is not attested before the fifth century.

[5] It may be of interest to note that the replacement of *quae* by *qui* occurs twice in an area (*Tarragona*) which belongs to present-day *Catalonia*, i.e. precisely in a region where the relative pronoun *qui* has survived to the present day, cf. Francisco de B. Moll, *Gramática Histórica Catalana* (Madrid, 1952), p. 198. That the use of *qui* for *quae* must have been more extensive seems to be evidenced by the fact that it occurs also outside this restricted region, e.g. V262, VII cent., *Cartagena (Southern Tarraconensis)* and survives in Old Spanish, cf. Menéndez-Pidal, *Gramática*, p. 263.

(our sampling being, unfortunately, too scanty to make a more definite statement in connection with this area) by the fifth century, and that by the sixth century the use of *qui* for *quae* may have been an accomplished fact in these areas, certainly in both areas of *Gaul*, encompassing also *Ce. Italy*, while this same development seems to have been somewhat slower in the areas of *Rome* and *So. Italy*.

It may be worth noting, furthermore, that in those areas in which we find the use of *qui* with a feminine antecedent, the masculine accusative singular form *quem* often appears where we would expect the feminine form *quam*, as illustrated in the following examples: [6]

> Fedula... cum quem v[ixi] (D2408) — *Narbonensis*
> arcam... quem emit (D494, IV/V cent.) — *No. Italy*
> Concordia... quem appellaverunt (D1578a III cent.) [7] — *Ce. Italy*
> subolem quem...re(li)quisti (D1464 a. 380) — *Rome*, etc.

There seems to be little doubt that, just as in the case of the use of *qui* for *quae*, the use of *quem* for *quam* is a morphological extension of the masculine form of the relative pronoun, cf. *supra*, Latin /ă/ in stressed position, p. 41, footnote #1. [8]

The only other monosyllable that occurs in our inscriptional material is the form *haec*, usually functioning as a feminine demonstrative adjective. It is found mainly on *Spanish* inscriptions and occasionally on *Italian* ones, but there is not a single occurrence of this form in the area of *Gaul*. When and where it does occur, it is usually spelled *hec*. Thus we find that of a total of nine occurrences in the three areas of the *Iberian Peninsula*, this demonstrative is spelled *haec* only once, whereas on inscriptions from *Rome* (where most instances are found outside of Spain) it is always spelled *hec*.

---

[6] The masculine form *quem* for the feminine *quam* also occurs on an inscription from *Baetica* (V159 a. 658) and *Lusitania* (V14, early V cent.), respectively, suggesting the extension of the masculine form of the relative pronoun in these regions as well.

[7] Probably the earliest attestation in a Christian inscription found in the St. Catherine cemetery at *Chiusi*. This cemetery is said to date back to the third century A.D., cf. Pauly-Wissowa, IV, pp. 115-116.

[8] For the survival of the masculine forms *qui* and *quem* in the Romance languages, cf. Menéndez-Pidal, *Gramática*, p. 263 (for Spanish); Ewert, p. 166 (for French); Pei, *Italian Language*, p. 89 and Rohlfs, II, pp. 229 and 233 ff. (for Italian).

1.2 The Diphthong /aj/ in Unstressed Syllable

In the following tables we have divided the treatment of the diphthong /aj/ into a pretonic and posttonic segment, the latter representing the genitive/dative singular and nominative plural endings of first declension nouns and adjectives.

As will be readily seen, the spelling *e* for *ae* is very frequent in both unstressed positions, so that only a few examples will be presented from each area under study.

A. *Iberian Peninsula*

(a) *Baetica*: *filius Emiliani* (V145 a. 543); *edificat* (V416)
   penitentia (V142 a. 536); *letentur* (V415)
   dedicata est... s̄c̄ē Marie (V301 a. 556)[9]
   ingredi paradisi ianue (V159 a. 658)

(b) *Lusitania*: *hunc edificium* (V311 a. 682?)
   sacrosancte aeclisiae (V93 a. 525)[10]
   fecit... uxori sue (V502/3 a. 634)

(c) *Tarraconensis*: *Cesaracosta* (V436): *edificata est* (V354)
   p̄r̄b̄. eclesie Romane (V268 a. 493)
   coniugi sue posuet memoria (V2 a. 362)
   sacrate sunt.... eglesie (V312 a. 691)

B. *Gaul*

(a) *Narbonensis*: *pref(ectus)* (D1806 a. 445)
   etatis sue (D1217 ca. VI cent.)
   secorales annus (D1670 a. 557/602)
   bone recordationis (D2454 a. 472)

(b) *Lugdunensis*: *magnas dum feneraris opis* (D1076 a. 633)
   Emellio nomine (D1218 a. 548/621)

---

[9] It is worth noting that the expected form *sanctae* either in a genitive or dative singular function, constantly appears in an abbreviated form s̄c̄ē. Because of this apparent scribal tradition, we have not included this form in our count.

[10] The occurrence of the spelling with *e* and *ae* side by side is frequent throughout our inscriptional material from all areas and will not be especially pointed out. Instances of this kind would seem to furnish good evidence of the fact that the digraph *ae* is merely used as an artificial graphic device.

> *in pace p(r)ecessit* (D1281)
> *bone memoriae* (D306 a. 488) [11]
> *sapiensie legis* (D1075 a. 630)

C. *Italy*

(a) *Northern*: *precepet* (D39 a. 528/29)
mani eius precidantur (D545 a. 394/402)
vite sue (D494 ca. cent.)
sancte aeclesiae (D503, early V cent.)

(b) *Central*: *prepositus* (D3827 a. 361)
coniugi... inextimabili (D4723)
basilica... edificavit (D659 a. 549)
dulcissime filiae... fecit (D323 a. 386)
viro... honestae fame (D255)

(c) *Southern*: *statuam [pr]esentem* (D1345a a. 425/50)
precessit... in pace (D649)
mire pietatis (D81 a. 385)
aecletiae catolicae sancte Brundisine
(D1026 ca. VII cent.) [12]

D. *Rome*

> *sine lesione* (D1603 a. 369); *heterna* (D277N a. 389)
> *equalis* (D4698 a. 359); *Cesario* (D3091A a. 397)
> *mortis sue* (D2805 a. 337); *fidei catolice* (D115 a. 462)
> *olografus propine Isidori* (D713 a. 536) [13]
> *p̄rī.* (=*primicerius*) *escole secundae* (D485b a. 480?)

---

[11] This genitive of quality followed by the name of the deceased is a very widespread formula in Christian inscriptions (cf. Diehl, ILCV, Vol. III (Index), p. 492) and is by no means limited to this area.

[12] For the assibilation of the consonant group /tj/ in Late Latin, as confirmed by the reverse spelling *aecletiae*, cf. Battisti, pp. 151-52.

[13] Worthy of interest is Diehl's quotation in the notes to this inscription from Isidore of Seville's *libri Originum* in re *propina*. It runs as follows: «'popina' graecus sermo est, qui apud nos corrupte 'propina' dicitur. est autem locus iuxta balnea publica, ubi post lavacrum a fame et siti reficiuntur. unde et 'propina' et 'propinare' dicitur.» This meaning should not be taken as the etymon of Spanish *propina* 'tip' which seems to go back to a Late Latin *propina* in the meaning of *donum*, *munus quodvis*, cf. Du Cange, VI, p. 532 and J. Corominas, *Diccionario crítico etimológico de la lengua castellana* (Bern, 1954), III, p. 434. Isidor's *popina* 'eating-house' comes from the Greek προπίνω

1.2a The Diphthong /aj/ in the Unstressed Pretonic Syllable

Area	Century	/aj/>ae	/aj/>e	%
Baetica	IV-VI	0	2	(100.0)
	VII	2	1	(33.3)
Lusitania	IV-VI	1	0	
	VII	0	2	100.0
Tarraconensis	IV-VI	1	3	75.0
	VII	0	3	100.0
Narbonensis	IV-V	0	1	(100.0)
	VI-VII	3	5	62.5
Lugdunensis	IV-V	2	0	
	VI-VII	1	5	83.3
No. Italy	IV-V	4	4	50.0
	VI	1	1	(50.0)
Ce. Italy	III-IV	3	2	40.0
	V	3	0	
	VI-VII	2	2	50.0
So. Italy	III-IV	4	1	(20.0)
	V	3	1	(25.0)
	VI-VII	0	0	
Rome	III-IV	18	13	41.9
	V	7	2	22.2
	VI-VII	4	7	63.6

1.2b The Diphthong /aj/ in the Final Syllable

Area	Century	/aj/>ae	/aj/>e	%
Baetica	IV-VI	0	3	100.0
	VII	4	17	80.9

---

so that *propina* would appear to be the correct form, cf. Lewis & Short, pp. 1398 and 1469, Cl. Latin *popina*, on the other hand, also in the sense of 'cook-shop', 'eating-house' (but apparently of a cheap sort) is a borrowing from Oscan and corresponds to the Latin *coquina*, cf. A Ernout — A. Meillêt, *Dictionnaire étymologique de la langue latine*, II (3rd ed. revised; Paris, 1951), pp. 923 and 954-955.

Area	Century	/aj/>ae	/aj/>e	%
Lusitania	IV-VI	3	6	66.6
	VII	1	4	80.0
Tarraconensis	IV-VI	11	8	42.1
	VII	0	11	100.0
Narbonensis	IV-V	18	4	18.1
	VI-VII	39	30	71.4
Lugdunensis	IV-V	10	12	54.5
	VI-VII	34	21	32.7
No. Italy	IV-V	26	11	29.6
	VI	2	0	
Ce. Italy	III-IV	13	11	49.1
	V	3	0	
	VI-VII	3	1	(25.0)
So. Italy	III-IV	11	12	52.1
	V	10	2	16.6
	VI-VII	3	8	72.7
Rome	III-IV	93	65	41.1
	V	18	6	20.9
	VI-VII	12	7	36.8

Instances of reverse spelling in both pretonic and posttonic syllables are not infrequent. A few examples follow:

(1) The spelling *ae* for Latin /ĕ/

    (a) *Lusitania*: *aeclisiae* (V93 a. 525); *Aliosae* (V393) for *Alogiose*, vocative of *Alogiosus*.

    (b) *Tarraconensis*: *praetioso marmore* (V292 VI/VII cent.?)

    (c) *Narbonensis*: *aelemosinis* (D1687 a. 527) *in pacae* (D1215 a. 559) and *passim indictionae* (D3038 a. 536)

    (d) *Lugdunensis*: *saepulchris* (D1676 a. 552); *aecclesia* (D1574) *in pacae* (D1317N)

DIPHTHONGS 251

(e) *No. Italy*: *maemoriae* (D1361A); *baenae* (D439 a. 434?)
saepulturae (D3473A); *in pacae* (D357)

(f) *Ce. Italy*: *in aeodem* (D3827 a. 361); *quaerella* (D3926)
Aerclanius (=*Herculanius*) (D4128C)

(g) *So. Italy*: *aepiscopi* (D1032 ca. V cent.)
daep. (=*depositio*) (D1204A a. 553)
maeritissimae (D1591)
aepist[ulae...] (D2163)
in pacae (D2935A a. 393) and *passim*
atquae (D4343 a. 366); *ideoquae* (D3862 a. 553)

(h) *Rome*: *Caeriale* (D2690N a. 358); *maerenti* (D1631a)
aessorcista (=*exorcista*) (D1258B)
in pacae (D2570 a. 398) and *passim*
sene ulla bilae (D161)
quinquae (D1527); *karerae* (inf.) (D1558)
quesquaet (=*quiescet*) (D3254)

(2) The spelling *ae* for Latin /ē/

This spelling occurs in all areas under investigation; however, with the exception of *praecipuae* (D2483 a. 601, *Lugdunensis*) and *Marcianae* (D3994C, *Rome*),[14] it is limited to the forms *diae* (abl. sg.), *pridiae* (adv.), as well as an occasional *diaes* (nom./acc. pl.). Hence, we felt that a list of examples was not necessary.

While reverse spellings for Latin /ē/ would seem to parallel the phenomenon observed in connection with Latin /ĕ/, it may be of some interest to note that we did not find any *ae* spelling for /ē/ in the pretonic syllable. The reason for this may be that the occurrence of this vowel in this particular position is far less frequent than that of /ĕ/; it is possible that, given a larger sampling, we might have found also instances of *ae* spelling for Latin /ē/ in the pretonic segment,[15] at least in those areas where reverse spellings for /ē/ in stressed position were found. It may be worth pointing out, however, that in some areas (the *Iberian* area, *Lugdunensis* and *Southern Italy*)

---

[14] The name *Marciane* would appear to be a Grecized form of *Marciana*, formed on the masculine *Marcianus*. For the final /ē/ in the nominative singular of Greek nouns of the first declension, cf. Allen and Greenough, p. 19.

[15] Niedermann (p. 61) quotes *aeorum* (CIL VI 2365), Sommer (p. 72) gives *aegisse* (CIL IV 2413) and Pirson lists *faeliciter* (XII 944 a. 513) and *Saeverianus* (XII 2966) as examples of reverse spellings in the pretonic syllable.

examples of reverse spellings for Latin /ē/ do not occur, except in final syllable, while in others (*Northern* and *Central Italy*, *Rome* and *Narbonensis*)[16] they occur frequently enough to be due to more than occasional misspellings and where they may, indeed, reflect, as suggested by Sommer, «(lokal begrenzte?) Artikulationsschwankungen (entweder engere Aussprache des aus *ae* entstandenen Lautes oder offnere des alten *ē*)» (p. 72).[17] But even if such were the case, these «Artikulationsschwankungen» would not be significant enough to speak of important dialectal differences.

The conclusion that we would seem to be able to draw from our inscriptional material is that by the time of the first appearance of Christian epitaphs (the primary concern of our study), the classical Latin diphthong /aj/, represented by the letters *ae*, has merged with the original Latin /ĕ/, as reflected in the high frequency of *e* spellings for *ae*, as well as the considerable number of instances of reverse spellings.

1.3 The Ending *as* for *ae* (*e*) in the Nominative Plural of First Declension Nouns and Adjectives

In classical Latin, in the plural of first declension nouns and adjectives, there was a formal opposition between the nominative endings in *ae* and the accusative in *as*. It seems, however, that a dialectal nominative plural form in *as* was in current usage at an early date, as attested by a line from one of the *Atellanae* of the poet Pomponius (ca. 100 B.C.), in which the forms *laetitias insperatas* has generally been interpreted as a nominative plural.[18] Lindsay states that «Dialectal -*as* Nom. Pl. is found in the old inscriptions of Pisaurum with the *s* dropped (C.I.L. i. 173 matrona Pisaurese dono dedrot;...» (p. 398).

---

[16] We found only one example from *Narbonensis*, but Pirson (pp. 19-20) gives quite a few from this area from non-Christian inscriptions.

[17] Certain developments in the Romance languages would seem to point, nevertheless, to the fact that in areas that do not give us any indication to this effect, the diphthong /aj/ may have merged with the original Latin /ē/. Thus, *laetus* gives It. *lieto*, Old Fr. *lie* (*liez*), but Old Sp. *ledo*, rather than *liedo* (Meyer-Lübke, REW, #4848, p. 349).

[18] Cf. Sommer, p. 329; Väänänen, p. 115; Lausberg, III, p. 18. In connection with the extension of the *as* ending to the nominative, the latter states: «Es handelt sich wahrscheinlich um einen fruhen Osko-Umbrismus des gesprochenen Lateins» (*ibid.*). For a similar view, cf. Väänänen, p. 116, with further bibliographical references.

The nominative plural ending in *as* is not infrequent in both Pagan and Christian inscriptions, nor is it limited to any particular area. Thus, the form *Asellinas* in a nominative function is found in a Pompeian inscription (cf. Díaz y Díaz, p. 32), while the much-quoted Christian epitaph reading, in part, *his quescunt duas matres duas filias... et advenas II parvolas* (D3476) originates from *Aquincum* in *Pannonia*. Diehl, *De m finali* (p. 204), quotes the forms *alumnas* and *collegas*, as well as *liberti libertasque* from pagan inscriptions found in *Central Italy* and *Dalmatia*, respectively.

The situation as far as our material is concerned is the following:

A. *Iberian Peninsula*

The nominative plural form, spelled with *e* in eight instances out of nine, never appears spelled with *as*.[19]

B. *Gaul*

There are only two occurrences of the nominative plural, spelled with *ae* and *e*, respectively, both found on inscriptions from the *Lugdunensis*. The spelling *as* in this function does not occur.[20]

C. *Italy*

(a) *Northern*: Two occurrences of the nominative plural were found, both spelled with *as*, as follows:

> *collegas sui conparaverunt* (D497 IV/V cent.)
> *bene quiescant reliquias* (D2101N)

(b) *Central*: No occurrence.

(c) *Southern*: A single occurrence of the nominative plural in *as* was found in an inscription from *Carales (Sardinia)*, namely

> *quen tumulant... patronas* (D753)

---

[19] Carnoy (p. 228) reports *filias matri posuerunt* from a pagan inscription that might be as early as the second century A. D. and the form *viduas* from an eighth century verse epitaph.

[20] It may be of interest to note that Pirson does not mention in his study a single instance of the use of *as* for *ae* in the nominative plural function. The extension of the *as* ending to this function, however, would seem to be evidenced by the frequency with which this spelling appears in Merovingian documents, where the classical Latin ending has just about been displaced by the *as* ending. Cf. Pei, *Texts*, p. 137.

D. Rome

The only occurrence in third/fourth century material is spelled with *ae*. The three occurrences of this case in fifth century material, on the other hand, are spelled with *as*, as follows:

> *requiescent... germanas... natas* (D1707 a. 461/482?)
> *filias intercedentes... quae* (D3753 a. 400/405?)

The number of nominative plural forms spelled with *as*, found in non-dated inscriptions, is not inconsiderable. A few examples follow:

> *Anastasia et Laurentia puellas dei quas* (D1472)
> *Petronia... et Martina depositas* (D2954)
> *que voluistis nobis esse inimicas* (D3887A)
> *duas sorores: Istercora... Marciane* (D4024)
> *filias matri pientissime in pace* (D4264G)
> etc.

It has been said that the derivation of the plural from the nominative rather than the accusative is one of the main features that separate the so-called «East» from «West» Romance speech, as a result of the fall of final /s/ which characterizes the languages of the «Eastern» group (i.e. Italian and Rumanian), as against those of the «Western» group (comprising the languages of the Iberian Peninsula and Gaul) which retain final /s/.[21] Sardinian, which lies outside this classification, follows the latter group in the matter of plural formation, while the Northern Italian dialects, with the exception of a small area around *Bergamo*,[22] conform to the Italian system.[23] Thus, the plural of first declension nouns in Spanish, Portuguese, Sardinian and Old Provençal ends in *as*, in Old French and Catalan in *es* (from the cl. Latin accusative plural ending *as*), while in both Italian and Rumanian the normal nominative plural ending is *e*, which is generally considered to be the continuation of the cl. Latin nominative in *ae*.[24]

---

[21] Cf. v. Wartburg, *Ausgliederung*, p. 21. For a discussion and critical evaluation of the criteria used for the division of the Romance domain into «East» and «West» Romance, cf. Pei, «Intervocalic Occlusives of «East» and «West» Romance,» *Studies*, pp. 85-99.

[22] Cf. Meyer-Lübke, *Grammaire*, II, p. 48.

[23] Cf. Pei, *Italian Language*, p. 155.

[24] Cf. Elcock, pp. 62-65; Bourciez, *Éléments*, pp. 227-228.

Looking at the evidence furnished by our inscriptional material, we find that the apparent morphological extension of the cl. Latin accusative plural in *as* to the nominative must have been very widespread, since this phenomenon is found in areas that would otherwise be classified under the «Eastern» group, such as *Pannonia* (had a Romance tongue survived there), *Dalmatia, Rome* and, with qualifications, *Northern Italy*. Leaving this latter area aside, seeing that traces of a nominative plural ending in *as* can still be found there, as well as *Dalmatia* where no Romance language is spoken any longer, our attention can be particularly focussed on *Rome*. Assuming that by the fifth century the formal opposition between the cl. Latin nominative and accusative plural had been obliterated (and our evidence would seem to give us some basis for such an assumption) and that the *as* ending had taken over both the subject and direct object functions, the question might be raised as to how this ending could have phonetically developed into modern Italian *e*.

In a *mise au point* entiled «On the origin of the Italian Plurals,» *Romanic Review*, XLIII (1952), 272-281, Robert Politzer re-examines the whole problem of the derivation of the Italian plurals on the basis of statistical evidence gained from original Late Latin documents from the eighth century. While it would be outside the scope of this study to discuss this scholar's line of reasoning, suffice it to say that Politzer advances some cogent arguments to support his conclusion that, for the first declension, the plural form in Italian derives not from the cl. Latin nominative but from the accusative in *as* (p. 280) by way of a «logical intermediary between -*as* and -*e*» which is a form ending in *es*, which seems to be amply attested in his documents (p. 276). [25]

We have no way, of course, to either confirm or reject Politzer's theory, seeing that our material shows no such intermediate stage in the development of the first declension Italian plural, but it would seem that our inscriptions could lend support to his contention that «at the beginning of the eighth century the nominative in -*ae* was quite dead also in the central Italian area, and could thus not possibly have furnished the Italian plural form» (*ibid.*). In fact, the nominative in *ae* may have been «quite dead» even before the eighth century.

---

[25] This possibility has quite recently been supported, not only for Italian but also for Rumanian plurals of the first declension, by Väänänen, pp. 115-116 and Lausberg, III, pp. 19-21.

2. *The Diphthong /oj/, represented by the letters oe.*

Authorities are agreed that the diphthong /oj/ became a closed [e] in pronunciation by about the same time the diphthong /aj/ merged with original Latin /ĕ/, i.e. about the first century of our era.[26]

The occurrence of this diphthong in our material is so sporadic that it would not be possible to draw any conclusions on the basis of our findings, even though the few examples of *e* spelling for an expected *oe,* in both stressed and unstressed syllables, would seem to be quite in line with the findings of other scholars.

2.1 The Diphthong /oj/ in Stressed Syllable

A. *Iberian Peninsula*

(a) *Baetica.*—Except for *cetu* found in a verse inscription (V286 a. 649), there are no occurrences of this diphthong in our material from this area.

(b) *Lusitania.*—No occurrence in dated material.
On a non-dated inscription we read *ceptum* (V311) for *coeptum.*

(c) *Tarraconensis.*—No occurrence.

B. *Gaul*

(a) *Narbonensis.*—The two occurrences found in dated material are correctly spelled.

In non-dated material we found one instance of an *e* spelling for *oe* in the proper name *Fedula* (D2408) (=*Foedula,* cf. Diehl ICLV, Vol. III, p. 71).

(b) *Lugdunensis.*—No occurrence of this diphthong.

---

[26] Cf. Niedermann, *Phonétique,* p. 63; Bourciez, *Éléments,* p. 44; Grandgent, p. 90; Sommer, p. 77 (who quotes *ceperint* appearing side by side with *coeperunt* in the same inscription, CIL II 1964 a. 81/4, which is also mentioned by Carnoy, p. 84); Battisti, p. 105; Väänänen, p. 34 (who quotes the forms *amenus, citaredus* and *Phebus* from Pompeian inscriptions).

C. Italy

(a) *Northern*.—The form *a penes* (=*poenis*) (D3879)[27] is the only instance of the occurrence of this diphthong, spelled with *e*.

(b) *Central*.—A single occurrence in dated material correctly spelled.

(c) *Southern*.—No occurrence.

D. Rome

No occurrence.

2.2. The Diphthong /oj/ in Unstressed Syllable

A. Iberian Peninsula

(a) *Baetica*.—A single occurrence of a form where we would expect the *oe* spelling appears spelled with *e*, namely *cenobi* (V286 a. 649) (cf. *supra*, the form *cetu* in same).

It may be of interest to note that in a non-dated inscription we find the spelling *moerore* (V65) for an expected *maerore*, suggesting that the graphic devices *ae* and *oe* were likely to be used for one and the same sound at a time when the diphthongs /aj/ and /oj/ had already been reduced to monophthongs. This spelling would also seem to lend additional support to Sommer's thinking that in some regions the [e] sound resulting from the monophthongization of these diphthongs may have been more similar in quality than is generally believed.[28]

---

[27] All *e*-s in this particular inscription are transcribed by *epsilon* without regard as to whether they represent originally long or short /e/.

[28] Pirson, p. 22, notes the occurrence of both *caelum* and *coelum* in his inscriptional material. Pei, *Texts,* p. 73, finds a similar spelling confusion in his own material and refers to other late Latin texts in which the spelling *oe* occurs for an expected *ae*, or vice versa, and concludes: «The replacement of *oe* by *ae* could not have taken place if *ae* had only had the sound of open *e*» (p. 74). It must be pointed out, however, that the *oe* spelling in our example occurs in the unstressed syllable where original Latin /ĕ/ and /ē/ merged anyway in this particular area, as shown by the subsequent development in Spanish, cf. Menéndez-Pidal, *Gramática*, p. 69. For the confusion of *ae* and *oe* spelling in classical Latin, e.g. *caelum* and *coelum*, cf. Lindsay, p. 44, and our footnote #1.

(b) *Lusitania*.—Except for the spelling *poenitentia* (V480 a. 588), rather than *paenitentia*, no occurrence of this diphthong was found. [29]

(c) *Tarraconensis*.—No occurrence in dated material.

In a non-dated inscription we read *cenobium* (V278) for *coenobium*.

B. Gaul

No occurrence of this diphthong.

C. Italy

(a) *Northern*.—Two correct occurrences of this diphthong were found in IV/Vth century material to one *e* spelling in *penalibus* (D3454 a. 488).

In non-dated material we read *de numero Misacorum* (D557) where the expected *oe* spelling (i.e. *Moesiacorum*) shows up as *i*. (For the *i* spelling for Latin /ē/ in initial position in this area, cf. *supra*, p. 131).

(b) *Central*.—The only occurrence in dated material appears spelled with *e*, namely *cimiterium* (D2000 ca. VIIth cent.). The same form is also found in a non-dated inscription (*iuxta cimiterium* D2163). [30]

(c) *Southern*.—No occurrence.

D. Rome

No occurrence in dated material.

In non-dated material we found two deviations, both in the forms *cimitero* (D2119) and *cymiterium* (D2149). [31]

---

[29] The only other occurrence of this word appears as *penitentia* (V66 a. 662), included in our table showing the treatment of the diphthong /aj/ in unstressed syllable, *supra*, p. 247.

[30] For the /i/ outcome in mod. Italian of cl. Latin /ĕ, ē, ĭ, ae, oe/ in the initial syllable. cf. Pei, *Italian Language*, p. 36; for the loss of yod after /r/, cf. *ibid*., p. 63.

Also cf. It. *cimitero*, Fr. *cimetière*, Old Sp. *cimiterio* and *ciminterio*, but Mod. Sp. *cementerio*, Pg. *cemiterio*, Prov.—Cat. *cementeri*, cf. Meyer-Lübke, REW, #2023, p. 163. For the Spanish development, cf. Corominas, I, p. 756.

[31] On the existence of an alternate form *cimiterium* side by side with the learned *coemeterium*, Battisti's comment is of interest: «[The Greek diphthong] οι diede normalmente *oe* anche nel latino della Chiesa: κοιμητήριον, *coemeterium*, ma accanto a questa soluzione di sviluppo dotto esistono tracce di iotacismo nelle grafie *cimiterium*, *cymiterium*, *cimeterium*.» (p. 127).

3. The Diphthong /aw/, represented by the letters au.

In connection with this classical Latin diphthong, Grandgent informs us that «*au*, pronounced *au*, generally remained in Vulgar Latin....» (p. 89), except that in the initial syllable *au* became *a* if there was an accented *u* in the next syllable» (*ibid.* p. 96). Väänänen calls it «la plus résistante des diphtongues latines» (p. 39), since it survives in some Romance languages to this day.

On the other hand, a feature of certain Italic dialects (particularly Umbrian), i.e. the monophthongization of the diphthong /aw/, seems to have been preserved in «rustic Latin» and even «in the Latin of the streets of Rome.»[32] Early inscriptional evidence of this phenomenon is found in Pompeian inscriptions,[33] and both Pirson (p. 27) and Carnoy (p. 85) report several instances of the spelling *Clodius, Clodia* and *Plotus* in their study of inscriptions from *Gaul* and *Spain*, respectively.

The situation as reflected in our material is as follows:

3.1 The Diphthong /aw/ in Stressed Syllable

The apparent reduction of this diphthong to /o/, as reflected in the *o* spelling for *au*, occurs only in the proper names *Pola*[34] and *Clodius/Clodia*.[35] Since the occurrences of /aw/ are mostly limited to proper names and there are no deviations to report in any common

---

[32] Lindsay, p. 40. According to the grammarian Festus, as reported by this scholar, the *rustici* pronounced *orum* for *aurum* and *oriculas* for *auriculas*. Pirson reports the occurrence of *Oricla* (CIL XII 5686) as a cognomen and the name *Oriclo* (dat. sg. *Auriculus*) occurs on a Christian inscription from *Africa* (D2522). Cf. also Probus' censure: *auris non oricla*. For evidence of the use of /o/ for /aw/ in the literary language, cf. Niedermann, *Phonétique*, pp. 65/66; Sommer, pp. 78/79; Kieckers, pp. 34/35; Battisti, pp. 106/107.

[33] Väänänen (p. 40) reports the occurrence of *Aulus* and *Olus* side by side, reminiscent of the doublet *Claudius* and *Clodius* (cf. Lewis & Short, p. 350), as well as forms like *ollam, coliclo* (=*caulic(u)lu(m)*) and *plostrari*.

[34] *Uxor Pola* (D3556 ca. V cent., *Lugdunensis*); *Cl. Polle coiugi* (D768, *So. Italy*). The diminutive *Politta* occurs once in *No. Italy* (D1431 a. 535) and in Rome (D4113B). The first inscriptional attestation of *Pola* (=*Paulla*) in CIL I 379 ca. 184 B. C. (Sommer, p. 79).

[35] D763 a/b from *Rome*.

noun, we felt that a tabular representation of this phenomenon was not necessary.

Concerning the forms *clusit* (D3532a a. 415) and *clusa* (D3534) (but *inclusa est* in D3535), both found in the area of *Rome*, there would seem to be little doubt that these are analogical reconstructions along the lines of the compounds *includere, concludere*, etc., and do not reflect the reduction of the diphthong /aw/ to /u/.[36]

3.2 The Diphthong /aw/ in Unstressed Syllable

Our inscriptional material seems to offer ample evidence of the apparent reduction of the diphthong /aw/ to /a/ before a stressed /u/ in the following syllable (cf. *infra*, p. 261), although this phenomenon is exclusively limited to the proper names *Augustus/Augusta* and the name of the corresponding month.[37]

In order to show the reader how widespread this monophthongization is in this particular form and in order to limit our examples to only a few instances, we include a table of correct occurrences and deviations.

3.2 The Diphthong /aw/ in Unstressed Syllable

Area	*Century*	*Augustus* etc.	*Agustus* etc.	*%*
Baetica	IV-VI	4	2	25.0
	VII	3	0	
Lusitania	IV-VI	3	3	50.0
	VII	0	2	100.0
Tarraconensis	IV-VI	4	2	25.0
	VII	0	0	
Narbonensis	IV-V	2	0	
	VI-VII	9	4	30.7

---

[36] For the occasional use of *cludo* for *claudo* in the literary language, cf. Lewis & Short, p. 351.

[37] For further examples of this phenomenon, cf. Lindsay, p. 38; Niedermann, *Phonétique*, p. 67; Battisti, p. 107. Väänänen, p. 40.

DIPHTHONGS

Area	Century	Augustus etc.	Agustus etc.	%
Lugdunensis	IV-V	3	0	
	VI-VII	2	2	50.0
No. Italy	IV-V	16	3	15.8
	VI	20	3	13.0
	III-IV	12	0	
Ce. Italy	V	4	0	
	VI-VII	6	0	
	III-IV	6	0	
So. Italy	V	5	4	46.6
	VI-VII	9	1	(10.0)
	III-IV	39	1	(2.0)
Rome	V	25	3	10.7
	VI-VII	15	5	20.5

Here are a few illustrative examples taken at random:

III kal. Ag. (V153 a. 578) — Baetica.
caln. Austas (V492 a. 543) — Lusitania [38]
Cesaracosta (V436 IV/VI cent.) — Tarraconensis [39]
kalendas Acustas (D3176D a. 532) — Narbonensis
III kal. Agusti (D2983A) — Ce. Italy
dierum Agustarum (D140 a. 552) — So. Italy
Agustinus (D1965A) — So. Italy
filiae Agustine (D2941AN a. 364) — Rome
dn. Arcadio Acusto (D2824A a. 406) — Rome

---

[38] This form offers an andditional interest in that it shows the fall of intervocalic /g/. However, this is not an isolated instance; in fact Carnoy (p. 127) reports the form *Austo* from a third century inscription from Asturias, Sommer (p. 199) notes *Austa* (=*Augusta*) from an African inscription (CIL VIII 9877) (cf. the name of the Italian city *Aosta*, the former *Augusta Praetoria*), while in Ce. Italy one finds *kl. Austas* (CIL XI 6811) and in our own material we find *kal. Aus.* (D2798) from *Rome*.

For the fall of pretonic /g/ in Italian, Spanish and Portuguese and its subsequent restoration in a few forms, such as *agosto* (as against Old Fr. *aost*), cf. Meyer-Lübke, *Grammaire*, I, p. 398 ff.

[39] For the consistent spelling *Cesaracosta* or *Cesaracusta* for *Caesaraugusta* on Visigothic coins, cf. our footnote #52, p. 90.

The evidence at our disposal, culled from both dated and non-dated inscriptions, would seem to show that the diphthong /aw/ in the word *Augustus* had probably been reduced to an /a/ by at least the sixth century in just about all areas under study. In *Ce. Italy* only a single example of this phenomenon was found in a non-dated inscription.[40]

Regarding the treatment of the diphthong /aw/ in stressed position, the fact that we found deviations only in such proper names where an *o* spelling for an expected *au* seems to represent an older alternative form (*Claudius — Clodius; Paulla — Polla*) and none in any common noun would seem to justify the conclusion that this diphthong is quite stable in our inscriptional material.

---

[40] This does not necessarily mean that in some regions the /aw/ may not have been reduced to /a/ at an earlier time. Väänänen (p. 40) reports an example of *Agusto* in Pompeian inscriptions and the earliest dated example found in *Rome* goes back to about the middle of the fourth century.

CHAPTER IV: SOME VOCALIC PHENOMENA

1. *Prothesis*

The prefixing of a front vowel before a word beginning with consonant groups whose first element is an /s/, is generally considered to be a characteristic feature of the vocalism of Vulgar Latin and seems to be well documented since early Christian times. [1]

This so-called prothetic vowel, which could be either /e/ or /i/, occurs first in Greek inscriptions, [2] but the first Latin example is attested in Pompeian inscriptions (e.g. *Izmurna* for *Smyrna,* cf. Väänänen, p. 48). Occasional examples of this phenomenon are to be found in the second and third centuries [3] and become quite frequent from the fourth/fifth centuries on, although it may be of interest to note that no mention of the prothetic vowel is made by Latin grammarians till quite late times, [4] which leads Lindsay to suspect that «however far it [viz. the prothetic vowel] had developed in Vulgar Latin, it did not threaten to encroach on the speech of the educated classes» (p. 106). That this phenomenon did, eventually, reach all classes of society would seem to be borne out by the fact that, as Pei puts it «....a prothetic

---

[1] Cf. Lindsay, p. 105; Bourciez, *Éléments,* p. 48; Meyer-Lübke, *Einführung,* p. 157; Battisti, p. 117; Sommer, p. 293. For a summary of various theories advanced in connection with the origin of the prothetic vowel, cf. B. Löfstedt, p. 107 ff.

[2] Cf. Grandgent, p. 98.

[3] These examples are not limited to a specific area. The form *izmara(g)dus* is found on a second century inscription from *Rome* and Carnoy (p. 115) reports *iscolasticus* from *Barcelona* dating back to the second century also. For further examples of an early date, cf. O. Prinz «Zur Entstehung der Prothese vor s impurum im Lateinischen», *Glotta,* XXVI, 97-115.

[4] Authorities give the time of S. Isidore, in the seventh century, Cf. Grandgent, Battisti, Lindsay, under footnotes #1 and #2.

e or *i*.... has attained full sway in French and Spanish (O. Fr. *escrire, espede, estable;* Sp. *escribir, espada, estrella*) and partial survival in Italian (*strada* but *per istrada, Svezia* but in *Isvezia*)» (*Texts,* p. 127).

The use of a prothetic vowel is, as might be expected, also attested in our inscriptional material, where it appears most frequently in inscriptions from *Italy,* particularly the area of *Rome.* On the other hand, this phenomenon is not particularly frequent in inscriptions from the *Iberian* area, whereas in the area of *Gaul* only a single trustworthy example was found, namely *bone memoriae Isp[es] nomene* (D1457N ca. VI cent.) from the *Narbonensis* area.[5]

The following examples of the use of a prothetic vowel were found in the *Iberian* area:

(a) *Baetica*:   *Domni Istefani* (V316, VI/VII cent.)
                      sacri Estepha[ni] (V328)
                      (but *ibid.* also *Stephani*)
(b) *Lusitania*:   *conmendavit ispiritum* (V86 a. 632)
(c) *Tarraconensis*: *Ispiritus Marturi* (V210, IV/VI cent.)
                      (but cf. *santus spiretus* (V211) from the same *Tarragona* region)
                      sci. Est[efani] (V307, VII cent.)
                      (but cf. *sco. Stephano* (V377))

A few examples from the *Italian* area are the following:

(a) *Northern*: *ispiretus [....requi]escat* (D2285A)
                quorum ispiritus (D3388)
                Sabino Istercoria.... amita (D4186)
(b) *Central*: *filio dulcissimo Istercorio* (D2997C)
(c) *Southern*: *cos. Istiliconsis* (D4181 a. 400)
                titulu... cot iscripserunt amici (D3851, VII cent.)
                Vernacla, ispiritus tuus (D3356A)
                inocenti ispirito (D3399)
                isce(ler)ata mater [f]e(ci)t (D4191A)

Occurrences of this phenomenon in both dated and non-dated inscriptions are quite abundant in the area of *Rome* (but let us also keep in mind that our material from this area is considerably more abundant than from any other!). Here are a few examples taken at random:

---

[5] Pirson lists about half a dozen examples from pagan inscriptions (p. 60). A doubtful example in the *Lugdunensis* is *amici is[cripserunt...?]* (D4462).

Clodia Ispes (D763a, assigned to the II cent. by Rossi)
tabulam isculsi (D4456B a. 371)
amicus dolis iscribet (D4177 a. 404)
Aetio et Istudio vv.cc. (D289 a. 454)
p̄r̄ī. (=*primicerius*) *escole secundae* (D485a a. 476)
...]*inus iscolasticus* (D732b a. 403)
(but ...]*co scolastico* in D732a)
bir ispectabilis (D198)
pax ispirito tuo (D2259)
que istetit in seculo (D2756)
Fl. Ursus istrator (D1632), etc.

Except for those scholars who suggest foreign influence to account for the appearance of a prothetic vowel (cf. our note #6), the consensus of those who see in this phenomenon a spontaneous development seems to be summed up by Niedermann, when he says: «À l'origine, la prothèse ne se produisait qu'à l'intérieur de la phrase après un mot terminé par consonne» (*Recueil*, p. 78), a state of affairs which is still reflected in modern Italian, where people say *la scuola* but *in iscuola*. Later, it seems, the prothetic vowel /i/ or /e/ came to be regarded as a regular part of the word, so that it could occur before a word ending in a vowel and at the beginning of a phonic group, i.e. after a pause. [6]

The examples of this phenomenon culled from our inscriptional material would seem to show that a prothetic vowel was likely to occur both after a consonant, a vowel or a pause. It would be of interest to try to determine the conditions under which prothesis occurs most frequently in each area under study but the only material that would lend itself to such an inquiry is our *corpus* from *Rome*. In fact, it was found that in this area, out of a total of 37 reliable examples of prothesis, 21 occur after a consonant, 10 after a pause or in absolute

---

[6] Cf. Grandgent, p. 98; Bourciez, *Éléments*, p. 156. In his special study on the genesis of the prothetic vowel, Prinz has examined inscriptional material and shown that this vowel occurs almost as often after a vowel as after a consonant, and that in sentence initial position and after a pause the frequency of occurrence is even higher (p. 109). His study is mainly based on inscriptions from the *Italian* and *African* areas (his argument in favor of a possible Semitic influence to account for the appearance of the prothetic vowel is based on its frequent occurrence of *African inscriptions*) since prothesis samplings from both *Gaul* and *Spain* are very scanty and inadequate for any conclusions to be drawn.

initial position and 6 after a vowel.[7] As to the nature of the prothetic vowel itself, our whole *Italian* material seems to point quite definitely to a preference of /i/; unfortunately, neither the *Iberian* area nor *Gaul* yield sufficient evidence to make any statement in this respect.[8]

2. *Apheresis*

This phenomenon, the inverse of prothesis, appears on a verse inscription from *Seville (Baetica), lapis ste* (V272 a. 641) and an epitaph from *Bolsena (Ce. Italy), maritus, curator r.p. (=rei publicae) stius civitatis stituit* (D365 a. 376).[9]

Although far from being a general Romance phenomenon, apheresis is quite extensive in modern Italian.[10] Bourciez, *Éléments*, quotes a few examples of this phenomenon from Late Latin texts from the Italian area and concludes: «La tendance qui favorisait à l'initiale s + cons. a été de bonne heure très forte en Italie» (p. 156). Unfortunately, the evidence that this scholar adduces in support of his thesis is rather scanty and, in the absence of comparative data from other areas, it would seem somewhat hasty to conclude that this apheretic trend, which is characteristic of modern Italian sound structure, is already perceptible in Vulgar Latin. In any event, our inscriptional material is far from sufficient to shed further light on this problem.

B. Löfstedt believes that in many instances apheresis is not a reflection of a spoken form but rather a hypercorrection and he argues as follows:

> man war sich dessen bewusst, dass man bisweilen vor s + Kons. ein *i* oder *e* zu Unrecht aussprach (und schrieb), und

---

[7] Cf. *supra*, inscription D732a/b from *Rome* where we find *iscolasticus* after a consonant but *scolasticus* after a vowel.

[8] In his study of *Eighth Century Texts*, Pei (pp. 127/28) shows a clearcut preference for /e/ as the prothetic vowel in the area of *Gaul*. On the other hand, in the eighth century *Forum Judicum*, Cooper finds that all instances of prothesis «show the form in is-» (p. 45), whereas in the *Cartulario de San Vicente*, written a century or so later, Jennings is in a position to state that «the predominance of *e* over *i* seems sufficient evidence that *e* has by the date of the *Cartulario* already gained the place it is to hold in Spanish» (p. 82).

[9] Further examples from non-Christian inscriptions will be found in Prinz, «Zur Entstehung...,» p. 104 ff.

[10] E. g. *stanotte, stasera, stamane*, as well as colloquial *sto libro, sta donna, sti libri*, cf. Pei, *Italian Language*, p. 39.

bei dem Bestreben, diesen Fehler zu vermeiden, ist man gelegentlich zu weit gegangen; ... (p. 114).

In the case of forms like *lapis ste* and *civitatis stituit* found in our material, the possibility of apheresis due to the identity of the preceding syllable might also be considered.

3. *Syncope*

Väänänen defines syncope, i.e. the fall of an unaccented vowel, as «un accident qui atteint l'économie phonique des mots en leur faisant perdre une syllabe» (p. 40) and lists conditions under which this phenomenon is most likely to occur (p. 41 ff.).[11] This scholar further states that it is «un phénomène d'aspect éminemment populaire et familier» (p. 42) and that out of 227 «mistakes» censured by the Appendix Probi, 25 instances refer to syncope (*ibid.*).

Of interest to the researcher in the field of inscriptional material is above all the comprehensive study by Ephraim Cross on Syncope and Kindred Phenomena in Latin Inscriptions, in which he establishes, on a comparative basis, «the actual status of Latin syncope as revealed by the inscriptions of various parts of the Roman world» (pp. 7/8). No less interesting is also the conclusion that this scholar reaches on the «actual status of Latin syncope,» namely that

> all portions of the Roman world are pretty much in agreement, that syncope is not noticeably more marked in one region than in another, ... (p. 100).

Although Cross does not list many examples from Christian inscriptions (Diehl's collection was not yet available to him), instances of syncopation found in our material are not much different from those given by Cross. A few examples follow:

---

[11] For the general phenomenon of syncope, cf. Lindsay, p. 170 ff.; Niedermann, *Phonétique*, p. 32 ff.; Grandgent, p. 98 ff.; Meyer-Lübke, *Einführung*, p. 153 ff.; Maurer, *Gramática*, p. 18 ff.

For a recent study which attempts to account for the occurrence of syncope with reference to the phonological system of consonantal distribution rather than by listing environments, either in specific or general terms, in which syncope is likely to occur, cf. James M. Anderson, «A Study of Syncope in Vulgar Latin,» *Word*, XXI (April 1965), 70-85.

A. Iberian Peninsula

Except for the forms *domnus* and *domna* which appear with some frequency in syncopated forms when referring to saints, kings and bishops (the full form *Dominus* being reserved for God, e.g. in *nomine Domini, in pace Domini,* or *Domine* in direct address), there are only a handful of examples, such as *per saecla* (V313 a. 637?) [12] as well as about half a dozen occurrences of *Acisclus*, the name of the Cordoban saint, both from *Baetica*, while the only reliable example found in *Tarraconensis* is *comtum* (=*comitum*, gen. pl. of *comes*) (V315 a. 737).

Although offered by Cross as evidence of the syncope of a pretonic vowel (p. 80), the form *klendas* (V165 a. 596, *Baetica*) (which is also found in other areas) might also be interpreted as some sort of abbreviation, in view of such other shortened forms as *kldas, klns* and *klnds* (*passim*).

B. Gaul

Examples of this phenomenon in Christian inscriptions are quite few in relation to examples found in Pagan epitaphs. (Cf. Pirson, p. 49 ff., who gives an impressive list of syncopated forms). Apart from the ever-present *domnus* used in connection with individuals (kings, consuls and *viri inlustri*), [13] examples of syncopated forms are just about limited to the following:

(a) *Narbonensis*: saecla (D148) and *passim* [14]
itrum (D2891A a. 529); bendictus (D3474)
bene merto (D3241)

---

[12] For the apparent syncope of forms ending in *culus, culum* representing the Indo-European instrumental suffix *tlom*, cf. Sommer, p. 228 and Lindsay, p. 174 ff. The forms *saeclum, periclum,* etc. seem to be the older forms and are used as doublets, as e.g. Plautus' line *periclum vitae meae tuo stat periculo* (quoted in Sommer, p. 140). A similar use of doublets is also found in many verse inscriptions, e.g. *felix luce nova saeclorum in saecula gaudet* (D60, Rome) and *extulit aeternum saeclorum in saecula nomen* (D61, Lugdunensis). On the analogy of these archaic forms, the diminutive suffix *culus, cula, culum* (always disyllabic in Plautus) were probably syncopated at an early time since, as Cross puts it «It was hardly likely that the spoken language would keep apart the instrumental suffix *clo* and the diminutive suffix *culo*» (p. 59).

[13] The syncope in *domnus* also seems to have been transferred to proper names, e.g. *Domnulus* (D1216 a. 496).

[14] It may be of interest to note that the syncopated forms occur mostly in verse inscriptions, whereas prose inscriptions generally show the forms *saeculum* or *saecolum*.

The form *depostio* (D1467) may deserve a special comment, since it would seem to show the syncope of a stressed vowel, which is a rather unusual phenomenon. Might we not, in order to account for this form, proceed from a hypothetical **depostionem* (=*depositionem*)[15] with a subsequent shift of accent in the nominative form, i.e. a sort of back formation?

Pirson connects up the form *depostio* with the past participle form *postus* «qu'on rencontre d'ailleurs assez fréquemment dans les textes vulgaires, et qui a été un des modèles sur lesquels les langues romanes ont créé de nombreux participes en *stus*» (p. 50).

(b) *Lugdunensis*: *occort* (=*occurrit*) (D1075 a. 630)
venturi saecli (D1072 a. 552)
Disderius (=*Desiderius*) (D1255 a. 517)
humlis (D1436 a. 643)

The original form *Lugudunum* and *Lugudunensis* exclusively appear in their syncopated forms *Lugdunum* and *Lugdunensis*, respectively, an apparently permissible doublet even in accordance with classical Latin standards (cf. Lewis & Short, p. 1084, where these forms are given in syncopated form only).

C. *Italy*

Examples of syncopated forms, besides the ubiquitous *domnus*/*domna* (as well as the inflected forms *domni*, *domno*, etc.) are not very numerous and can be listed in their entirety, as follows:

(a) *Northern*: *vetranibus* (D515, IV/V cent.)[16]
(also *vetranus* (D555) and *betranus* (D463)
Domnulae (D538B) and *seclo* (D4341) from non-dated material.
(b) *Central*: *Felicla* (D2698); *depostio* (D3006A)[17]
Aerclanius (=*Herculanius*) (D4128C)
all from non-dated material.

---

[15] The form *depossione* (=*depositione*) is attested in *Tarraconensis* (V199, IV/VI cent.) and in the area of *Rome* (e.g. *abet depossione* (D3047) and *passim*), while the nominative form *depossio* is quite frequent in the whole *Italian* area.

[16] In connection with this form, Väänänen states the following: «fréquent dans les inscr. depuis le 1ᵉʳ s. ap. J.-C.; roum. *batrîn*, it dial. *vetrano*, frioul. *vedran*» (p. 41).

[17] Cf. our note #15.

(c) *Southern*: *deposio* (D1145 a. 368); *Lepusclus* (D2792 a. 404)
magistra (v)ercundiae (D615)
oclos (D4692); *Vernacla* (D3356A)
(d)εposte (=*depositae*) (D2948A)

D. Rome

At first glance it would appear that the number of syncopated forms in this area is considerably higher than in the other areas under study. However, this is more apparent than real, since (a) we have more material from *Rome* than from any other region and, hence, the possibilities of the occurrence of syncopated forms are much higher, and (b) by classifying the conditions under which syncope occurs, we find that these are not any different from those in *Spain*, *Gaul* and the rest of *Italy*.

Thus, we find the frequent occurrence of *domnus/domna* when referring to persons, as well as a great number of syncopated forms ending in *culus/cula*, e.g.

> *a(d) lacu(m) cunicli* (D775 a. 375) [18]
> loc. *Erclanes* (=*Herculanae*) (D3500 a. 387) [19]
> *acuclarius* (D643), [20] *oclu* (D3877)
> *artis ispeclararie* (=*specularariae*) (D688), etc.

Examples of other syncopated forms are as follows:

> *calda, porge* (=*porrige*) (D1569a) [21]
> *ispirto* (D3877); *teglata* (D2143) [22]
> *depostio* (D158 ca. III cent.); *depostus* (D2951A)
> *agneglus* (=*agniculus*) *dei* (D2481), etc.

Discussing the phenomenon of syncope in connection with modern Italian, Pei, *Italian Language*, states the following:

---

[18] Cf. It. *coniglio*, Sp. *conejo*, Old Fr. *conil* (Meyer-Lübke, REW, #2397, p. 190).

[19] For the nominative singular *e* ending of Graecized Latin feminine *cognomina* and the use of the Greek declension *es* ending in the genitive singular, cf. Hehl, *op. cit.*, pp. 6 and 17.

[20] Cf. Sp. *agujero*, Fr. *aiguillier* (Meyer-Lübke, REW, #121, p. 9). For **acuc(u)lat*>It. *agucchia*, cf. Pei, *Italian Language*, p. 63.

[21] Cf. *calida non calda* in the Appendix Probi.

[22] For the triple development of cl. Latin *tegula* to It. *tegola*, *tegghia* and *teglia*, cf. Pei, *Italian Language*, p. 56.

It is definitely a popular phenomenon and goes much further in French and Spanish than it does in Italian, where cultured and urban influences in pre-Romance times appear to have been fairly strong (p. 37).

This statement seems to be in conflict with the conclusions reached by Cross who postulates a lack of noticeable difference in syncope throughout Romania (cf. *supra*, p. 267).

In his study on the inscriptions from *Gaul*, Pirson already raises the question of a possible dialectal differentiation between the area of *Gaul* and the rest of the Roman world, when he states

> Le provençal et le français se différencient surtout des autres langues romanes en ce qu'ils ont généralement supprimé toutes les voyelles posttoniques ou protoniques non initiales. On est, par conséquent, en droit de se demander si une certaine prédilection pour les formes syncopées ne distingait pas déjà le latin de la Gaule du latin des autres provinces (p. 48).

The French scholar has to leave the question open, since his study is not based on comparative data but he, nevertheless, suggests that a comparative study of inscriptional material and other Vulgar Latin texts might supply the answer as to whether «les inscriptions de Gaule renferment un nombre relativement plus considérable de formes syncopées» (p. 49).

Cross, as we have seen, has undertaken to supply an answer to this question as regards inscriptional material but it would seem to us that his conclusions might be re-examined. Indeed, this scholar bases his thesis on actual syncopated forms found in the inscriptions from all provinces of the Roman world, and to that extent his findings would seem to be accurate. Nevertheless, it would seem to us that syncope is closely related to the weakening of the vowels in intertonic and penult positions, a phenomenon that, from about the sixth century on, is most marked in the area of *Gaul* — as illustrated by the frequent *e* spelling for Latin /ĭ/ and *o* spelling for Latin /ŭ/ in these positions — and less so in *Northern Italy* and the *Iberian Peninsula*, while in the rest of the *Italian* area (including *Rome*) it is much less frequent. (Cf. *supra*, pp. 151, 154, 212/213, 214/215).

Since this strong paroxytonic trend observed in the area of *Gaul* is, we believe, closely related to and, indeed, inseparable from the phenomenon of syncope, especially as regards the general «agreement as to the loss of the vowel of middle syllable or proparoxytones» (Cross, p. 93), the conclusions of Cross would seem to need modification to the effect that, at least as far as our inscriptional material goes, the syncopating trend is indeed most marked in *Gaul* and that *Rome* does lag behind.[23]

4. *Anaptyxis (Vowel Epenthesis)*

This phenomenon, the opposite of syncope, is due to the speaker's desire to avoid a difficult consonant cluster by introducing a «parasitic» vowel between two consonants to facilitate pronunciation.

For the use of an epenthetic vowel in the older Latin loanwords from Greek and in archaic Latin, in general, mainly between a stop and a lateral, e.g. I.E.*-*tlo*>Lat. -*clo,* cf. Lindsay, p. 145 ff. For the subsequent syncope of many originally anaptyctic forms (cf. *stabulum non stablum* in the Appendix Probi), cf. Kieckers, p. 74. For the widespread phenomenon of anaptyxis in Oscan, often accompanied by syncope, cf. Carl D. Buck, *A Grammar of Oscan and Umbrian* (Boston, 1904), p. 50 ff.

As regards the phenomenon of anaptyxis in the Vulgar Latin period, Sommer notes that

> Die spätere Volkssprache zeigt in weiterem Umfang Anaptyxe, wobei die Färbung des neuen Vokals oft durch die benachbarten Silben bestimmt wird: ... (p. 139).

and offers examples like *cerescenti* (CIL III 4908a), *digina* (CIL VI 25741) and *reipubulice* (XII 5519) from inscriptional material.

A few examples can also be found in our material, although the occurrence of this phenomenon is far from frequent.

A. *Iberian Peninsula.*

The form *offeret* occurs quite frequently throughout our material from this area. Even though at first sight it might be taken for an

---

[23] Cross, indeed, states that «Rome by no means lags behind Gaul» in the matter of the loss of the penult vowel (*loc. cit.*).

example of anaptyxis, we rather believe that it is to be interpreted as an analogical third person singular present active indicative form.

B. *Gaul*

The following spellings were found in this area:

(a) *Narbonensis*: *tempulo* (D1303, ca. V cent.)
(b) *Lugdunensis*: *domesitiqus* (D44, ca. V. cent.)
  Dafinis (D3080N)
  reqisicit (D3566N); *requiesecit* (D3543A)

Pei notes that in his Northern French texts anaptyxis is fairly general (p. 130) and that a conflict may have existed between syncope and anaptyxis in the formative period of Romance, which was resolved, in Northern France «into a victory for syncope and the almost total disappearance of anaptyxis» (p. 132). Our material from *Lugdunensis* would seem to show this anaptyctic trend observed by this scholar.

C. *Italy*

(a) *Northern*: *geloriam, facoletaten* (D811c)
  predicabili discipulinae (D4324)
(b) *Central*: *sεpitε* (=*septem*) (D4011)
(c) *Southern*: No example.

D. *Rome*

There are only two examples found in this area:

superistitem (D1464 a. 380);
quiesquenet (D3095A)

Quoting the Italian scholar Bertoni, Pei, *Texts,* informs us that «anaptyxis is a very widespread and very ancient phenomenon in the south-central Italian dialects» (p. 132). While there is no question that it is a very widespread phenomenon in modern Southern Italian dialects, [24] our material does not give any evidence of its extension in Vulgar Latin; if anything, and keeping in mind the ratio of inscriptional material from the various areas under study, it would seem that the strongest anaptyctic trend obtained in the *Lugdunensis*.

---

[24] Cf. Pei, *Italian Language*, p. 157.

PART III

SUMMARY OF FINDINGS AND CONCLUSION

In may be convenient at this point to summarize the phenomena found in our inscriptional material and to bring under one heading the conclusions reached in the body of the work.

I. Accented Vowels (pp. 41-101)

1. In both open and closed syllables Latin /ă/ gives no evidence of any change.

2.1 Latin /ĕ/ in open syllable remains unchanged and there is no evidence of diphthongization.

2.2 In closed syllable, an inconclusive example of a possible diphthongization was found in *Baetica*. In the areas of *Gaul* and *Italy* (including *Rome*) there are no indications of diphthongization but sporadic *i* spellings occur, particularly before the /nt/ consonant group. A sporadic *i* spelling for Latin /ĕ/ in monosyllables (e.g. *et*) may be due to proclitic position.

3.1 Examples of *i* spellings for Latin /ē/ in open syllable are found in all areas; our percentage figures would seem to indicate that the area of the *Lugdunensis* —with 15.3 % in IV/V century and 27.2 % in VI/VII century material— is most «innovating» in this respect.

3.2 In closed syllable we also find the greatest number of deviations in the area of Gaul, with percentage figures in IV/V century material from both *Narbonensis* and *Lugdunensis* as high as 46.1 % and 31.6 %, respectively. During the same period, we find 5.1 % *i* spellings in the *Northern Italian* area and 9.0 % in fifth century material from *Rome*, while significant deviations from the rest of *Italy* do not seem to occur before the sixth century. There are no significant deviations from the *Iberian* area. These figures would, furthermore seem to show that Latin /ē/ in closed syllable was more likely to be spelled with *i* than in open syllable.

Significant deviations for Latin /ē/ in monosyllables occur only in the area of *Rome* where *se* changes to *si* in a ratio of 4:3 in VI/VII century material.

4.1 The most significant percentage figures showing *e* spelling for Latin /ĭ/ in open syllable are found in the area of *Gaul* (40.6 % and 37.5 % in VI/VII century material from *Narbonensis* and *Lugdunensis*, respectively). In the *Italian* area (including *Rome*) the highest percentage of deviations is found in the *Northern* region, while in the *Iberian* area the *Tarraconensis* would seem to point to a more frequent *e* spelling than the other regions.

4.2 In closed syllable the area of *Gaul* would again seem to set itself apart from the others as far as frequency of deviations go.

4.3 An occasional *e* spelling for Latin /ĭ/ in monosyllabic words, particularly the preposition *in*, is found here and there, without limitation as to a particular area.

4.4 Hiatus /ĭ/ very seldom is spelled with *e*.

The summary table concerning the merger of Latin /ē/ and /ĭ/ seems to indicate quite clearly that by the fifth century this merger is an accomplished fact in the area of *Gaul*, with a better than 15 % differential over most of the *Italian* and *Iberian* areas. Within the *Italian* area (including *Rome*) the *Northern* region is about 5 % ahead of the others for the same period, while in IV/VI century material from the *Iberian* area the *Tarraconensis* (particularly the eastern part since most of our inscriptions come from the *Tarragona* area) shows a lead of about 4 % over the others. (The fact that the fourth, fifth and sixth centuries are taken together for lack of material makes exact comparison with *Gaul, Italy* and *Rome* difficult).

5.1 Latin /ī/ in open syllable seems quite stable.

5.2 Isolated instances of an *e* spelling for Latin /ī/ in closed syllable occur in *Gaul* and in the general *Italian* area but seem to be limited to *vexit* and *benegnus* only.

6.1 Latin /ŏ/ in open syllable remains unchanged and there is no evidence of diphthongization.

6.2 In closed syllable sporadic *u* spellings for Latin /ŏ/ are found mainly in the *Italian* area, particularly before a nasal consonant.

7.1 Instances of *u* spelling for Latin /ō/ in open syllable are less frequent than the *i* spelling for /ē/ in the same position. By the sixth century deviation figures seem to be significant enough to point to a merger of Latin /ō/ and /ŭ/ in all areas, except the seemingly conservative *Southern Italian* and *Iberian* ones. It may be worth noting, however, that the only area in which there seems to be a significant percentage of *u* spellings for /ō/ before the sixth century is the *Central Italian*, suggesting that the back vowels may have merged earlier in this particular region than in the others.

7.2 The occurrence of Latin /ō/ in closed syllable is very infrequent. Sporadic *u* spellings found in the areas of *Gaul* and *Italy* (including *Rome*) occur before a nasal consonant, particularly the /ns/ group.

7.3 Latin /ō/ in monosyllabic words, particularly the demonstrative *hōc* (ablative) and possessives, occasionally appears spelled with *u*. With a single exception (*No. Italy*) this phenomenon seems to be limited to the area of *Gaul*, particularly the *Lugdunensis*.

8.1 Latin /ŭ/ in open syllable appears very often spelled with *o* in the area of *Gaul* and the *Tarraconensis* (although reservations must be made in connection with the latter on account of a small sampling and the fact that some deviations occur on the same inscription), with 52.4 % and 33.3 % deviations in VI/VII century material from the *Narbonensis* and *Lugdunensis* areas, respectively. In the general *Italian* area, although occurrences of this vowel are rather infrequent, there are few deviations.

8.2 In closed syllable, Latin /ŭ/ is rather infrequently spelled with *o*. This spelling is not found in the *Central* and *Southern Italian* areas nor in those of *Baetica* and *Lusitania*, the last three being particularly conservative since no deviations were found in open syllable either.

8.3 The preposition *cum*, being virtually the only instance of Latin /ŭ/ in monosyllables, frequently appears written as *com* or *con* in the whole *Italian* area, once in *Tarraconensis* but is always correctly spelled in the area of *Gaul*.

The summary table on the merger of Latin /ō/ and /ŭ/ would seem to indicate that in the area of *Gaul* this merger is an accomplished fact by the sixth century, as evidenced by an increase in percentage figures (18.5 % and 19.3 % in *Narbonensis* and *Lugdunensis*, respectively) as against the previous century (3.4 % and 4.3 %). A comparable, albeit less of a jump is also noticeable in the *Northern Italian* area (1.3 % vs. 6.6 %) and *Rome* (2.6 % vs. 6.0 %), while in the *Central Italian* area the consistently increasing pattern of percentage figures (5.5 % — 7.4 % — 9.3 %) would seem to point to the possibility of a merger of these vowels at an earlier time than in other areas. The most conservative area regarding this phenomenon is *Southern Italy*, with *Baetica* and *Lusitania* a close second. The situation in *Tarraconensis* is somewhat inconclusive, seeing that some deviations occur in the same inscription; however, it would seem that of the *Spanish* areas it is the least conservative.

The purpose of the table comparing percentage figures obtained for the relationship of the merger of Latin /ē/ and /ĭ/, on the one hand, and Latin /ō/ and /ŭ/, on the other hand, is to attempt to ascertain not only the chronology of merger but also to test the widely accepted theory to the effect that front vowels universally merged before back vowels in those areas of Romania where these mergers took place. Our conclusion based on the evidence offered by our material is that the merger of the front vowels does not seem to have preceded that of the back vowels in all areas.

9. In both open and closed syllables Latin /ū/ generally remains unchanged. The form *orna* found in several areas may be due to analogy, while the *o* spelling before a nasal, found in the *Northern Italian* area, is said to be a regionalism that has survived there to this day.

SUMMARY OF FINDINGS AND CONCLUSIONS 279

II. The Unaccented Vowels (pp. 102-239)

1. Latin /ă/ appears written as *a* in our material, except in a few cases when preceded by a palatal consonant, such as *jenuarius*, a form that is not limited to any specific area.

2.1 In the initial position, Latin /ĕ/ occasionally appears spelled with *i*, primarily in the areas of *Rome* and *Southern Italy* (taking also non-dated inscriptions into account) but deviations do not seem to be significant in terms of percentage figures. A few examples of *i* spelling in the *Iberian* area may be due to umlaut.

{ 2.2 Sporadic *i* spellings in both intertonic and penult positions
  2.4 occur here and there but deviations are not significant enough to draw any conclusions as to their frequency in one area over another.

2.3 For Latin /ĕ/ in hiatus we find a few *i* spellings in the *Central, Southern Italian* areas and *Rome*, in both dated and non-dated material. It must be pointed out, however, that our material from both *Gaul* and the *Iberian Peninsula* is very scanty and makes any conclusion in this connection very difficult.

2.5 In the final syllable (non-morphological endings), Latin /ĕ/ is spelled with *i* in several non-dated inscriptions from *Lugdunensis*, which may point to the fact that in this position and in this area Latin /ĕ/ was likely to merge with /i/.

2.6 In the nominative and accusative singular of third declension nouns sporadic *i* spellings occur, especially in the area of *Lugdunensis*. As to the *i* spelling in the ablative singular, of which a number of examples were found, particularly in the area of *Rome*, this would appear to be the reflection of a morphological phenomenon, namely a hesitation between the ablative ending in /ĕ/ and /ī/ (of I-stem nouns and adjectives).

2.7 The *et* ending of the third person singular present active indicative of second conjugation verbs often appears spelled *it* in all areas where verb forms belonging to this class are found.

Since it was also observed that the *it* ending of the third person singular present active indicative of third/fourth conjugation verbs often appears spelled with *et* (the trend being towards the replacement of *it* by *et*), it would seem that this hesitation reflects a free variation of two formal devices. In *Lugdunensis*, furthermore, the third person singular present active subjunctive form appears as *it*.

3.1 Except for the *Iberian* area, an occasional *i* spelling for Latin /ē/ in initial position is found everywhere. However, the only clear pattern of what would seem to be a progressive merging of the front vowels appears in the area of *Rome* (5.8 % — 9.4 % — 13.6 %).

3.2 Latin /ē/ in intertonic position occurs very infrequently. A sporadic *i* spelling is found in the *Southern Italian* area and *Rome*.

3.3 In the final syllable (non-morphological endings) there are a number of *i* spellings for Latin /ē/ in the area of *Gaul*, particularly the *Narbonensis*, although an occasional adverbial ending also appears as *i* in a few inscriptions from the *Italian* area.

3.4 The most noteworthy deviation in morphological endings is the spelling *is* for *es* in the accusative plural of third declension nouns, found in all areas, except the *Baetica* and *Lusitania*. An extension of the *is* ending to the nominative plural occurs in the areas of *Gaul* and *Italy*, particularly the area of *Rome* where, despite the infrequent occurrence of this case, the number of deviations would seem to be important enough to suggest that this morphological extension may be the origin of the plural of third declension nouns in modern Italian. The fifth declension ablative singular in /ē/ generally appears spelled with *e*.

3.5 Although verb forms ending in /ē/ are very infrequent in our material, a few *is* spellings for *es* (in the second person singular present indicative active of second conjugation and the second person singular present active subjunctive of first conjugation verbs) are found in non-dated inscriptions from the *Italian* area also.

SUMMARY OF FINDINGS AND CONCLUSIONS 281

Our comparative table concerning the treatment of /ĕ/ and /ē/ in unstressed syllable, on the basis of which it was attempted to ascertain whether a separate treatment of these vowels was justified or whether, as some scholar suggested, the merger of these vowels had occurred at such an early time in the postclassical period that a separate treatment is unnecessary, would seem to suggest the following:

(a) A separate treatment seems to be justified only in the *initial* syllable, particularly in the area of *Rome,* where there appears to be a clear pattern of separation between /ĕ/ and /ē/ at least through the fifth century, and possibly even later, as reflected in the frequency of *i* spellings for the latter vowel, as against few deviations for /ĕ/ (our criterion for establishing a qualitative difference between the originally long and short Latin vowels). A similar situation may also obtain for the areas of *Gaul* and *Northern Italy,* although our material from these areas is not sufficient to draw definite conclusions in this respect.

(b) In the *final* syllable, several *i* spellings for Latin /ē/ as against none for /ĕ/ may point to a qualitative difference between originally short and long vowels in the *Narbonensis,* as late as the sixth century.

(c) Apart from the exceptions noted under (a) and (b), our material does not yield sufficient evidence to justify separate treatment of Latin /ĕ/ and /ē/ in unstressed syllable.

4.1 Latin /ĭ/ in the initial syllable appears spelled with *e* mainly in the areas of *Gaul, Northern Italy,* and *Rome.* Examples of deviations in the other areas are mostly limited to foreign (Germanic) proper names.

4.2 In both intertonic and penult positions the inscriptions from
4.3 *Gaul* show the greatest number of *e* spellings for Latin /ĭ/ with, in the sixth century, 28.0 % and 46.8 %, respectively, in the *Narbonensis* and 44.4 % and 55.5 %, respectively, in the *Lugdunensis*. It is likely, as has been suggested, that these figures reflect a weakening of the vowel in these position into a *shwa,* as a prelude to total disappearance by syncope. A similar trend, particularly in the penult, is also

found in the *Northern Italian* area —which, in this respect, seems to set itself apart from the rest of *Italy* and *Rome*— as well as the *Iberian* area. This indication of a very important phonological rift within the so-called Western Romance languages, i.e. the essentially proparoxytonic syllable structure of standard Italian and Sardinian as against the paroxytonic structure of the Northern Italian dialects and languages like Spanish, Portuguese, Catalan, Provençal and Old French (modern French being essentially oxytonic), would seem to us to be the most significant dialectal feature that can be detected in our inscriptional material.

4.4 Latin /ĭ/ in hiatus very seldom appears spelled with *e*.

4.5 In the final syllable (non-morphological endings), the *e* spelling for Latin /ĭ/ is found only in the area of *Gaul*. In view of the fact that both /ĕ/ and /ē/ were found spelled with *i* in this area also, there would seem to be good evidence, for the phonological merger of these phonemes in this position, even in the case of morphological endings.

4.6 There are instances of frequent *es* spelling for *is* in the nominative and genitive singular of third declension nouns and adjectives, particularly in the areas of *Gaul* and *Italy* (including *Rome*).

4.7 On the free variation of the ending *it* and *et* in the third person singular present active indicative of second/third/fourth conjugation verbs, cf. *supra*, No. 2.7. It was also found that the replacement of the ending *it* by *et* is much more frequent in the present tense, except for the areas of *Gaul* and *Northern Italy*, where this replacement is quite frequent in the third person singular of the perfect active indicative as well.

5.1 Latin /ī/ is stable in all positions, save for morphological endings.

5.2 An occasional *e* spelling for the genitive singular of second declension nouns and adjectives is found only in the area of *Gaul*. Noteworthy also is the occasional appearance of an *o* ending in this case in the areas of *Gaul, Northern Italy* and *Rome* (and a single example from the *Central Italian* area), pointing, it would seem, to the creation of a single

SUMMARY OF FINDINGS AND CONCLUSIONS 283

oblique case in the singular of these nouns and adjectives. An occasional *e* spelling for the dative and ablative singular (I-stem nouns and adjectives), occurring in all areas, would also seem to point in the direction of a morphological merger of these two cases and the concomitant development of a single oblique case.

The accusative plural ending in *is* (totally absent in the *Iberian* area) very frequently appears spelled *es,* but it is worthy of note that there is a sharp decrease of deviations in most of the *Italian* area (*Central, Southern* and *Rome*) over the centuries, so that by the sixth century the *is* spelling is the only one found. Since, during a comparable period, there are frequent *is* spellings for *es* in both nominative and accusative plural of third declension nouns and adjectives (cf. *supra,* No. 3.5), the facts would seem to suggest the morphological extension of the *is* ending to the detriment of *es*. The correlation between the frequency of this phenomenon and later developments in standard Italian, furthermore, would seem to lend strong support to Pei's theory to the effect that the /-i/ outcome of the third declension Italian nouns is the «continuator of classical Latin -īs.»

6.1 Latin /ŏ/ in the initial syllable very infrequently appears spelled with *u*.

6.2 In the intertonic position, the sporadic *u* spelling appears mostly in proper names beginning with *Theo-* and may be a reflection of the semi-vocalization of Latin /ŏ/ in hiatus.

6.3 The few *u* spellings in the penult, which occur in the Greek loan words *diaconus* and *episcopus,* may be an attempt to represent the close quality of Greek *omicron*. A couple of deviations in Latin words appear in the *Lugdunensis* only.

6.4 Occurrences of Latin /ŏ/ in the final syllable (non-morphological endings) are very infrequent. The only *u* spelling appears in the numeral *quattur* (alternating with *quator*) in the area of *Rome*.

6.5 Latin /ŏ/ in noun-adjective endings is frequently spelled with *u* in forms of the *or* type in the area of *Gaul*. The dated examples do not occur before the VI/VII centuries, so that this phenomenon may, indeed, reflect the blurring of final vowels in the sixth and seventh centuries, as suggested by some scholars. The *u* spelling also appears sporadically in the *Italian* area (including *Rome*) but it is limited to words where there is little doubt of analogical support from second declension nouns.

7.1 A few examples of *u* spelling for Latin /ō/ are found in the areas of *Gaul* and *Rome*, in the latter particularly before /r/ plus consonant and the consonant group /ns/.

7.2 Occurrences of Latin /ō/ in intertonic position are infrequent. Except for the *Iberian* area, a few *u* spellings occur here and there, but it may be worth noting that the only occurrences of this vowel in dated material from *Lugdunensis* appears spelled with *u*.

7.3 Occurrences of this vowel in the final syllable (non-morphological endings) are very infrequent and there are no deviations.

The attempt to ascertain a qualitative difference between Latin /ŏ/ and /ō/ in the unstressed syllable by means of a similar comparison employed in connection with /ĕ/ and /ē/ (cf. *supra*, p. 281) has yielded only negative results. There would seem to be no valid reason, therefore, not to treat the originally long and short /ō/ under the same heading in unstressed syllable.

7.4 The most noteworthy phenomenon involving Latin /ō/ in morphological endings is the frequent *us* spelling for *os* in the accusative plural of second declension nouns and adjectives. Except for two examples from the *Iberian* area, this phenomenon is very widespread in the areas of *Gaul* and *Italy* (including *Rome*), possibly reflecting an intermediate confusion, on the formal level, due to the declensional shift of nouns and adjectives from the fourth to the second class, which is said to have taken place in the post-classical period. In the ablative singular, the *u* spelling for /ō/ also occurs with some frequency in all areas, except *Baetica* and *Lusitania*. Since whenever Latin /ō/ appears in a dative case function it is virtually never represented by *u*, there seems to be little doubt that this phenomenon is of a morphological nature and would seem to reflect the neutralization of a formal opposition between the second and fourth declension ablative singular, as a result of the general reshuffling of the classical system of declension.

8.1 Latin /ŭ/ in the initial position infrequently appears spelled with *o*; furthermore, some deviations occur only in Germanic proper names.

8.2 The *o* spelling for Latin /ŭ/ in the intertonic position occurs with some frequency in the areas of *Gaul* (particularly *Narbonensis*), *Northern Italy* and *Rome*.

8.3 In the penult, the *o* spelling, which occurs almost exclusively in words of the *ulus* type, is particularly frequent in *Gaul*, with 70.9 % and 54.8 % deviations in VI/VII century material from *Narbonensis* and *Lugdunensis*, respectively, with *Northern Italy* a fairly close second. In the *Iberian* area this spelling appears with some frequency (especially in *Baetica*), whereas the rest of the *Italian* area and *Rome* seem to be quite conservative. In view of the parallelism with the treatment of Latin /ĭ/ in the same position, particularly for what concerns the area of *Gaul*, we believe that this orthographic confusion reflects a weakening of the penult as a first step towards syncope, cf. *supra*, Nos. 4.2/4.3.

8.4 Latin /ŭ/ in hiatus is occasionally spelled with *o* and, in some instances, also disappears altogether, especially in the form *febrarias*, which is found throughout our material. The loss of this vowel before an unstressed /u/ (and even /o/ or /a/) (e.g. *mortus* - *morta*) is amply attested in *Roman* inscriptions, while short forms of the possessive (*sus*, *tum*, *so*) are found in several areas, although they are entirely absent in *Gaul*.

8.5 In both *Gaul* and *Northern Italy* there is an occasional *o* spelling for Latin /ŭ/ in the final syllable of non-morphological endings, particularly in the adverb *minus*, appearing generally as *menos*.

8.6 An occasional *o* spelling for /ŭ/, i.e. the spelling *os* for *us* and *om* for *um* in the nominative and accusative singular of second declension nouns and adjectives is found primarily in the areas of *Gaul* and *Northern Italy* where this spelling also occurs in non-morphological endings.

The *us* ending of the nominative is occasionally replaced by *o* in virtually all areas under study, pointing, it would seem, to a morphological extension of the oblique case in the singular. However, this phenomenon is very sporadic and our figures would seem to indicate that the *us* ending in the nominative singular function is still quite stable throughout the period covered by our inscriptional material.

An orthographic *o* is occasionally found for the *um* ending in the classical accusative singular (direct object function) in *Tarraconensis*, *Gaul* and *Rome*. Although the occurrence of this case is far from frequent, our figures would seem to indicate that this apparent extension of the oblique case may have been more widespread in the area of *Gaul* than one might think in the light of the subsequent development of a two-case system in Old French and Old Provençal.

The spelling *oro* for *orum* in the genitive plural of second declension nouns and adjectives is found mainly in the area of *Rome*, with an occasional occurrence in the *Northern* and *Central Italian* areas as well. This phenomenon would seem to be a characteristic feature of inscriptions from these areas. The purely morphological phenomenon of the use of the ending *ent* for *unt* in the third person plural present indicative active of third/fourth conjugation verbs is attested in all areas in both dated and non-dated inscriptions. In view of the fact that in these same areas it was also found that the third person singular ending appears as *et* for *it*, i.e. a classical Latin second declension for a third declension ending, an analogical extension of the free variation of two formal devices in the singular to the plural may be envisaged. A couple of examples of *or* spelling for *ur* in the present passive indicative were found in the area of *Gaul* where, conversely, the nominal suffix *or* occasionally also appeared as *ur*.

9. Latin /ū/, except for morphological endings, occurs almost exclusively in the initial syllable. A sporadic *o* spelling is found in proper names in the *Iberian* area; the same spelling before a nasal consonant found in the *Northern Italian* area may reflect a regionalism.

9.1 Latin /ū/ occurs most frequently in the accusative plural of fourth declension nouns and the sporadic *os* spelling for *us*, found in most areas, would seem to be an analogical extension of a second declension ending, as a result of the declensional shift in post-classical Latin already referred to, cf. *supra*, No. 7.5. This same analogical pull would also seem to be responsible for the hesitation between *o* and *u* spellings in the ablative singular.

III. Diphthongs (pp. 240-262)

(1.1 Our figures would seem to show rather clearly that by the
(1.2 time of the appearance of Christian inscriptions the diphthong /aj/, spelled *ae*, has merged with original Latin /ĕ/ and, occasionally, also /ē/, in both stressed and unstressed syllables. The sporadic use of *qui* for *quae*, i.e. the morphological replacement of the feminine relative pronoun by the masculine form, is attested as early as the middle of the fourth century in Roman inscriptions. This use of *qui* with a feminine antecedent seems to be particularly widespread in the areas of *Gaul* and *No. Italy* by the fifth century, increasing in frequency by the sixth century also in the rest of the *Italian* area. Our material from the Iberian area is extremely scanty, although the use of *qui* for *quae* is attested in the *Tarraconensis* region.

1.3 The morphological extension of the accusative plural *as* ending of first declension nouns and adjectives to the nominative form in *ae (e)*, which is said to be characteristic of the so-called «Western» Romance languages, seems to have been a very widespread phenomenon, encompassing areas otherwise classified under the «Eastern» group where final /s/ has not survived, e.g. the area of *Rome*, suggesting the loss of a formal opposition between the classical nominative and accusative, with the *as* ending taking over both subject and direct object functions.

2. The occurrence of the diphthong /oj/, spelled *oe*, is most infrequent in both stressed and unstressed syllables, but the occasional *e* spellings would seem to point in the direction of a monophthongization also.

3. Except for certain proper names where the reduction of the diphthong /aw/ seems to represent an earlier alternative (e.g. *Claudius* — *Clodius*), no indication is found in our material to the effect that it had undergone any change.
In the unstressed syllable the reduction of /aw/ to /a/ occurs in the form *agustus* (either used as a proper name or the month of August) exclusively, in all areas under study.

IV. *Some Vocalic Phenomena* (pp. 263-273)

1. Prothesis is well attested in our material from *Italy*, particularly the area of *Rome*, while in the *Iberian* area this phenomenon is quite infrequent and it is just about totally absent in *Gaul*. Our *Italian* material clearly seems to point to a preference of /i/ as a prothetic vowel (as borne out by subsequent developments), whereas in the material from the *Iberian Peninsula* one finds both /i/ and /e/. On the basis of our material, no statement can be made with respect to *Gaul*.

2. Apheresis is very rare and is shown only in two examples from *Baetica* and *Central Italy*, respectively.

3. Syncope is found in all areas under study; except for the area of *Rome*, it is not particularly widespread, although the phonological environment in which this phenomenon occurs is the same as that observed in the other areas, so that it is only the number of similar examples that is greater in this area. (For the weakening of the vowel in intertonic and penult positions, indicating strong syncopating trend, cf. *supra*, Nos. 4.2/4.4 and 8.2/8.3).

4. Anaptyxis is illustrated by a few examples, but the phenomenon is far from frequent. On the basis of our evidence, the strongest anaptyctic trend would seem to obtain in *Lugdunensis*.

Looking back over our inscriptional material, it would seem that it can furnish information as to

(a) changes that the Latin language may have undergone with respect to classical standards, i.e. the Latin reflected in the authors of, say, the first century B.C. and the Augustan age, and

(b) closeness to classical Latin, as evidenced by traditional spelling.

Some areas, such as *Baetica* and *Lusitania*, would, indeed, seem to be quite conservative as far as closeness to classical Latin standards go. Whether this is due to the supposed «purity of Latin in Spain»[1] or to a particularly careful training of its scribes and stonecutters, or both, is a matter of conjecture. In any event, it would seem fair to state that even inscriptions of the funeral type, considered to be the most «popular» in nature,[2] are, on the whole, couched in correct Latin. While it may be an exaggeration to state, as Cross does, that the language of inscriptions is not diferent from Cicero's literary prose (p. 98) (except, possibly, for official inscriptions), it is, nevertheless, true that the language found in our material from all areas is such as to be perfectly understandable even to a person trained in Ciceronian school Latin exclusively.

As to the question whether the inscriptions represent the actual spoken language of the people or only an artificial written language, the views expressed by Cross seem to be quite appropriate:

> Now, in the inscriptions either we have the popular speech or we have not the popular speech. If the inscriptions do represent the actual spoken language of the people, then both the popular speech and the literary language are virtually identical. If the inscriptions are not monuments of the actual speech, then we have nothing but meagre and scattered indications of that elusive tongue. But the inscriptions must represent some language once in use. This language can hardly have been totally artificial and purely «literary.» (pp. 99/100).

Would, indeed, a grieving parent or spouse really have resorted to an «artificial» and «literary» language or would he have rather written, or cause someone to write, the way he would have expressed himself in the spoken language, with due allowance for traditional orthography and technical phraseology?

---

[1] Cf. M. N. Ramsey who in this Introduction to his *Textbook of Modern Spanish* (revised by R. K. Spaulding) (New York, 1956) states: «Latin of the purest type was spoken in Spain» (p. xii).

[2] Cf. Vives, p. 6.

The above summary would seem to show that, despite the strongly formulaic nature of our inscriptional material and the fact that deviations from the classical Latin norm do appear to be more or less identical in all areas, it *is* possible to cull information as to the language in which Christian inscriptions are written, by means of the kind of statistical analysis that we have attempted to undertake. Unsatisfactory as this method may be in relation to other documentary material which offers more abundant language, it, nevertheless, does seem to enable us to detect certain features (or shall we call them «mistakes»?) that occur more frequently in one area as against another, thus pointing to regional differentiations in the Vulgar Latin period covered by this material, i.e. roughly the fourth, fifth and sixth centuries.

* * *

As stated in our Introduction, the primary purpose of this study is to investigate dialectal differences as they may be reflected in the orthography of Latin Christian prose inscriptions, as far as the vocalism is concerned. Indeed, the problem surrounding what v. Wartburg has called «die Ausgliederung der romanischen Sprachräume» and its ancillary, the local variations in Latin, particularly the Vulgar Latin of the imperial and post-imperial periods has given rise to a great deal of discussion and theorizing, ranging all the way from an attempt to trace differences in the Romance Languages to the influence of Italic dialects (Mohl) to a general unity of the Vulgar Latin *koiné* until at least the end of the eighth century of our era (Muller).[3]

There is little doubt that regional differences in speech must have arisen in the various Provinces of the Roman Empire virtually as soon as the Latin language became the vehicle of communication, if for no other reason than that

> dialect varieties are inherent in all speaking groups.... due to the natural tendency of language, which is centrifugal....[4]

---

[3] The controversy, of course, is far from settled. «Il problema del passaggio del latino al neolatino resta sempre quello piu importante e piu difficile della linguistica romanza» is the opening sentence of the article by Alfredo Schiaffini. Incidentally, his article is of interest also on account of the rich bibliographical references.

[4] Pei, *Linguistics*, p. 146.

St. Jerome himself testifies to changes taking place daily when he says, in his letter to the Galatians, «...et ipsa latinitas et regionibus quotidie mutetur et tempore.» [5]

The question may be legitimately raised, nevertheless, as to just how important these dialectal differences were; for there are degrees of regionalism as, for instance, between a speaker of New York and Boston, on the one hand, and a Milanese and Neapolitan dialect speaker, on the other hand. It is this degree of difference which seems to prompt Väänänen to ask:

> Mais s'agissait-il vraiment de différences telles qu'on pourrait les qualifier de dialectes? (p. 21)

seeing that, despite regionalism like the use of *apud* in the sense of 'with' in Merovingian texts (surviving in Old Fr. as *ab, od,* Prov. *ab*), or *iumentum* 'mare' (cf. Fr. *jument*), or else *tata* 'father' and *monumentum* 'tomb' found in Balkan inscriptions, surviving in Rumanian as *tată* and *mormînt,* [6]

> ce qui caractérise ces textes [viz. those of the «époque impériale et surtout du haut moyen âge], c'est le parallélisme des particularités populaires destinées à survivre en roman. (*ibid*).

This fact was already underscored by Schuchardt when he said

> Dieses [viz. das rustike Latein] erscheint nämlich auf den Denkmälern aller Gegenden eigentlich immer also ein und dasselbe. (p. 92),

and it now seems generally recognized that so-called Vulgar Latin texts give little or no indication of local variations until about the seventh century. [7]

---

[5] Quotation taken from Löfstedt, *Late Latin,* p. 39.

[6] In his discussion of the Rumanian forms, Väänänen refers to the study of H. Mihăescu on the Latin of the Danube Provinces (*Limba latina in provinciile dunarene ale imperiului roman.* Bucarest, 1960). It must be pointed out, however, that *monumentum* in the meaning of 'tomb' is found in Christian epitaphs from all areas (cf. Diehl, ILCV, Vol. III, pp. 555/556) while *tata* is found in inscriptions from *Southern Italy* and *Rome* and is still used in Southern Italian dialects today in the meaning of 'daddy', coexisting with forms derived from Lat. *pater.* In Rumanian, however, the latter has been displaced by *tată,* cf. Rohlfs, *Diferenciación,* pp. 23/24.

[7] Cf. Löfstedt, *Late Latin,* p. 50 ff. Let it be said, however, that this scholar bases himself almost exclusively on syntactic and lexical phenomena.

If we have, nevertheless, attempted to learn something about local variations as they may be reflected in the orthography of inscriptional material, it is because we believe that these are primarily differences in frequency of occurrence of the same type of phenomenon, provided both the correct forms and deviations therefrom are compared in various areas. It is the failure to show this kind of relationship among the various provinces of the Roman Empire that would seem to weaken Sittl's thesis of an «African,» «Gaulish,» «Hispanic,» etc. Latin, which has been subjected to searching criticisms and nowadays seems to have little more than historical interest. [8]

At the opposite end of the pole, so to speak, there is the theory of the Franco-American scholar H. F. Muller, who suggested in his *Chronology* that Vulgar Latin had remained the spoken language of the whole of Western Romania until well into the latter part of the eighth century and that at this late period there still existed

> a general unity of speech with a few regional characteristics which do not by any means interfere with the unity of language but are perfectly compatible with it. (p. 53).

His son, B. Löfstedt, on the other hand, specifically underscores the same unity in matters of orthography, (p. 209).

[8] Cf. Wilhelm Hartel's review in *Philologischer Anzeiger*, Band XIII, Supplementheft II (1883), p. 782 ff.

Sittl's main concern is to demonstrate that some linguistic, particularly syntactical peculiarities in some Late Latin authors like Fronto, Apuleius, Tertullian, etc. are due to their African origin and should be interpreted as good evidence for an African dialectal variant of spoken Latin. His thesis of an «Africitas» was subjected to severe criticism by W. Kroll, «Das afrikanische Latein», *Rheinisches Museum für Philologie*, LII (1897), 569-90, and was shown to be a figment of his imagination. In this connection, cf. also Max Bonnet's comment: «M. Sittl.... a tenté de démontrer l'existence de traits distinctifs du latin des différentes provinces. Il a complètement échoué (*Le latin de Grégoire de Tours* (Paris, 1890), p. 40, note #3).

It does not seem to be generally known that Sittl himself retracted his thesis in his *Jahresbericht*, p. 226, for insufficient sifting of the evidence. A subsequent study of the language of African inscriptions undertaken by Bernhard Kubler («Die lateinische Sprache auf afrikanischen Inschriften», *Archiv für lateinische Lexicographie und Grammatik*, XIII (1893), 162-202 has indeed shown that the evidence yields very little information as to specific «Africanisms.»

As to the extent of these regional features, Muller feels that

> they never went so far as to make the speech of one region difficult to understand for the people of another region... (*ibid.*)

This linguistic unity was a consequence of and closely corresponded to the political and social conditions of Western Romania, the good system of communications and the highly developed commerce between the different towns and regions even after the fall of the Roman Empire, as well as the spiritual unity and cohesion brought about by Christianity, which Muller calls

> the real foundation of the linguistic unity of Romania through the whole Merovingian period. (p. 26) [9]

Muller's thesis, which rests on his insistence on the identity of spoken and written language, particularly as reflected in Merovingian documents, [10] advanced at a time when it was the consensus that the fate of Vulgar Latin was subordinated to the existence of the Empire, [11]

---

[9] For a further development of Muller's thesis concerning the influence of Christianity as a factor of linguistic cohesion and the direct relationship between linguistic evolution and social conditions, cf. his *Époque mérovingienne*.

On the importance of Christianity in the historical development of Latin, cf. Löfstedt, *Late Latin*, pp. 68-87, where the important studies by the Dutch scholars Jos. Schrijnen and Christine Mohrmann concerning Christian Latin are discussed.

For the «influenza dissolutrice del cristianesimo», i.e. a view radically opposed to that of Muller, cf. Vidos, pp. 267-274.

[10] For a summary of various theories regarding two conflicting views as to whether the language of these documents is a fair representative of the spoken language or whether it merely represents an artificial mixture of the classical and the popular, written by scribes who were striving to imitate the classical language but unconsciously made «slips» due to the influence of the «vulgar» tongue which they spoke, cf. Pei, *Texts*, p. 352 ff. and Sas, p. 2 ff. Pei concludes that the evidence favors the reliability of his texts from the standpoint of the spoken language, a theory subsequently supported by the latter.

For dissenting views expressed more recently, cf. Löfstedt, *Late Latin*, p. 3 («There could be no sharper contrast than that between the conservative character of officialdom's language and the tendencies of popular speech») and E. Pulgram, *The Tongues of Italy* (Cambridge, Mass., 1958), pp. 311-343, who differentiates between spoken and written Latin.

[11] With the fall of the Roman Empire the erstwhile unity of Vulgar Latin broke up and evolved separately in the various regions of Romania, cf. Bourciez, *Éléments*, 32; v. Wartburg, *Ausgliederung*, p. 65 ff.

gave rise to both favorable and unfavorable critical comment. Despite the acceptance of Muller's views by such eminent names as Meillet, Meyer-Lübke, Pirenne and Lot, [12] they came under sharp attack on the part of a number of scholars, [13] particularly H. Meier, [14] J. Brüch, [15] and more recently, A. Tovar, [16] R. Politzer, [17] and B. E. Vidos, [18] as

---

[12] «...en ce qui concerne la date où s'est brisée l'unité romane, les faits semblent donner raison à l'auteur... les changements qui devaient aboutir à constituer les langues romanes distinctes n'apparaissent dans les documents écrits qu'au VIIIe siècle... M. Muller a réussi ainsi à présenter avec la nuance exacte ce qui s'est passé du VIe au IXe siècle... la christianisation, sur l'importance de laquelle M. Muller a très justement insisté, a sans doute achevé la généralisation de la lingua romana...» (A. Meillet).

«...ein inhaltreiches, anregendes, manches Rätsel lösendes Buch...» (W. Meyer-Lübke).

«Dans la vie courante le latin est encore plus abâtardi que dans la littérature... mais... n'en est pas moins du latin authentique. C'est ce que les lettres appellent le latin rustique. Mais ils s'y prêtent et l'emploient, surtout en Gaule, parce qu'il est la langue populaire, celle de tous... C'est sans doute ce latin-là qu'on enseignait dans les petites écoles... la langue subsiste et c'est elle qui fait, jusque dans le courant du VIIIe siècle, l'unité de la Romania.» (H. Pirenne).

«Le latin parlé avait prodigieusement évolué depuis la fin de l'Empire romain. Or les hommes instruits, même dans le clergé, le prononçaient comme la masse de la population et ils l'écrivaient à peu près comme ils le prononçaient.» (F. Lot).

The quotations are taken from Pei, *A reply to Robert A Hall, Jr.'s Review of* «*The Italian Language*» (Language, 17.3 (1941), 263-269) (New York: by the author, 1945), p. 16, footnote #11.

[13] Cf. *Zeitschrift für romanische Philologie*-Bibliographie. 1927/35, No. 1191.

[14] «Über das Verhältnis des Lateins zu den romanischen Sprachen», *Romanische Forschungen*, LIV (1940), 183-194, where the author seems to take more exception to Muller's insistence on the identity of the spoken and written language based on the Latin of the Merovingian documents, than on the late date of the break-up of Vulgar Latin unity.

[15] *Zeitschrift für französische Sprache und Literatur*, LIV (1931), 357-382. This is, no doubt, the most extensive (and devastating) criticism of Muller's *Chronology*. Essentially, this reviewer reproaches Muller for making aprioristic assumptions and drawing conclusions insufficiently supported by facts and also objects to the emphasis that this scholar places on the cohesive force of Christianity in linguistic matters and «the direct relationship existing between the respective characteristics of the linguistic evolution in each of the main regions of Western Romania and the social conditions prevalent therein» (*Chronology*, p. 7).

[16] «La sonorisation et la chute des intervocaliques, phénomène latin occidental,» *Revue des études latines*, XXIX (1951), p. 106, where this scholar particularly objects to Muller's statement that «no real dialects are to be discovered before the literary period of the Romance languages» (p. 5).

[17] In Politzer's *Romance Trends*, p. 49, discussed *infra*.

a result of which one often reads in manuals, monographs and articles that Muller's theory has been generally rejected by Romance scholars.[19] But is not the fact that this scholar's views are still being discussed, either in connection with the late survival of the Vulgar Latin *koiné* or dialectalization, in itself good evidence that they have left a strong imprint on the thinking of researchers concerned with this crucial, and enigmatic, period of the language?

Speaking of the problem of dialectalization in the Vulgar Latin period, B. Löfstedt makes the following statement:

> Es ist Müller als Verdienst anzurechnen, dass er mit grosser Energie auf diese Einheitlichkeit des späten Lateins sowohl in der Lexikographie und Syntax wie in der Orthographie hingewiesen hat, ... (p. 211).

Nevertheless, this scholar feels that Muller overlooked the fact

> dass es im Mittellatein etwa vom 7. Jh. an trotz allem möglich ist, gewisse Unterschiede aufzuzeigen, die die Differenzierung der rom. Sprachen präludieren, und zwar mit Hilfe der S t a t i s t i k . Wenn auch dies Mittellatein immernoch insofern einheitlich ist, als kaum irgendwelche orthographischen (oder anderen) Abweichungen n u r in einer gewissen Provinz vorkommen, in einer anderen überhaupt nicht, kann man beobachten, dass gewisse «Fehler» im Latein einer Provinz häufiger als in dem einer anderen auftreten. (p. 212).

A comparison of seventh and eighth century Vulgar Latin documents from Italy and France, undertaken by the Politzers,[20] indeed shows dialectal divergences, however small they may be, a fact that would seem to weaken Muller's thesis of a «general unity of speech» through the eighth century. Hence, Politzer's stand:

---

[18] Pp. 210-212. Among his various objections, let us just mention the one which concerns dialectalization: «Il punto più debole linguisticamente della sua argomentazione è tuttavia l'affermazione insostenibile che... in questa κοινή latina volgare non si fossero veramente prodotte differenziazioni degne di considerazione fino alla fine dell'VIII sec....» (pp. 211/212).

[19] Thus Vidos, *loc. cit.;* Sofer, p. 22; Silva Neto, p. 6, to name just the most recent ones.

[20] Although the study on the Romance trends in 7th and 8th century Latin documents has been published as a joint undertaking, the first part presents primarily the results of research undertaken by Frieda Politzer, while parts II and III are the contributions of Robert Politzer.

Muller in his *Chronology of Vulgar Latin* insists on the identity of the spoken and written languages, but steadfastly denies any possibility of the existence of dialectalization, and thereby weakens his own point. For while cohesion within the Roman Empire must have kept dialectal variations to a minimum, it is impossible to believe that in such a vast domain and as late as the 6th or 7th centuries they could have been practically non-existent; and if the written language does not show any indication of dialectalization it cannot be identical with the spoken language. The point we wish to make here, is precisely that the documents do show dialectal divergences. (*Romance Trends*, p. 49).

The question arises in our mind as to whether Muller indeed meant an *absolute* unity of speech throughout the Western Roman world, with practically nonexistent dialectal variations, as his critics seem to think. After all, within what he calls «a general unity of speech,» this scholar does make room for «regional characteristics,» even though they «never went so far as to make the speech of one region difficult to understand for the people of another region.» Furthermore, an absolute unity of speech with regional characteristics would be a contradiction and anyone familiar with Muller's writings would find it a little hard to conceive that this scholar should have failed to recognize the true nature of the spoken language which is to change in time and space, despite «the failure of the various attempts at finding proof of important dialectalization before the Carolingian period» (*Chronology*, p. 7).

Is it not conceivable, therefore, that Muller may have had in mind the kind of *relative* unity of speech that has been attributed to American English,[21] the Spanish and Portuguese languages in South America[22] and, generally speaking, to all languages of colonization?

---

[21] Cf. Albert C. Baugh, *History of the English Language*, (2nd ed.; New York, 1957), p. 412 ff., where the author speaks about the high degree of uniformity of English spoken in America in contrast to the pronounced dialectal differences that mark the popular speech of different parts of England. Also cf. the chapter on «The Dialects of American English» by Raven I. McDavid, Jr., in W. Nelson Francis, *The Structure of American English*, (New York, 1958), pp. 480-543, particularly this scholar's conclusions: «Thus, we conclude with the observation that the two important characteristics of American English, from the point of view of the linguistic geographer, are its relative unity and homogeneity, and the persistence of variety at the standard level» (p. 540).

SUMMARY OF FINDINGS AND CONCLUSIONS 297

In this connection, B. Löfstedt's remarks seem to be quite appropriate:

> Uniformität ist überhaupt ein für diejenigen Sprachen, die sich ausserhalb ihres ursprünglichen Gebiets in andere Territorien verbreiten oder verpflanzt werden, charakteristischer Zug. Das Paradebeispiel ist ja die Weltsprache des Hellenismus, die Koiné... (p. 210).

Even one of Muller's most recent critics, B. E. Vidos, concedes that

> L'unità del latino volgare non può essere in alcun modo negata a causa delle sue ineguaglianze. Malgrado il fatto che, p. es., nel III sec. d.C. un contadino romano pronunciava *i* come *e*, un Sardo invece come *i* ..., che un abitante della Gallia diceva *manducare* e *plus bellus*, uno dell'Iberia invece *comedere* e *magis formosus* ..., essi parlavano tutti latino volgare. (p. 209).

And as to the late date of this «general unity of speech,» it may be instructive to refer to a similar opinion advanced more recently by

---

For a comparison of linguistic conditions prevailing in the Western portion of the Roman Empire at the time of its greatest extent and those of present-day United States, cf. Pei, *Italian Language*, p. 15.

[22] For the Spanish language in South America, cf. Max Leopold Wagner, «Amerikanisch-Spanisch und Vulgärlatein», *Zeitschrift für romanische Philologie*, XL (1920), 286-404, where this scholar refers to the «unleugbare Einheitlichkeit der spanischen Sprache in Amerika» (p. 389) and draws a parallelism between the uniformity of Vulgar Latin and the Spanish superstratum, as follows: «Man muss sie [viz. what he calls «eine amerikanisch-spanische Koiné»] auf die nach Amerika verpflanzte Volkssprache der Conquistadorenzeit zurückführen und dabei nicht vergessen, das die Militärkolonien bei ihrer Verbreitung, wie bei ihrer Vereinheitlichung sicher eine grosse Rolle gespielt hat, so wie die Veteranenansiedlungen, die Heiraten römischer Soldaten mit einheimischen Frauen und der ausgeglichene sermo castrensis der aus allen Teilen des Reiches stammenden Legionäre anerkanntermassen die Ausbreitung des Lateinischen und die Bildung einer römischen Koiné gefördert haben» (p. 388). Wagner subsequently incorporated his thesis in his book *Lingua e dialetti dell'America Spagnola* (Firenze, 1949), in which he sums up the characteristics of Spanish-American with the words: «varietà nell' unità e unità nella differenziazione» (p. 147).

On the Portuguese language in Brazil, cf. Serafim da Silva Neto, «Le portugais dans le nouveau monde,» *Orbis*, II (1953), 143-156. Concerning «l'unité linguistique brésilienne,» this scholar makes the following observation: «Il faut tenir compte, toutefois, de ce que unité n'est pas égalité; il y a certainement dans le tissu linguistique brésilien des gradations de couleur... Mais ce qui est certain c'est que l'ensemble des parlers brésiliens se conforme au principe de *l'unité dans la diversité et de la diversité dans l'unité*» (p. 155).

the Finnish scholar Väänänen who —in observing the fall of final /s/ in Late Latin texts from the French and Spanish areas also, and not only the Italian area as would be expected on the basis of subsequent Romance developments— states

> C'est encore le cas de nombreux traits «vulgaires» qui par la suite devaient se répartir entre les divers idiomes romans et qui encore à la veille de l'avènement de Charlemagne surgissaient dans divers coins de la Romania, ce qui indique une différentiation locale du latin relativement tardive. [23]

Whether we accept the view of a relative unity of Vulgar Latin or choose to side with those who advocate an early disruption thereof, [24]

---

[23] «À propos de l's final dans les langues romanes,» *Boletim de Filologia*, XI (1950), p. 36.

[24] In the field of phonology, the theory of a Vulgar Latin unity has come under attack by E. Richter and G. Straka, in their respective studies on the relative chronology of phonetic changes («relative chronology» being based on the interdependence of various linguistic changes in a given language, rather than the succession of changes as is the case with «absolute chronology»). Richter states that «Die chronologische Darstellung erweist, dass viele Veränderungen früher eingetreten sind, als im allgemeinen angenommen wird. Sie zerstört die Vorstellung einer einheitlichen lateinischen Sprache, einer lateinischen Koiné, die viele Gelehrte als Ausgangspunkt der romanischen Sprachen voraussetzen» (p. 4), without however, specifying a time when this supposed break-up of unity took place (possibly because this scholar limits her study to historical phonology of French). G. Straka, on the other hand, after examining those changes that are common to all Romance languages and those that appear in specific areas only, reaches the conclusion that «ces faits prouvent que la différentiation du latin parlé selon les régions et, en conséquence, les débuts de l'individualisation et de la formation des divers idiomes romans remontent jusqu'au IIe siècle de notre ère, sinon encore plus haut» (p. 254).

Against these views, Menéndez-Pidal, in his *Orígenes*, raises a critical voice: «Hay que desechar la falsa creencia de que los cambios lingüísticos se realizan rápida y casi momentáneamente, a modo de una revolución decidida y arrolladora, muchos errores se cometen en la cronología relativa de los fenómenos fonéticos por seriarlos simplistamente como etapas sucesivas que no se entremezclan ni superponen sus fenómenos unas con otras...» (p. 535).

To reconcile the two opposing views, Robert de Dardel, *Le futur fort en roman commun* (Genève, 1958), proposes, as a common denominator, the Saussurian distinction between *langue* and *parole*: «De pareilles divergences de vues n'ont en somme rien d'étonnant tant qu'on n'adopte pas une commune mesure pour évaluer le degré d'unité ou de diversité des langues; cette mesure, nous pourrions la trouver dans la distinction saussurienne entre la parole et la langue. Tant que les faits de parole ne changent rien au système, nous avons affaire à une même langue; en roman commun, il y avait un système qui était cohérant, mais il y avait des différences de réalisation dans la parole, entraînant des variantes secondaires» (p. 25).

there is no denying the fact that, at least in its written form, the Latin language on inscriptions, texts and documents of the Vulgar Latin period appears as very much the same in all provinces of the Roman world. On the other hand, comparative studies, such as those undertaken by the Politzers as well as the present one, would seem to show that despite the obvious shortcomings ot written material as a true reflection of speech, it is possible to detect from the orthography dialectal features or, at least, certain trends, not only in the morphological and syntactical but also in the phonological aspect of the language. [25]

There is little doubt that the expansion and development of Latin throughout the Empire presents a complex problem and that the difficulties faced by the researcher who wishes to catch a glimpse of linguistic developments during this period are considerable. Professor William Diver has very aptly summed them up in these words:

> The difficulties that confront the historical linguist are many and complex, but chief among them is the essentially fragmentary nature of his data. Whether he is trying to reconstruct the dynamics of a prehistoric evolution or to deduce linguistic reality from the baffling inconsistencies of inscriptions or manuscripts, he is acutely aware of the importance of every scrap of information. [26]

If this study has succeeded in contributing another «scrap of information» to the controversial and much debated problem of Vulgar Latin, it will have fulfilled its purpose.

---

[25] On the information concerning pronunciation that can be culled from scribal errors, cf. Lehmann, p. 73.
[26] Review of *Historical Linguistics*, by Winfred P. Lehmann, *Word*, XIX (April 1963), p. 106.

www.ingramcontent.com/pod-product-compliance
Lightning Source LLC
Chambersburg PA
CBHW030610230426
43661CB00053B/1917